Pillsbury's B E S T

Pillsbury's B E S T

Pillsbury's B E S T

Pillsbury's B E S T

Pillsbury's B E S T

Pillsbury's B E S T

Pillsbury's B E S T

Pillsbury's B E S T

Pillsbury's B E S T

Liz Keeler

Pillsbury's BEST

**A Company History
From 1869**

William J. Powell

The Pillsbury Company • Minneapolis • 1985

Managing editor: Ellen B. Green
Jacket and book design: Seitz Yamamoto Moss, Inc.
Page layout: Ellen B. Green
Indexing: Suzanna Moody
Printing: Viking Press, Inc.

Illustrations are from the files of The Pillsbury Company unless otherwise noted.
Illustrations from the Minnesota Historical Society are on pages 12, 14, 24, 27, 29
(Floyd, Minneapolis, original at Northwest Area Architectural Archives), 37 top,
38 both, 46 (*Northwestern Miller* 37:77), 47, 51 bottom, 56 top (*Northwestern
Miller* 50:605), 61 (*Northwestern Miller* 51:260), 63 (*Northwestern Miller* 32:July
31, 1891), 64, 65 (Stafford & Co., Minneapolis), 67 top, 68 bottom (*Northwestern
Miller* 60:279), 74, 77 (Hibbard), 78 bottom right, 81 (William de la Barre Papers,
D 332, Division of Archives and Manuscripts), 84, and 96 top (Norton & Peel
Photo, Hubbard Studios, Minneapolis). Illustrations from the Richard L. Ferrell
Collection are on pages 20, 23, 30 (Chas. A. Tenny, Winona), 33 bottom, 34 both,
37 bottom, 40, 43 left, 44 bottom, 48 both, 51 top, 54, 55 both, 57 bottom, 58 both,
67 bottom, 68 top, 70 all, 71, 87, 91, 94, 99 all, 100 both, 103 both, 104 top, 106
all, 108 bottom, 110, 112, 114 bottom, 118 bottom, 123, 133 both, and 140 top and
bottom right. Illustrations from Leo Burnett Co., Inc., are on pages 128, 137, 157,
163 top left and right, 216 top left and right and bottom left, and 217. Illustration
page 78 is from Faegre & Benson; page 83 is from Touche Ross & Co; and
page 214 top is from the *St. Paul Pioneer Press and Dispatch*. Charts and graphs
were generated by the author.

Eric Mortenson provided copy photography for illustrations on pages 20, 30, 33 bottom, 34 both, 37 both, 38 both, 40, 43 left, 44 bottom, 49, 51 top, 54, 55 top, 57
both, 58 top, 59, 68 top, 70 top and left bottom, 71, 78, 83, 87, 91, 94, 99 all, 100
both, 103 top, 104 top, 106 all, 108 bottom, 110, 112, 114 all, 118 bottom, 121,
123, 133 both, 139, 141 top, 142, 143, 145, 146, 178, 183, 194, 200, 204, 212 bottom left and right, 216 top left and right and bottom left, 217, and 221.

Library of Congress Catalog Card Number: 85-6112

ISBN: 0-926208-01-2

Manufactured in the United States of America

To the employees of The Pillsbury Company who are responsible for its success—past, present, and future

Contents

Foreword   9
Acknowledgments   11

1. From the Bottom of the Heap, 1869–1889   13
2. So Many Eggs In One Basket, 1889–1908   41
3. A Nice Mess, 1908–1911   75
4. A New Beginning, 1909–1940   95
5. Buckling Down, 1940–1952   129
6. At the Threshold, 1952–1972   157
7. A Bold New Strategy, 1973–1984   195

Epilogue   231
Pillsburys Active in the Company   234
Governance of the Company   235
Notes   238
Index   246

Foreword

When histories such as this one are written, people and events naturally become intertwined. Sometimes they become inseparable. Still, it is people who are the impelling force in history, for it is their spirit, dedication, and vision that ultimately lead to progress.

Nowhere is this more true than in business. And at no time in America has this been more evident than in the late 1800s, when entrepreneurial spirit soared. It was a time of unparalleled growth and expansion, duly recorded by those who experienced it.

Charles Francis Adams, who returned to the United States in 1868 after seven years abroad as minister to Great Britain, wrote that the most noticeable change ''is perhaps to be found in a greatly enlarged grasp of enterprise . . . the great operations of war, the handling of large masses of men, the influence of discipline, the lavish expenditures of unprecedented sums of money, the immense financial operations, the possibilities of effective cooperation were lessons not likely to be lost on men quick to receive and apply new ideas.''

One of those men was Charles A. Pillsbury, who in 1869 founded The Pillsbury Company by purchasing a one-third interest in the Minneapolis Flouring Mill for $10,000. The milling industry was soon to embark on a phenomenal growth path. By 1882 Minneapolis had become the foremost flour milling center in the United States, providing 25 loaves of bread annually for every person in the nation. That same year C. A. Pillsbury & Co. became the largest flour milling firm in the world.

Of course, the decades to follow were not without obstacle. Like any business with a long history, The Pillsbury Company has had failures along with its successes, disappointments along with its joys. But, overall, it has been a positive story.

I think this is an appropriate time to look back on how that story has evolved and to examine the people and events that have made Pillsbury a highly prominent, international company. One reason for doing this now is that several of the people who built the foundation for Pillsbury's prosperity were able to contribute their personal accounts in the preparation of this book.

Pillsbury today is a well-defined company with a clear direction for the future. Its sole commitment is to the food and restaurant businesses. It is a commitment that has been formed over more than 100 years and that represents a far-reaching, almost limitless extension of that fledgling flour mill operated by Charles A. Pillsbury on the banks of the Mississippi River.

On the National Archives Building in Washington, D.C., is inscribed the statement: ''The past is prologue.'' If so, then perhaps this book provides an encouraging insight into what the next century holds for The Pillsbury Company and the people it serves.

WILLIAM H. SPOOR

Acknowledgments

The preparation of this book has been aided immensely by the research and ideas of Doniver C. Lund and by a number of individual interviews by Kenneth D. Ruble.

William H. Spoor has been the catalyst for the book. Two former chief executive officers of The Pillsbury Company, Paul S. Gerot and the late Philip W. Pillsbury, also gave unstintingly of their time to furnish information about and insight into events within their experience or knowledge.

Edward C. Stringer, executive vice-president of the company, is responsible, or perhaps chargeable, for my opportunity to write this history. He patiently read and commented on its successive drafts and responded immediately to every request for assistance.

Richard Ferrell, senior electrical engineer and former A Mill plant manager, probably knows more about the early history of Minneapolis flour milling than any person living today. He is a discriminating collector of photographs and memorabilia related to the company's early years and an engaging writer concerning that period. His contributions from his personal library and his advice add greatly to this book.

The list of current and former Pillsbury employees who gave help is a long one. I do, however, want to record my particular thanks to Ronald E. Lund, Michael D. Ellwein, Nancy Ehlert, Kathy Frey, Allan E. Fonfara, Sig Nyline, Rachel Berry, Toni Hammond, Don A. Osell, Judith A. Belter, Graham Hatcher, Robert J. Lewis, George S. Pillsbury, Paul J. Kelsey, Everett A. Blasing, and Bernard L. Adomeit.

The Pillsbury Company was fortunate to secure for this book the services of Ellen Green, a gifted, experienced, and perceptive editor. It is she who assembled the extensive illustrations. Without her contributions this book would not have been published.

The resources of the Minnesota Historical Society have been invaluable, as has the encouragement and advice of its director, Russell W. Fridley, and his recently retired associate, Lucile M. Kane. The archives of Northern States Power Company and the assistance there of Charles P. Quinn were also helpful.

On a personal and practical note I owe my greatest thanks to Meredith B. Powell for her keen, constructive criticism and great forbearance during the course of this project.

1 From the Bottom of the Heap
1869–1889

The Minneapolis flour milling industry was in a depressed condition in 1869. Mills at other locations were producing better flour, and local millers were hard pressed to earn satisfactory returns. On the surface at least, the industry was not a promising one when 26-year-old Charles A. Pillsbury arrived from the East that year in search of a new career. Nonetheless Charles, his father, and his uncle acquired in the summer and fall of 1869 a one-half interest in one of the young city's small, unprofitable flour mills. None of the three had any flour milling experience. Yet in 13 years the family partnership, managed by Charles, would become the largest flour milling firm in the world. Charles would be hailed as the foremost miller of his time.[1]

Minneapolis owed its existence to the Falls of St. Anthony, a magnificent cataract on the Mississippi River, fast gaining recognition as one of the nation's great waterpowers. In 1805, Lieutenant Zebulon Pike had been ordered to explore the Mississippi from St. Louis to its source and to seek permission from the Indians to build forts and trading houses along its course. Pike obtained from the Sioux (Dakota) a grant of land nine miles on each side of the Mississippi running north past the falls from the confluence of the Mississippi and Minnesota rivers. The government established a military reservation on part of the ceded lands and in 1820, as part of its program of frontier defense, built Fort Snelling on a promontory seven miles below the falls. Soldiers from the fort constructed a sawmill and a gristmill on the west side of the river in the early 1820s. Located a few rods below the brink of the falls, the mills represented the first use of the falls' immense power.[2]

Separate treaties with the Sioux and Chippewa (Ojibway), signed in 1837 and ratified in 1838, opened to settlement all the territory from the Mississippi east to the St. Croix. When news of ratification reached Fort Snelling, army officers and frontiersmen alike rushed to the falls to file claims along its east bank, an area the army had excluded from its reservation. By 1848 a dam was completed across the river's east channel. Almost immediately a line of waterpowered sawmills sprang up on the east side to saw into lumber the great logs floated downstream from northern Minnesota's pine forests.

It took Charles A. Pillsbury and his partners only 13 years to develop their flour milling company into the largest in the world. This poster, showing mills on both sides of the Mississippi, was used in store windows, ca. 1888.

Minneapolis was photographed (left) from the east side of the Mississippi River around the time the Pillsburys got into the milling business. The Minneapolis Flouring Mill is the tall peaked building facing the river at top, center. It was flanked by the Alaska (left), later the Pillsbury B, and what was then the Empire Woolen Mill (right).

In 1849 the settlement of almost 250 people was platted as the townsite of St. Anthony. A gristmill built alongside the row of saw-mills in 1851 was joined three years later by the area's first merchant flour mill, built to supply the demands of an expanding local popula-tion and the logging camps to the north. Because nearby wheat pro-duction was negligible, Iowa and Illinois wheat was brought by boat to St. Paul and then by wagon to St. Anthony so that the merchant mill could operate at a 100-barrel-per-day capacity.[3]

The growth of the flour and sawmilling industries on the east side of the falls and the increasing population led to the incorporation of St. Anthony as a city of the territory of Minnesota in 1855. The bus-tling young community had grown in 17 years to a city of 3,000 people.

On the west side of the falls, development proceeded more slowly. Unlike the St. Anthony side, the west bank was part of the military reservation. Nonetheless, settlers did their best to establish preemptive rights to the land, first through formal leases from the government, then by permits obtained from the Fort Snelling com-mand, and finally by staking out claims and squatting on the land. The first permanent home was built on the west side in 1849, and soon dwellings of all descriptions stood on the reservation lands. Bowing to the inevitable, Congress in 1852 passed a bill severing more than 26,000 acres from the military reserve. In 1855 it followed with a preemption bill granting settlers, including the more than 1,000 people living on the west bank, the first right to buy the home-sites they had claimed.

And so it was, in 1855, when 28-year-old John S. Pillsbury, Charles's uncle, became the first of his family to move from New Hampshire to Minnesota. John had journeyed extensively throughout the western United States before deciding to open a hardware store and settle at St. Anthony. The Minnesota Territory was experiencing its largest immigration to date, and the falls at St. Anthony powered a thriving sawmilling business, by then in its eighth season. The place bore no resemblance to the quiet New England villages and estab-lished cities John had known. Instead, St. Anthony was a noisy, rough, untidy frontier town where "Houses built of green lumber cured on their foundations to the annoyance of housewives who mopped up the oozing moisture. 'Nasty, piratical looking pigs' roamed at will, and streets were filled with stumps. Stagecoaches, carts and wagons rumbling in from St. Paul—the head of Mississippi River navigation where steamboats carrying people bound for St. Anthony tied up—spilled out passengers with mountains of baggage and freight. Indians wandered through the town, strangers to the noise and bustle around them. Piles of logs and lumber from the saw-mills dotted the landscape, and the whine of the saws could be heard above the roar of the falls."[4]

John S. Pillsbury, described as a man of imagination, iron will, and resourcefulness, was the first three-term governor of Minnesota and widely acclaimed as "Father of the University of Minnesota."

Changes came rapidly, however, most of them conducive to the business that would perpetuate the Pillsbury name. The single most important development was an increase in the number of farms, as waves of pioneers poured into the territory. Spurred by the well-publicized richness of the prairielands, the passage of the Homestead Act in 1860, and the availability of attractively priced railroad land grant acreage, the population of Minnesota exploded from 6,077 in 1850 to 172,023 in 1860, and to 439,076 in 1870. Most newcomers settled on lands that they could quickly clear and plow. Improved farmland in the state jumped from 556,250 acres in 1860 to 2,322,102 acres in 1870. Wheat became the chief crop almost immediately, with 60 percent of the tilled land in wheat by 1865. New machinery, notably mechanical reapers and harvesters, facilitated the harvest. Minnesota wheat production in 1850 was a grand total of only 1,401 bushels. By 1860 it reached 2,186,993 bushels and, a decade later, 18,866,073 bushels.[5]

The fast-growing wheat supply, coupled with an ever-increasing number of consumers, offered an attractive opportunity to millers. In 1855 there were two small mills at the falls, grinding a total of about 200 barrels of flour per day. By 1869, nine mills operated on the west side of the falls and four on the east; flour production had increased to 3,380 barrels per day. This quantity greatly exceeded local needs, and some 70 percent was shipped to outside markets. Still, as one flour milling authority notes, "None of the Minneapolis mills or millers . . . had more than a local reputation up to 1870."[6]

Between 1855 and 1869 a second element essential to development of a major milling center emerged. Before Minnesota became a state in 1858 the territorial legislature had granted charters to 27 railroad companies. The Panic of 1857 and difficulties in raising capital had stalled construction, but finally in 1862, the St. Paul and Pacific laid the first line of railroad, stretching ten miles from St. Paul to Minneapolis. Over the next few years, the St. Paul and Pacific and four other railroads built slowly but steadily, and by the end of 1869 there were 764 miles of rail in operation in the state. Construction of a transportation network, so important to the growth of flour milling and other manufacturing businesses, was well under way.[7]

The Falls of St. Anthony provided the third essential ingredient for a successful flour milling industry—plentiful and inexpensive waterpower. In 1856 the territorial government chartered two water-power companies—the Minneapolis Mill Company on the west side of the falls and the St. Anthony Falls Water Power Company on the east. Poorly organized and financed, the east-side operators began with "thirteen years of chaos," during which little was done to make full use of the falls' power. The Minneapolis Mill Company, however, did well from the start. In 1857 it began construction of a power canal that ran inland and parallel to the river, making power available

George A. Pillsbury (top) won acclaim as a civic businessman and church leader in both Concord, New Hampshire, and Minneapolis. He was mayor of Concord in 1876 and 1877 and of Minneapolis from April 1884 to April 1886. Charles A. Pillsbury (bottom) learned the milling business thoroughly as the company's managing partner. Easily accessible, generous, and charming, he became one of the most popular businessmen in the city.

to industries that could not locate waterwheels on the river. As a result the west-side manufacturing district developed so rapidly that in 1869 it turned out five times the flour and more than twice the lumber produced by the east side.[8]

Thus when Charles Pillsbury arrived in Minneapolis most of the pieces necessary for a highly successful flour milling industry—ample wheat production, readily available low-cost power, and a good transportation network—were falling into place.

By 1869 John Pillsbury was one of the community's most successful and respected citizens. His retail and wholesale hardware business had prospered, and he had branched out. He made substantial investments in timberlands and other real estate, participated in a number of manufacturing and mercantile businesses, and became a director of various railroad, banking, and other enterprises. He devoted a great share of his time to public service, beginning with his election in 1858 to the St. Anthony City Council. By 1869 he was a prominent member of the state senate, to which he had first been elected in 1864.

John's brother, George A. Pillsbury, was a leading citizen of Concord, New Hampshire. Born in 1816, he had a public school education, followed by employment in retail and manufacturing enterprises in Boston and in his native New Hampshire. He then operated in the mercantile business on his own until 1851, when he was appointed purchasing agent for the Concord Railroad Corporation, a position he held for 24 years.

George's son Charles was born in Warner, New Hampshire, in 1842. He was educated in New Hampshire, first in Warner's public schools, then at the New London Academy, and finally at Dartmouth College, where he graduated in 1863. His college course of study concentrated heavily on languages—three years of Greek and Latin, and a year of French and of German. Other courses included civil engineering, physics, and chemistry. A classmate described Charles's life at Dartmouth: "He did not seek to attain high scholarship; he did a good deal of general reading; he was a good talker and kept the fact constantly in mind that he meant to be a successful 'business man'; and this fact he did not conceal from others. He was generally popular with the students and the faculty; no one would have selected him as the one member of the class who was to gain a world-wide reputation, as there was nothing specially brilliant to indicate it by the traits he manifested."[9]

After graduation Charles went to Montreal as a clerk for Buck, Robertson & Co., a produce commission company. To avoid interrupting his business career, he exercised the option of providing a substitute when he became eligible for the Civil War draft. In 1865 he became a partner in the Canadian firm. Years later Charles commented on the long hours, sometimes through the night, that he de-

Memorandum of Agreement made this fourth day of June 1869 between George A Pillsbury of Concord in the County of Merrimack and State of New Hampshire and Charles A. Pillsbury of Minneapolis in the State of Minnesota as follows

The Said Geo. A. and Charles A. Pillsbury having purchased one third of a Flouring Mill at Minneapolis in the State of Minnesota Known as the Minneapolis Flouring Mill for the sum of Ten Thousand Dollars, the same to be conveyed to the said Geo. A. Pillsbury, and the further sum of Two Thousand dollars being required as one third of the working capital to operate said Mill; It is hereby agreed by and between the said Geo. A. and Chas. A. Pillsbury, that the said Geo. A. Pillsbury, shall furnish within one year from date the sum of eight thousand dollars, and the said Charles. A. Pillsbury shall furnish four thousand dollars, making in all the sum of Twelve thousand Dollars for one third interest in the mill fixtures and personal property therewith connected, including also the two thousand dollars for one third part of the working capital of the company. now it is hereby agreed between the said Geo. A. and Chas. A. Pillsbury, that in consideration of the said Chas. A. Pillsbury devoting his entire time to the business shall first receive at the rate of one thousand dollars a year for his services and the balance of profits over and above one thousand dollars that may be derived from the one third interest in said mill shall be divided equally between the said Geo. A and Chas. A. Pillsbury, It being understood that the interest on the money invested as above specified shall not be claimed by either party

Geo. A. Pillsbury
Chas. A. Pillsbury

This contract, handwritten in June of 1869, was the beginning of Pillsbury involvement in the flour milling business.

voted to his work in Montreal. But according to an early biographer, "It is stated by good authority that his business venture in Montreal, before going to Minneapolis, came near being a total failure. When he left that city for Minnesota, all that he had to carry with him was $1,500 in cash and a keenly disciplined business mind."[10]

No one knows for sure why Charles Pillsbury decided to move to Minneapolis or why he entered the flour milling business, though he was probably encouraged in both decisions by his uncle, John, who had witnessed the course of milling in the area. Shortly after his arrival in Minneapolis, Charles and his father, George Pillsbury, purchased a one-third interest in the Minneapolis Flouring Mill, on the west side of the falls. Undaunted by their lack of flour milling experience, they signed an agreement on June 4, 1869, under which George furnished $8,000 and Charles, $4,000. With this they paid a purchase price of $10,000 and contributed $2,000 to the mill's working capital. The agreement provided that George would take title to the one-third interest and that Charles would devote full time to managing the mill. Their share of profits would first pay Charles's $1,000-per-year salary and then be divided equally between them.

The Minneapolis Flouring Mill, built by Frazee and Murphy in 1864, stood on the second lot south of what is now the southeast corner of First Street and Sixth Avenue South. In 1869 it employed seven people, and its capacity was estimated at from 200 to 300 barrels of flour per day, not much more than that of the first merchant mill built at the falls. When Charles and George purchased their one-third interest, "the townsmen thought they had been sold a turkey, a business as shaky as its machinery." Charles himself said, "Up to that time Minneapolis flour was way down at the bottom of the heap, and the mill had been losing money almost steadily . . . The other fellows in the business rather pitied me, and said that another poor devil had got caught in the milling business of which he would soon get enough."[11]

Charles immediately threw himself into learning the flour milling business. One of his grandsons wrote in 1950 that "from a little wooden shack near the five year old 'Minneapolis' mill . . . Charles began dealing with farmers personally for their little wagon-loads of wheat, and was always watching the mill."[12]

In October 1869 Charles's uncle John purchased a one-sixth interest from George M. Crocker, another Minneapolis Flouring Mill partner, bringing Pillsbury ownership to one-half. Early in their first year with the mill, the partners advanced additional funds for working capital and improvements, and the property began to operate at a profit.

This 1884 photograph shows (left to right) the Minneapolis Flouring Mill, the Pillsbury B, and the Excelsior, all reconstructed on their original sites following an 1881 explosion. The railroad tracks on First Street were constructed on a platform level with the second story.

Meanwhile, the Taylor Brothers' mill adjoining the Minneapolis Flouring Mill on the south was floundering. Built in 1866 and 1867 with a 200-barrel-per-day capacity, the Alaska mill, as it was known, was put up for mortgage foreclosure sale in April 1870. Encouraged by the early success of the Minneapolis Flouring Mill, Charles and his Uncle John acquired the Alaska from the purchaser at the foreclosure sale. On April 12, 1871, the young firm of C. A. Pillsbury & Co., with Charles as its manager, gained its first full title to a flour mill and immediately changed the mill's name from the Alaska to the Pillsbury. Later Charles and John sold a one-third interest in the mill to George, who continued his equal partnership in the firm.[13]

One of the first things Charles learned about the country's flour milling was that despite Minneapolis access to wheat, waterpower, and railways, St. Louis was the center of the industry. In St. Louis flour was made from the soft winter wheat grown in surrounding states. This wheat, sown in the fall, could not be grown in the colder climate of the "Northwest" states like Minnesota, where the main crop was a harder wheat planted as soon as farmers could get into their fields in the spring. With contemporary flour milling techniques it was impossible to produce as high quality a flour from the hard Northwest spring wheat as could be ground from winter wheat. As a result, Minneapolis flour sold at a substantial discount.[14]

The art of flour milling, which had changed little in the United States since the end of the eighteenth century, consisted of three main steps: separating the wheat from the chaff, grinding the clean wheat between a pair of millstones, and bolting, or sifting, the ground wheat through a fine cloth to permit the passage of the flour but not of the bran coating.

It was the second step, dating back to several centuries before Christ, to which spring wheat did not lend itself as well as did winter wheat. Because of its much harder coating, millers of spring wheat placed their stones close together and turned them at a high speed. This method of "low grinding" scorched the flour and pulverized portions of the hard, brittle bran coat so much that they could not be separated from the flour in the sifting step. If the miller set his stones farther apart to avoid the scorching and pulverizing of the outer coat, incomplete separation of the glutenous mass of cells just below the bran caused much of the gluten to remain with the bran and be lost to the flour. These so-called middlings contained some of the most nutritive elements of the wheat as well as the gluten that provides the strength, or rising properties, of flour. Consequently, the usual result of milling spring wheat was some combination of a discolored, unattractive product with less nutritional value, less gluten, and a shorter shelf life than winter wheat flour. The preference of merchants and consumers for St. Louis winter wheat flour was a serious obstacle to the growth of Minneapolis milled flour.

In the late 1860s, when Minneapolis flour "was away down at the bottom of the heap," several small mills in southern Minnesota produced a spring wheat flour enjoying stronger acceptance in the eastern market. Charles, along with most of his fellow Minneapolis millers, believed that the Faribault mill, the Ames mill at Northfield, and the Gardner mill at Hastings had access to better wheat than they did. From a visit to the Ames mill he took home a sample of wheat for testing. Informed that it was no better than what was used in his own mills, Charles then decided that the southern millers were employing better milling practices.[15]

He was right. The southern Minnesota millers had been experimenting with various devices and methods to "purify" the middlings. The objective was to separate more of the middlings from the bran, allowing them to be milled into the flour and allowing the tiny particles of bran to be removed. Foremost among the experimenters were two Frenchmen, Edmund N. LaCroix and his brother Nicholas, who helped build and operate the Faribault mill in the 1860s. In 1868, they built their own mill nearby, installing a crude middlings purifier after the design of a French patent. They abandoned the mill when a flood washed away its dam and bridge, and in 1870 Edmund came to Minneapolis. There he visited the Washburn mill, constructed on the west side of the falls in 1866 by C. C. Washburn, a highly successful businessman from LaCrosse, Wisconsin. LaCroix persuaded George H. Christian, the mill's managing partner, to let him fabricate and install one of his machines. The purifier, installed in March or April of 1871, was then materially improved by Christian and George T. Smith, a stonedresser Christian had hired from the Hastings mill.[16]

The new machine purified the middlings by running them through a vibrating sieve, where a strong current of air pulled out the lighter particles of bran while the flour passed through the sieve and the middlings tailed off at the end. The purified middlings were run through millstones again and resifted, resulting in a white, high-gluten flour that produced 12 percent more bread than winter wheat flour. In the new "high-grinding" process, the millstones, set farther apart, ran more slowly and caused a better separation of the middlings from the bran.[17]

Charles Pillsbury watched the developments at the Washburn mill closely. Wasting no time, he immediately recruited Smith as Pillsbury head miller and directed him to install the new process in the newly acquired Pillsbury mill and the Minneapolis Flouring Mill. The results were dramatic. Other millers quickly adopted the middlings purifiers, and spring wheat flour became supreme in the chief markets of the country, very quickly adding as much as three dollars per barrel to the profits of Minneapolis millers.[18]

The middlings purifier (top) revolutionized the milling industry.

This early postcard's "Instantaneous View of Pillsbury's Store House" (right) shows the huge sacks and barrels that were the consumer sizes of the 1880s.

The Anchor mill was destroyed by fire in 1878. This undated photograph shows the reconstructed Anchor (taller building, right foreground) and (to its left) the later-constructed Anchor annex. The railroad tracks are on Second Street, and the Pillsbury B elevator, built on the site of the old Empire mill, can be seen in the left background.

Fred C. Pillsbury, who joined the partnership in 1875, was closely associated with his brother Charles in operating the mills. He had a strong interest in agriculture, maintaining a model farm on the shores of Lake Minnetonka near Minneapolis.

Shortly after the middlings purifiers were installed, on October 12, 1872, a fire destroyed the Minneapolis Flouring Mill. Although winter approached, reconstruction of the mill commenced immediately, and it was completely rebuilt in 100 days with an increased capacity of 350 barrels a day. The speed of reconstruction reflected what the *Northwestern Miller*, the area's milling journal, described as "the palmiest days our millers have ever seen."[19]

Anxious to obtain maximum benefit from the sudden heavy demand for Minneapolis flour, the Pillsburys added two more west-side mills to their operation in 1873 and 1875. The first was the Empire, originally a woolen mill, which the company leased and converted to a 500-barrel-per-day flour mill. The second was the Anchor, acquired by John and leased to the company when he sold his hardware business in 1875 to begin the first of three consecutive terms as Minnesota's governor. The Anchor, constructed in 1874 with a 500-barrel-per-day capacity, faced Second Street, west of and across the canal from the Pillsbury mill. The Empire was on the southeast corner of First Street and Sixth Avenue South, immediately north of the Minneapolis Flouring Mill. During this same period the three Pillsburys, wishing to have full control of their own holdings, sold their one-half interest in the Minneapolis Flouring Mill, and Charles's management of that mill came to an end.

A fourth family member, Fred C. Pillsbury, joined the partnership in 1875. Ten years younger than his brother Charles, Fred had worked for several years in John's Minneapolis hardware business. When that was sold, Fred acquired a one-seventh interest in C. A. Pillsbury & Co., and the three original partners each became an owner of two-sevenths of the company. In October the firm completed construction of a new office building, probably located directly across First Street from the Empire. It was proclaimed in the *Northwestern Miller* as "in all its appointments one of the finest business offices in Minneapolis."[20]

While the rest of the country suffered through the Panic of 1873 and its aftermath, the Minneapolis milling business grew and prospered. In 1874 Minneapolis millers witnessed the start-up of the new Washburn A,* a 3,000-barrel-per-day mill built on the west side of the power canal. The country's largest flour mill, its life was to be short. Four years later, on May 2, 1878, the Washburn A exploded in Minneapolis's first great industrial accident. Fire quickly jumped the canal and spread through the clustered milling district, burning down three other mills. The Pillsbury mills, more than a block away from the burning buildings, escaped undamaged. The Washburn A was rebuilt, but mill explosions caused by the combination of a flame or spark with an accumulation of flour dust in a confined space were to plague flour millers even in the twentieth century.[21]

---

* Custom designated different mills of identical ownership alphabetically, in order of erection or acquisition. Pillsbury and Washburn mills, however, designated their mills alphabetically by size. Thus the original Washburn mill became the Washburn B, and when the Pillsbury A was built in 1881, the smaller west-side mill became the Pillsbury B.

The facilities of C. A. Pillsbury & Co. continued to expand along with those of others. In 1878 the partnership leased the new Excelsior mill built immediately south of the Pillsbury by Dorilus C. Morrison, a cousin of C. C. Washburn. The Excelsior had a daily capacity of 500 barrels. Later in the year, after the Washburn A explosion, the Anchor burned and was promptly rebuilt with an increased capacity. In the late 1870s the capacities of the Pillsbury and Empire mills were enlarged, and by the end of the decade Pillsbury's total production approximated 3,000 barrels per day.[22]

Continuing rapid expansion in Minneapolis milling capacity brought on by the middlings purifier would have been troublesome had it not been for the development of an export flour market in the late 1870s. Even though the population of the United States was increasing along with per capita consumption of flour, the country's demand for flour could not keep pace with the increasing supply. Almost all sales were of "family flour," that is, flour used for baking in the home, as a commercial baking industry had not yet developed. The discovery of new markets was imperative.

Minneapolis millers first substantially entered the export market in 1877, when Washburn's William H. Dunwoody persuaded a Liverpool firm to place a small order for his company's flour. The next year area millers shipped out about 107,185 barrels of flour, mostly to Europe, and the export business began a period of rapid growth. Exports reached 1,181,322 barrels in three years, and for the remainder of the 1880s, roughly 35 percent of Minneapolis flour was sent out of the country. Customers in the United Kingdom were the principal purchasers, although most other European countries bought as well.[23]

A second major technological development almost immediately followed the opening of the export market for Minneapolis flour. Local millers, including Charles Pillsbury and George Christian, observed on an 1873 visit to Europe that many millers in Hungary and France had totally replaced millstones with chilled iron or porcelain rollers. In this process, the wheat was ground gradually by running it through six or seven sets of rollers. The rollers in each set turned against each other to break the wheat. After each break the product was sifted and graded before it passed through the next set of rollers. Because so many similar steps were taken, this was called the "gradual reduction" process. While as early as 1875 a few Minneapolis mills made a limited use of rollers to crush wheat before it went through the millstones or to grind bran, millstones were still central to the milling process. In fact, reliance on millstones was still so prevalent that the *Northwestern Miller* reported on November 4, 1881, that "only a year or two ago all of our mills were comparative strangers to the roller system."[24]

The roller mill, shown in the Pillsbury A in 1897, was second only to the middlings purifier in revolutionizing the flour industry.

It was not until the fall of 1879 that W. D. Gray, a leading American mill builder during the last quarter of the nineteenth century, prevailed upon C. C. Washburn to install a small, experimental all-roller mill in an unused corner of his new Washburn C. Conducted under closely guarded secrecy, installation was completed in mid-1880, about the time the first half of the rebuilt Washburn A started operating. Although the experimental system was judged a success, there was no time to install it in the Washburn A.[25]

William de la Barre, a young Austrian engineer who assisted Gray in the all-roller experiment, recalled: ''Soon after the starting of the Washburn A, Charles A. Pillsbury and his brother, Fred C. Pillsbury, called at my home one day while I was eating dinner. Charles A. Pillsbury said that he would like me to answer just one question, if I thought it was fair to do so . . .

'' 'Just tell me,' said he, 'from what you know about this Hungarian way of milling, if, in your opinion, we will all have to come to it. Consider the question well, as a good deal depends upon it.'

''I told the Messrs. Pillsbury that I was fully convinced that a change would have to be made from the old way to the new by all the mills, sooner or later. Mr. Pillsbury looked at me sharply for a minute, then shook hands with me, saying 'Many thanks to you; I believe you are right.' ''[26]

That same fall when Charles contracted with Gray to supervise a crew of millwrights to adjust the machinery in the Excelsior mill of C. A. Pillsbury & Co., Gray suggested that he be authorized instead to convert the mill to the roller system. Later Gray wrote: "After a good deal of talk he very reluctantly told us to go ahead and change the mill, and added, 'Go quick, for fear I'll change my mind.'

"He did not have to wait long. It was then the middle of the afternoon; and I went over to the mill, stopped the work of lining up, and set the workmen to tearing out. We kept them at work all night, and in the morning I found the millstones and iron hurst frames standing on the platform at the front door. The next day it would have cost Mr. Pillsbury a good deal of money to put them back again, had he changed his mind."[27]

With conversion complete in the spring of 1881, the Excelsior became the first merchant mill in Minneapolis, and one of the first in the country, to operate without millstones.[28]

The roller system provided major manufacturing economies. While eliminating the cost of dressing millstones and requiring less power and mill space than the old system, it increased by at least 3 percent the amount of flour produced from a given quantity of wheat. Charles Pillsbury wrote later, that, as a result of the 1873 trip to Europe, "Some of the Minneapolis mills adopted the Hungarian process bodily, middlings purifier and all, and in a few years were compelled to throw away some of the complex machinery with which they were loaded. The Pillsbury mills, however, adopted only what seemed to be the best features of the Hungarian process, such as the rolls, made modifications all along the line, and retained the American middlings purifier invented by Mr. Smith." Charles promptly converted the three other Pillsbury mills to the roller system, although for many years he made a limited use of millstones to reduce fine middlings, even in the Pillsbury A, then under construction.[29]

The building of the Pillsbury A mill was the high point of the early years of C. A. Pillsbury & Co. In 1879 the partners, no doubt delighted by the results of their first ten years, decided to construct a 5,000-barrel-a-day mill that would more than double the company's capacity and establish it as the nation's foremost flour miller. In February 1880 the company purchased lands on the southeast corner of Main Street and Third Avenue Southeast, only a block away from the site of John Pillsbury's first hardware store.

According to one respected milling historian, the crowded westside district lacked waterpower and a sufficiently attractive site for the new mill. But John Pillsbury, who had started his career on the east side, cited a different reason for locating the new mill there. Recalling his continuing desire to help east-siders, he said, "It was this idea of mine which led to building the Pillsbury A Mill on the east side, while all the other mills are on the west side of the river. My partners objected to separating the Pillsbury flour mills, but I stood out for the East Side, and the mill was built where it would benefit East Side working men."[30]

The Pillsbury A was the first flour mill in the world to be designed by an architect. This is L. S. Buffington's rendering.

In anticipation of the decision to build, Charles had toured both Europe and the United States extensively, acquainting himself with the latest advances in milling technology. The new A mill, he decided, would be designed as two separate units, each with its own machinery and crew and capable of operating independently. Both units would use roller mills, incorporating the best available middlings purifiers.

Excavation for the new mill began in the spring of 1880. In November the building was ready for roofing, and installation of the milling machinery began. The east unit, completed first, commenced production on July 5, 1881. On August 12 the *Northwestern Miller* announced that ''The Pillsbury A mill is said to have made 2,200 barrels of flour per day the latter part of this week and 2,500 will be an easy task for it when cooler weather comes and better wheat can be procured.''

According to the press, the A mill was the first in the district to use electricity for lighting. The July 22, 1881, *Northwestern Miller* reported that a couple of trial runs of the new lighting system ''did not prove just satisfactory, the jar of the mill affecting the light, but it is hoped this difficulty can be overcome.'' At first the A mill did not have a separate wheat storage facility, and wheat was brought to it

each day by rail and horse-drawn wagon. In 1883 and 1884 the company constructed a 100,000-bushel brick elevator adjacent to the A.

On December 4, 1881, at the time the A mill was being completed, disaster struck. A fire in the basement of the Pillsbury B touched off an explosion that completely destroyed Pillsbury's B, Empire, and Excelsior mills, as well as Crocker & Fisk's Minneapolis Flouring Mill. The December 9, 1881, *Northwestern Miller* reported four persons killed and many more severely injured and burned. Whether to get away from the congested milling district or for other reasons, the company moved its headquarters downtown the next year to the Windom Block on the corner of Washington and Second avenues.

For a time, only the Anchor (which the partnership had purchased from John in 1881) and the east half of the A mill produced the company's flour. Finally, on July 10, 1882 the west unit of the A mill started up, and on October 12 the mill attained a world record run of 5,107 barrels in one day. With this, the Pillsbury A became the largest mill in the world, a distinction it held for decades. The London *Times* carried a report in 1883 declaring, "This mill stands in relation to the American flour trade, as Niagara does to waterfalls."[31]

The Pillsbury B was rebuilt by October 1882 with a 2,500-barrel-per-day capacity, but because of a slow-down in business, its milling machinery was not installed until the summer of 1885. At the same time the Empire mill site remained vacant until the partners purchased the property and constructed a building to house a mill in 1885. The partners never did install milling machinery there, however; in 1889 the company bricked up the windows and converted the building into a 200,000-bushel grain elevator. Dorilus Morrison decided to rebuild and operate the Excelsior himself, ending the lease to Pillsbury. Meanwhile, the Pillsbury A was setting new production records, and on October 21, 1884, it produced 6,197 barrels of flour in 24 hours.[32]

Charles Pillsbury was very proud of the company's level of production, and when announcement of the A's latest record drew skepticism, the *Northwestern Miller* reported: "C. A. Pillsbury says that if any one discredits that the Pillsbury 'A' made 6,197 bbls. [barrels] of flours in 24 hours, he will wage 1,000 to 5,000 bbls. of flour with any party that it can make 6,000 bbls. in a day, and let a competent committee come in and oversee the operations of the mill, the loser's flour to be given to the poor."[33]

In the winter of 1883–84 Charles had steam engines installed in the Pillsbury A and Anchor mills as an auxiliary source of power during periods of low water in the late fall and winter months. Low water the previous winter had caused area mill operators to establish a schedule under which, on a rotating basis, one-fourth of the mills shut down for a specific time so that the others could operate at full capacity. The arrangement included appointment of an inspector "to see that the agreement is lived up to by all."[34]

Another concern of the industry was the need to earn better returns from its by-products. Historically the offal (the parts of the wheat consisting chiefly of hulls, bran, and germ) had been thought of little or no value, and was either dumped into the river, burned, or hauled away by neighboring farmers. When introduction of the new process brought large increases in milling capacity, the volume of offal reached major proportions. The new A mill facility included an adjoining stone building called the bran house, to which offal was

The original Pillsbury logo (above) was blown up to half-page size for an ad in the *Northwestern Miller* on February 6, 1901.

carried by conveyor belt from the mill for storage. Some was shipped in carloads to the eastern United States, and part was sacked or sold in bulk to local farmers as animal feed. [35]

During the mid–1880s Fred Pillsbury, convinced that the bran had unexploited value as cattle feed, began a series of experiments to prove its worth. He purchased a small herd of cattle, kept careful records, and clearly demonstrated bran's effectiveness as a cattle food. His findings were confirmed by studies at the University of Minnesota, and the Minnesota millers published and distributed a pamphlet advertising the merits of bran as a stock fattener and enhancer of milk production. From this beginning, when the science of animal nutrition was just developing, millfeed rapidly gained acceptance as an important feed commodity. According to the *Northwestern Miller*, sales from the A mill's bran department aggregated almost $200,000 in 1889. [36]

Charles constantly strove for greater production to obtain economies of scale, coupling this thrust with an aggressive marketing program. He began in 1872 to indicate the superior quality of his flour with the label Pillsbury's Best® and the XXXX mark, rooted in the symbolism of the Middle Ages. Bakers then had marked their best flour, for use in the preparation of communion bread, with three crosses. In 1875 the company registered these now-famous trademarks, and it vigorously prosecuted infringers in cases such as the 1885 New York *Pillsbury v. Skidmore and Bull*, in which the court enjoined a Pillsbury competitor from using "Best" and "XXXX" in combination with its own name. [37]

Like other Minneapolis milling companies, Pillsbury used newspaper and magazine advertising in the 1880s to promote sale of the company's flour. Charles was quoted as saying, "In a business making a staple product, advertising cannot build the business alone—it takes more than that—but, advertising can earn a good return on the investment. If our advertising can keep enough housewives thinking of Pillsbury's Best® Flour, so that they will give it a trial, that is all we can ask. Then it is up to the flour itself to carry the burden." [38]

On October 12, 1883, C. A. Pillsbury & Co. became the first miller to buy space in the *Northwestern Miller*, probably to reach that publication's readers in the flour export trade. The first Pillsbury ad included the names of the four partners, declaring that they were the "Manufacturers of Finest Brands of Flour from Choice Selected Hard Spring Wheat." The firm's daily capacity was stated as 7,500 barrels, and the brands listed were Patent, Pillsbury's Best®, Bakers', Kanabec, Pillsbury, Crown, Reform, and Carleton. Prominently featured was the notice: EXPORT TRADE A SPECIALTY. Of the brands named, Kanabec, Crown, Reform, and Carleton were used only in the export trade; the other four were used in both domestic and export markets. [39]

This advertisement, originally published in the *Northwestern Miller* on October 12, 1883, was the first by a milling company to appear in that journal. The company's invoice (right) also refers to its daily capacity of 7,500 barrels, a figure substantially exceeded in 1884.

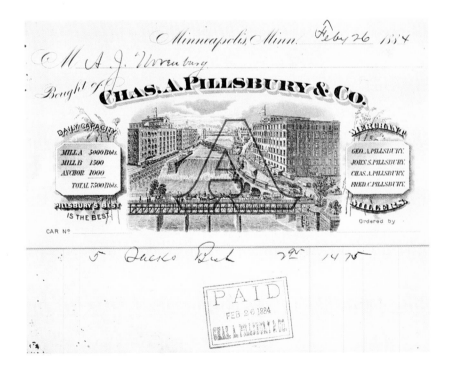

COMPLIMENTS OF
✳ A. M. GARBER. ✳
Selling Agent for the GREAT PILLSBURY FLOUR,

C-754 SALUNGA, LANCASTER CO., PA.

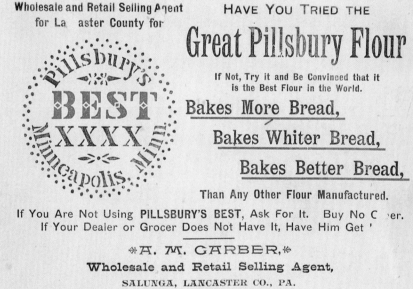

Wholesale and Retail Selling Agent
for La aster County for

HAVE YOU TRIED THE

Great Pillsbury Flour

If Not, Try it and Be Convinced that it
is the Best Flour in the World.

Pillsbury's
BEST
XXXX
Minneapolis, Minn.

Bakes More Bread,

Bakes Whiter Bread,

Bakes Better Bread,

Than Any Other Flour Manufactured.

If You Are Not Using PILLSBURY'S BEST, Ask For It.   Buy No C er.
If Your Dealer or Grocer Does Not Have It, Have Him Get '

✳ A. M. GARBER. ✳

Wholesale and Retail Selling Agent,

SALUNGA, LANCASTER CO., PA.

THE NEW ERA PRINT.

Postcard-size trade cards, printed in color, were popular in the late 1800s. The agent's name and product appeared on both sides of this 1887 card (left).

Obtaining enough wheat to make flour for such a large market was not a simple matter. Some people questioned whether the supply available would be great enough to run both the Pillsbury A and the Washburn A mills. As early as 1869 the principal Minneapolis millers had formed an organization to buy wheat from Minnesota and Dakota farmers. In 1876 this led to incorporation of the Minneapolis Millers' Association, which made purchases for and distributed wheat to member mills in proportion to their production. The arrangement drew the wrath of farmers, who believed it was depriving them of the best price for their wheat, and the practice became one of the burning political issues of the day. The controversy ended in 1881 when a group of businessmen established the Minneapolis Chamber of Commerce (later the Minneapolis Grain Exchange), and it became the principal market where Minneapolis millers purchased their wheat.[40]

The Pillsburys, however, ultimately decided to have on hand sufficient wheat of their own to protect against the vagaries of market price and supply. On July 13, 1882, they incorporated the Pillsbury and Hulbert Elevator Company to conduct a general grain and elevator business along the line of the Great Northern Railway Company in Minnesota and North Dakota. The Pillsburys' company, which changed its name in 1885 to the Minneapolis and Northern Elevator Company, was ultimately to own and operate 47 elevators and warehouses in North Dakota and 33 in Minnesota.[41]

Also around 1882, the mills began to mix various wheats in their flours. In *The Development of the Flour Milling Industry*, Charles Kuhlmann notes: "The English millers, having to deal with a wide variety of different kinds of wheat, were the first to make a study of wheat mixing. As early as 1880 American milling journals began to print extracts from scientific articles by European experts on this topic. In America, C. A. Pillsbury seems to have taken the lead in adopting new methods. In 1889 it was stated that he had two men constantly employed in testing wheat as it came into his mills. By this means he was able to mix low grade wheats with higher and still maintain a certain standard of strength. Incidentally, it was possible by this method to preserve a uniformity of quality in the flour."[42]

Charles's early insistence on quality went beyond the testing of wheat, and he required that baking tests of the flour be conducted as well. The *Northwestern Miller's* 1875 account of the company's new offices said the one-story building included a "doughing room" in which tests of flour were made. According to the report, "The entire arrangement of the room is with reference to securing the best possible light in order that tests of flour may be perfectly made."[43]

Pay scales offered by Charles and other millers to Minneapolis mill employees were higher than those of their local counterparts in other industries. Among skilled labor wages in other manufacturing establishments, the average daily wage was $2.31 for blacksmiths, $2.15 for carpenters, $2.17 for engineers, $2.45 for machinists, and $2.21 for painters. The average wage for grinders and machine tenders at Pillsbury was $3.25. The average daily wage for common laborers in all manufacturing establishments in Minneapolis was $1.32, or $.58 lower than for unskilled labor at Pillsbury.[44]

Charles and his partners had a high regard for the performance of their employees, and in 1883 the company established an employee profit-sharing plan, one of the first in American industry. At first it included all employees with five or more years of service; the eligibility requirement soon was reduced to two years. During five of the plan's first eight years, the company made distributions to the employees. The *Northwestern Miller* estimated a total of $150,000 disbursed in the five years, affording an employee "at the end of the year a check for a sum greater rather than less than a current annual interest upon his total yearly salary." A description of the plan in the September 1891 *Review of Reviews* quoted Charles as saying: "I was first led to adopt the system of profit-sharing from a desire to enter into some plan which would more equitably divide the profits between capital and labor. Of course the continual agitation of the labor question called my attention to the subject; but there was no disaffection among my own employees, so far as I was aware . . . As to the details of a profit-sharing scheme, I was not influenced by what others had done, and at that time knew absolutely nothing of the experience of others or the results of any kindred experiments."[45]

We do not know exactly what the profits of C. A. Pillsbury & Co. were; in those days business enterprises rarely divulged their profits or their sales. We do know that the Minneapolis milling industry was modestly profitable at best as the 1870s began, and that in the ensuing 20-year period Minneapolis millers experienced substantial swings in profit. Widespread installation of the new middlings purifier in the early 1870s had produced a period of major prosperity, stimulating rapid expansion. The *Northwestern Miller*, reporting on that period on November 8, 1889, noted: "With the flour . . . commanding $10 per bbl at the mill, and the price of wheat fluctuating from 60¢ to $1.25 per bu, it is readily to be seen how Mr. Pillsbury laid the foundation of his present fortune." Profits appear to have fallen again in the early 1880s, however, primarily due to an excess of supply. Herman Steen, for many years the secretary of the Millers National Federation, wrote of the substantial profits made during the early years of the new process: "It may well have been the most lucrative period in the industry's history, although by no means the only one. Earnings through most of the 1880s were perhaps drab in comparison with the

PLATE 2

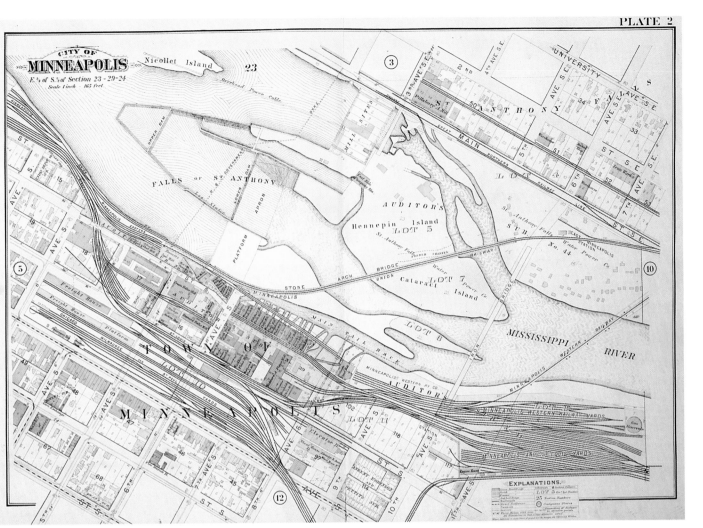

An 1892 *C. M. Foote Atlas* plate (above) included the west-side milling district as well as a portion of the east bank. See page 38 for detailed plats.

This battered photo (right) of the Anchor day crew, taken in 1889, was featured 32 years later in the Pillsbury employee publication, *Carry-On*.

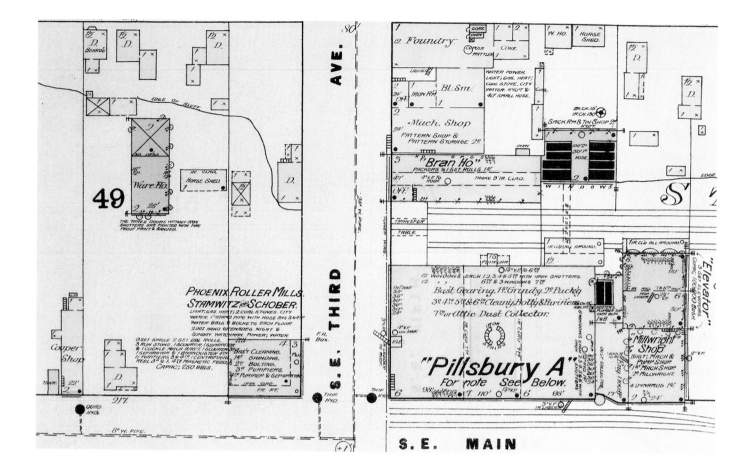

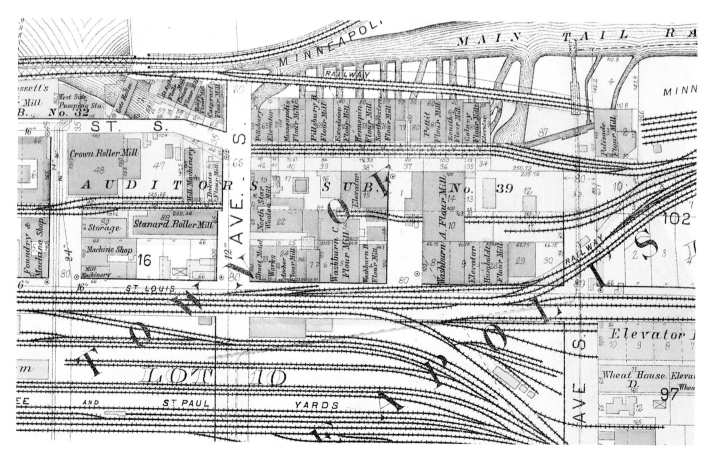

An 1885 *Sanborn Atlas* plate (left, top) depicts the Pillsbury A mill complex at that time. The *C. M. Foote Atlas* plate (bottom) shows the west-side milling district in detail in 1892.

opulent years, but they could hardly have been really unsatisfactory. However as the decade neared the end, several Minneapolis mills were experiencing losses, and the same condition prevailed elsewhere. For the first time millers were faced with a condition that continued nearly all the time for the next sixty-five years—an excess of milling capacity."[46]

While the precise amount of their earnings remains unknown, Charles and his partners in C. A. Pillsbury & Co. achieved remarkable results. Starting almost from scratch in 1869, the Pillsburys had emphasized quality, efficiency, and marketing, recognition of good ideas and good people. This and their uncanny sense of timing resulted in the largest flour milling business in the United States. Their magnificent new A mill produced more flour than any other mill in the world. They had carefully consolidated their position, and in 1889 they were unsurpassed in the industry. N. G. Ordway, territorial governor of Dakota from 1880 to 1884, capsulized the partnership's accomplishments: "The Pillsbury family . . . have collectively had more to do with the breadstuffs of this country than any other family, or any other set of men of the same number, in the world . . . this family have, by the erection of elevators and mills, and by introducing new milling processes, placed it within the power of the farmers of Dakota and Minnesota, and of the New Northwest, to get the best prices for their product, I only state what is acknowledged all over the world."[47]

The Minneapolis flour milling business underwent a complete change in that 20 years. In 1869 an aggregation of small flour mills produced a mediocre product consumed almost entirely in the surrounding region. In the 1870s the introduction of new milling techniques totally revolutionized the flour milling process, not just in Minneapolis but in the rest of the nation as well. The changes enabled Minneapolis millers to produce an excellent flour from the area's abundant supplies of spring wheat, and by 1882 the thriving young city was the foremost flour milling center in the country. But by 1889, according to Charles, "The business of making flour had been brought to so close a point by competition that it is only possible to succeed by using the latest machinery and adopting the best system. It is purely a matter of business and must be conducted scientifically." With the profits per barrel of flour closer to a dime than a dollar, successful companies were those, like Pillsbury, that produced a high volume of product at a low cost and marketed it successfully in both national and export markets.[48]

2 So Many Eggs in One Basket
1889–1908

Rumors that English capitalists were looking into the purchase of several of Minneapolis's largest flour mills began circulating in the spring of 1889. The stories had a certain plausibility. Wealthy investors in Great Britain, dissatisfied with the low rates of return on their British and American securities, were known to be exploring acquisition opportunities in the United States. Flour milling, which led all American industries in the value of its annual product, was an attractive and logical target. Minneapolis flour, in particular, was well known in Great Britain, for both its fine quality and its share of the market in that country.[1]

On July 4, 1889, a featured story in the *Minneapolis Tribune* related that three English visitors were in Minneapolis, reportedly to investigate its flour mills and waterpower companies. The story said it was hard to find a Minneapolis man who would go on record as believing that any purchases would occur, and it quoted Charles Pillsbury: "For the past two or three months there have been several parties here asking prices on different milling and elevator properties, and I understand there has been some figuring with water power companies. I have not yet learned that any of these negotiations have amounted to anything. No doubt, nearly all the property in Minneapolis, whether manufacturing or other property, can be bought if people are willing to pay the price at which the owners will sell, but I have not heard that anyone has received any money or absolute promise of any from any parties who have been here."

A week passed and the *Northwestern Miller*, without revealing its sources, reported that "An option on several valuable plants has been given to certain financiers, representing outside capital. The properties included in the proposed syndicate are those of C. A. Pillsbury & Company, Washburn Mill Company, the Washburn Flouring Mills Company, the East and West side water powers and the Pillsbury system of elevators." The story went on to say that "Should the deal be consummated, C. A. Pillsbury will manage the entire business." No date was given for either the grant or the exercise of the purported option.[2]

With English acquisition came a new look and the first mention in advertising of Pillsbury's Best® as a family flour. For the other side of this leaflet, see page 43.

The two Washburn companies referred to in the July 12 story were separately owned. The Washburn Mill Company was owned and operated by William D. Washburn, C. C. Washburn's younger brother, and consisted of the Palisade mill, located a block south of the Pillsbury B, and the Lincoln mill at Anoka, several miles upriver from the falls. The other company referred to by the *Northwestern Miller* was the C. C. Washburn Flouring Mills Company, which took title to the Washburn A, B, and C mills following the death of C. C. Washburn in 1882. These were operated in 1889 by Washburn Crosby Company.

Speculation continued on July 23, when a *Minneapolis Tribune* reporter noted a number of leading Minneapolis businessmen visiting the Pillsbury offices. He connected their visit to a prevailing rumor that options to buy the mills would expire that day, and he asked Charles whether the matter of a sale would be settled one way or the other during the day. Charles replied, "No, not necessarily. Under the strict terms of the option, I suppose either party could declare the deal off after today, but it is probable that today will not settle it. There is nothing new in the situation and it is impossible to say just when an official statement that the mills are or are not to be sold can be made." The next day's *Tribune* carried the reporter's conclusion that "the millers" had extended "the option" to October 1 or November 1.[3]

The first solid evidence that sale of the Pillsbury properties might be near came on Sunday, September 29, in a *Minneapolis Tribune* article with a Chicago dateline. Levy Mayer, a prominent Chicago lawyer, was quoted as announcing several important acquisitions made by two English syndicates he represented. Mayer said that title had been taken to a number of eastern and midwestern breweries, several northwestern grain elevator systems, and a few iron mines in Michigan. He added that arrangements had been made to purchase other businesses, including "the Pillsbury flour mills, of Minneapolis, Minn." and "the Washburn flour mills, of Minneapolis, Minn." He said that the syndicates he represented included a great number of British bankers and trustees of large estates in Great Britain, and that each business acquired by his clients had paid at least 12.5 percent for the past five years.

Responding to inquiries from the Minneapolis press about the Mayer announcement, George Pillsbury said that an option on Pillsbury properties had expired September 1 and had not been renewed. Charles added that "Very few people who were interested in the option given upon our plant are interested in it now." Charles denied knowing Mayer but said, "He may represent parties who have money enough to carry the deal through. All I can say is that the Pillsbury mills are not sold."[4]

The prospectus (the first page of which is shown at right) ended speculation about a sale to the British. Charles A. Pillsbury and product ingredients were featured on company advertising after the English acquisition. Above is the backside of the leaflet on page 40.

PROSPECTUS.

THIS Company is formed to acquire as a going concern and carry on the following Flour Mills, Businesses and Properties at Minneapolis, in the State of Minnesota—the heart of the wheat-growing area of the United States of America :—

1. CHARLES A. PILLSBURY & CO.
2. WASHBURN MILL CO. (The Palisade and Lincoln Flour Mills).
3. MINNEAPOLIS AND NORTHERN ELEVATOR CO.
4. MINNEAPOLIS MILL CO.
5. ST. ANTHONY FALLS WATER POWER CO.
6. 1,340 Shares (being the majority) of the Capital Stock of the ATLANTIC ELEVATOR COMPANY.

Flour Milling is the staple industry of Minneapolis, and the population of the City, which in 1880 numbered 46,000, now exceeds 200,000.

1.   Messrs. Charles A. Pillsbury & Co., own three freehold Flour Mills—the "Pillsbury A," which is by far the largest Flour Mill in the world, and is equipped with the best modern machinery and appliances, including Elevators, Machine Shops, and Electric light plant the "Pillsbury B," and the "Anchor," with a united capacity of about 10,900 barrels per day.

2.   The Washburn Mill Company, own two freehold Mills—the "Palisade" and the "Lincoln" (the latter being situated at Anoka), with a united capacity of about 2,500 barrels per day.

     The annual output of the Mills of Minneapolis, which is the greatest flour manufacturing centre in the world, is about 7,361,680 barrels. The Mills to be acquired by this Company turn out nearly 3,750,000 barrels per annum, being about half of the actual output.

     The flour produced at these Mills has a world-wide reputation.

3.   The Minneapolis and Northern Elevator Company own about 130 Elevators and Warehouses, spread over a large extent of country ; the land on which they stand being leased from Railroad Companies. At each of these depots grain is purchased from the farmers of the surrounding districts, or stored for their account. The total storage capacity is nearly 6,000,000 bushels. This Company has worked under arrangement with, and consequently acted as a feeder to, the Pillsbury Mills. Nearly the whole of the buildings have been erected within the last five or six years ; some are worked by steam, others by horse power. In addition, the Company owns a number of Dwellings at the various stations.

4 & 5.   The Minneapolis Mill Company and The St. Anthony Falls Water Power Company control the whole water power of the Mississippi River at Minneapolis, except the right to use a very small quantity of power which was ceded by these companies some years ago. Certain lands of these Companies not available for mill sites are excepted from the purchase.

6.   The Atlantic Elevator Company owns a terminal Elevator, with a capacity of about 500,000 bushels, fitted with working machinery and Electric Light plant, about seventeen acres of land attached, and forty-two Country Elevators and Warehouses, with a total capacity of about 740,000 bushels. All these Elevators, may be said to be quite new. The terminal Elevator is freehold ; the others stand on land leased from Railroad Companies and are worked by horse-power.

     The foregoing particulars have been supplied by the Vendors.

     The whole of the above properties have been valued on behalf of the Company by Mr. C. H. PETTIT and Mr. W. HOWARD WHITE, who were selected by Messrs. MORTON, BLISS & CO., of New York, and report as follows :—

GENTLEMEN,
     In accordance with instructions received from you, we have investigated and valued the Property and Plant of the following concerns :—

         (1.)   CHARLES A. PILLSBURY & CO.
         (2.)   THE "PALISADE" AND "LINCOLN" FLOUR MILLS.
         (3.)   THE MINNEAPOLIS AND NORTHERN ELEVATOR CO.
         (4.)   THE MINNEAPOLIS MILL CO.
         (5.)   THE ST. ANTHONY FALLS WATER POWER CO.
         (6.)   THE CONTROLLING INTEREST IN THE ATLANTIC ELEVATOR CO.

and report that the Properties to be acquired are of an aggregate value of $5,254,048, exclusive of goodwill.
     This valuation is made as the Property stood on the 1st July last, and includes the value of the two Water Power Companies which we have estimated at $1,603,515. This estimate is based upon the present net incomes and upon the value set by the City tax assessors upon the unused real estate of the two Water Power Companies, and upon general best information obtainable.
     The machinery, plant, buildings and everything connected with the Mills, Water Power Companies and Elevators, are well constructed and in excellent condition. The Mills are massively built of limestone upon rock foundations, with the exception of the "Lincoln" Mill, which is of wood covered with corrugated iron.
     The value of the property of the two Water Power Companies will in our opinion certainly increase with the growth of the City of Minneapolis, because these Companies own all the land suitable for Mill sites which can be reached by the water power furnished by the St. Anthony Falls.
     We consider the expenditure in the past on the Elevators, under the head of renewals and repairs, is sufficient to cover any depreciation. The only parts that depreciate, except in a very long and practically indefinite period, are the Sills and the Shingling. The former will need renewal perhaps once in seven or eight years, the latter after a somewhat longer period ; the expense of which renewals can be paid out of ordinary repair account.
     Every precaution has been taken to prevent damage by fire or by explosion, and all the Mills are provided with automatic sprinklers and with hose connected with abundant water supplies, and of course the property is kept insured. All the Mills are heated by steam and lighted by electric light.
     The amount of working capital which can be advantageously employed in the business intended to be taken over is estimated by us at $1,750,000.
     We believe, if we may forecast the future of the new Company, that taking into consideration the unique position of the Mills, the extensive Railroad connections which have grown up around them and the monopoly of the extensive water power which it will possess, hardly any other Milling Company, wheresoever situated, could enjoy the same advantages.
     The fullest enquiries have been made into the position and value of the concerns to be taken over, and no effort has been spared to base the valuation upon a sound and conservative footing.

Yours respectfully,

C. H. PETTIT,

W. HOWARD WHITE.

     PETTIT & WHITE have advised that, by the expenditure of about $1,200,000 the value of the Water Power may ʼsed by upwards of $2,000,000, and the Directors have therefore reserved power, should they hereafter decide recommendation of the Valuers, to issue additional Debentures to an extent necessary to provide funds

The Palisade, one block south of the Pillsbury B, and the Lincoln, in Anoka, had been owned by the Washburn Mill Company, part of the English acquisition. They are shown at the turn of the century and in 1916, respectively. The Pillsbury A mill can be seen across the river from the Palisade.

Whether the statements of the two Pillsburys were part of the bargaining process or intended to accommodate the desire of the English for secrecy, serious negotiations to sell the company were clearly under way. One month later the four owners of C. A. Pillsbury & Co. signed an agreement dated October 29, 1889, selling their three flour mills and the Minneapolis and Northern Elevator Company to a newly formed English company, Pillsbury-Washburn Flour Mills Company, Limited. The agreement provided for the purchaser to begin operations on November 1.

In addition to Pillsbury's mills and elevator system, Pillsbury-Washburn contemporaneously acquired from William D. Washburn the Washburn Mill Company, the majority interest in the Atlantic Elevator Company, and all the capital stock of Minneapolis Mill Company, which controlled waterpower rights on the west side of the falls. From James J. Hill, founder of the Great Northern Railroad, it purchased the capital stock of the St. Anthony Falls Water Power Company, owner of the waterpower rights on the east side of the falls. With these acquisitions, the English company gained control of five flour mills that produced about half the output of all Minneapolis mills, approximately 170 elevators and warehouses spread throughout the Minnesota and Dakota wheatlands, and the waterpower rights on both sides of the Falls of St. Anthony. Thus began a period of English ownership that would continue until 1923, when another generation of Pillsburys would form a United States corporation to reacquire the Pillsbury properties.[5]

With one important exception, the properties acquired by the English were identical to those that the July 12 *Northwestern Miller* reported as optioned to an English syndicate. The English company did not acquire the C. C. Washburn Flouring Mills Company. While it was generally believed that an English syndicate had obtained an option on the company, no sale was ever consummated, and later attempts to acquire the company for Pillsbury-Washburn were unproductive. According to one report, "the old rivalry" between the Pillsbury and C. C. Washburn interests prevented their joining forces.[6]

C. A. Pillsbury & Co. remained in existence after the sale. Its three surviving partners and the heirs of Fred Pillsbury retained the non-flour-milling assets of the partnership. They also continued to own and operate two Minneapolis grain elevators under Charles's management.[7]

The Pillsbury-Washburn Flour Mills Company, Limited, was capitalized for £1,635,000, the equivalent of $7,929,750 at the then-current rate of exchange of $4.85 to the pound. The capital was divided into 50,000 8-percent cumulative preference shares of £10 each,

50,000 ordinary shares of £10 each, and £635,000 in 6-percent first mortgage debentures. Provision was made for increasing the debenture issue at a later date by an amount not to exceed £240,000.

The four Pillsburys received $4,325,000, of which $3,225,000 was paid in cash, $500,000 in debentures, and $600,000 by delivery of 6,185 preference and 6,185 ordinary shares. Washburn was paid $1,525,000, also divided among cash, debentures, and shares, and Hill received $300,000 in cash and $100,000 in debentures. As a part of the agreement, the Pillsburys paid a total of $500,000 to the underwriters of the company's stock and debentures, as did Washburn.

Pillsbury-Washburn Flour Mills Co., Ltd., retained Charles A. Pillsbury (left, at his desk in 1896) as managing director, and William D. Washburn (above) as one of the "Committee of Management in America."

Contemporary observers offered a variety of reasons for the decision to sell, some attributing it to the price, some to the advanced ages of John and George, and others to the partners' desire to be free from the risks, hard work, and heavy capital demands of the flour milling business. Charles himself, testifying a little more than a year later before a U.S. Senate subcommittee investigating the effects on the American workman from foreign acquisition of American properties, said simply that the Englishmen offered a good price, and as they had so many eggs in one basket, the partners thought it desirable to make the deal. It is probable that several factors contributed to the decision, including the excellent sense of timing that had characterized the firm's history.[8]

Pillsbury-Washburn had about 300 stockholders. Its first board of directors consisted of four London businessmen. Richard H. Glyn, a bank director, was chairman; the other directors were J. Flower Jackson, a member of a firm of hops merchants; Sydney T. Klein, a flour merchant whose firm handled Pillsbury flour sales in Great Britain; and E. T. Rose, who was associated with the investment banking firm that underwrote the company's debentures and shares of stock.[9]

In addition to the board of directors, the company's articles provided for a "Committee of Management in America." The board appointed to the committee Charles A. Pillsbury, chairman, John S. Pillsbury, and William D. Washburn, thereby retaining the managements of the acquired companies. Washburn, then 58 years old, was a prominent figure in the Minneapolis business and financial community. Shortly after coming to Minnesota in 1857, he became secretary and agent of the Minneapolis Mill Company, organized by C. C. Washburn and others. In succeeding years he was active in flour milling, lumbering, real estate, railroad promotion and organization, and other businesses. Washburn served three terms in Congress before being elected to the U.S. Senate in 1889, where he served one term. Defeated for reelection in 1895, he returned to his various business and philanthropic pursuits in Minneapolis.[10]

The purchase agreement with the Pillsburys stipulated that Charles would act as "managing director" of the company in Minneapolis for a period of five years. His salary was fixed at $15,000 per year, plus a bonus of 10 percent of the profits after a 12-percent dividend was paid to ordinary shareholders. The agreement specified that Charles and John "shall in the conduct and management of the affairs of the company conform to the directions of the English Board of Directors."

The prospectus issued by Pillsbury-Washburn included a report by its chartered accountants that the profits of C. A. Pillsbury & Co. and Minneapolis and Northern Elevator Company, together with the

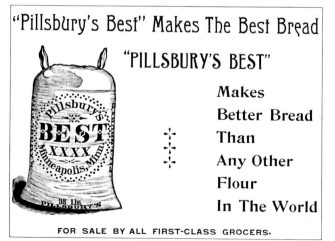

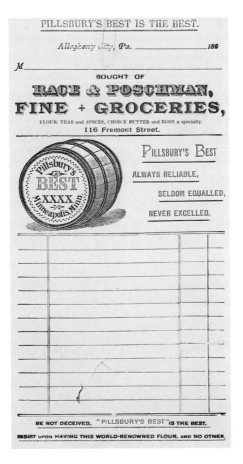

Pillsbury-Washburn lost no opportunity to tout its flour. In the 1890s it ran ads in the University of Minnesota's *Gopher Yearbook* (left, top 1892, bottom 1896) and advertised on its order forms (above) as well. The 196-pound barrel was the standard consumer size. The 98-pound sacks were known as "halves."

two Washburn mills, had averaged $808,152 per year in the six-year period from 1883 through 1888. Adding the most recent year's actual or estimated profits of the Atlantic Elevator Company and the two waterpower companies, the accountants projected total annual profits for all the acquired companies of about $900,000, which the prospectus said would enable the company to pay the interest on its debentures, the dividends on its preference shares, and a *15-percent* (prospectus italics) dividend on its ordinary shares, leaving $128,000 for management expenses and reserves. The prospectus included this statement from the appraisers of the properties: "We believe, if we may forecast the future of the new Company, that taking into consideration the unique position of the mills, the extensive railroad connections which have grown up around them and the monopoly of the extensive water power which it will possess, hardly any other milling company, wherever situated, could enjoy the same advantages."

The glowing promise of the prospectus notwithstanding, London's *Financial Times* soon published a rumor that the public subscription for the company's shares and debentures raised somewhere around $2 million, leaving the underwriters with an obligation to supply about $5 million of the company's capital.[11]

The sale was part of a major shift in the flour milling industry. From an industry characterized by a large number of small, individually owned mills, the structure rapidly changed to one dominated by a few large, publicly owned companies. The economics of the industry forced many small mills into combination, as survival became dependent upon sales volumes large enough to absorb the increasing costs of operation. Three years after the sale of the Pillsbury mills, 80 percent of the Minneapolis production was concentrated in three companies: Pillsbury-Washburn with five mills and a capacity of 14,800 barrels per day, Northwestern Consolidated Milling Company with six mills and 10,050 barrels, and Washburn Crosby Company with three mills and 9,900 barrels.[12]

The change in structure of the flour milling business was accompanied by a sharp rise in the amount of flour produced in the United States. Emphasis was on increased production, as the large concerns worked to establish market dominance. In 1894, the Duluth Imperial Mill ran a full-page ad in the *Northwestern Miller*, exulting about its record 7,905 barrels in one day. The Pillsbury A quickly responded with 24-hour totals over 9,000 barrels. During Pillsbury-Washburn's first ten years, its flour production rose from about 2,500,000 barrels to nearly 5,300,000 barrels of flour annually. In the same period flour exports from Minneapolis alone jumped from 1,557,575 barrels to 4,593,000. Such huge volume increases of a commodity product led to even stronger competition and, all too often, to dangerously low profit margins for such a capital and labor intensive business.[13]

Nevertheless, the new company's start was auspicious. Net earnings for its first fiscal year, actually a ten-month period ending August 31, 1890, were $691,876. On an annualized basis this exceeded the amount cited in the prospectus as necessary for a 15-percent dividend on the ordinary shares. After paying the debenture interest and the preference dividend, however, the directors declared only a 10-percent dividend on the ordinary shares and placed $184,000 in a surplus reserve. One shareholder, who questioned the amount of the ordinary share dividend at the October 30 annual meeting, was advised by Chairman Glyn that the board thought it best to establish a large reserve in order to maintain dividends in the future.[14]

The first year's annual report showed expenditures of about $125,000 for ordinary repairs and renewals, together with $153,000 for capital improvements, including about $73,000 to bring the two Washburn mills to a par in efficiency and quality of flour with the Pillsbury mills. Chairman Glyn predicted that the same level of expenditures for repairs and renewals would continue. Part of this expense, as in succeeding years, went to expand production capacity.[15]

The second year's profits were $573,120, a considerable drop. The directors acted to pay the debenture interest, the preference dividend, and with about $28,000 from the reserve, a 6-percent dividend on the ordinary shares. Before the end of 1890, Fred Pillsbury left the company to join the management of Northwestern Consolidated Milling Company, and Pillsbury-Washburn extended Charles's management contract to ten years. Fred's 17-year milling career ended tragically when he died from diphtheria on May 15, 1892.

The company moved its Minneapolis headquarters in 1891 to the prestigious Guaranty Loan Building, later the Metropolitan Life Building. The new 14-story building, described as the first skyscraper west of Chicago, also housed the offices of the rival Northwestern Consolidated Milling Company. Despite the proximity of the Minneapolis milling companies, competition was intense, a fact frequently mentioned in the Pillsbury-Washburn reports to shareholders. Two responses by C. A. Pillsbury & Co. to an 1889 *Northwestern Miller* survey suggest that this degree of competition was not necessarily appreciated. The company stated that combinations of millers to regulate output were practicable and desirable, and that ''the greatest evil of the trade consisted of believing what your eastern correspondents say as to the price your neighbors are selling their flour for.''[16]

The subject of wheat speculation and excessive purchases of wheat during Charles's management would receive recurring attention in the next several years. Rumors abounded that the second-year drop in Pillsbury-Washburn's earnings was caused by speculative losses in wheat, but according to the stenographic record of the

In August 1890, the Pillsbury-Washburn office staff gathered in front of the Second Avenue entrance to the Windom Block (top). The next year the company moved its Minneapolis headquarters to the Guaranty Loan Building (bottom).

annual shareholders' meeting in 1891, Glyn said: "It is not true, as has been reported all over the place, that the company's shortage has arisen from speculation in wheat. (Hear, hear.) Nor has it arisen from any excessive purchases of wheat beyond what was necessary for the requirements of the company. We have not gambled in any way, either directly or indirectly, in the buying or selling of wheat."

Speculation in the purest sense consists of trading in a commodity for the sole purpose of profiting from the trade, and in that sense Glyn undoubtedly was correct in denying that the company had been speculating in wheat. Few public companies engage in such speculation, since the practice could cause large swings in earnings from year to year, adversely affecting stock prices and jeopardizing the regular payment of dividends. Usually a mill buys wheat some months before grinding it into flour. For example, in March a mill may buy a million bushels of wheat intending to sell the flour in September or October. To hedge, the mill immediately enters into a futures contract to sell an equal amount of wheat for delivery in September. When September arrives, any gain or loss in the price of wheat in inventory is offset by an opposite gain or loss in the futures contract. The result is that the mill's profits will be little affected by fluctuations in wheat prices between the time the wheat is purchased and the time it is ground into flour and sold.

Losses just as real as those from pure speculation, however, could follow from a practice of carrying large inventories of unhedged wheat. Accepted accounting procedures required a company's fiscal year-end wheat inventory to be valued at market price. Consequently, if unhedged wheat purchased during the fiscal year by Pillsbury-Washburn at $1.00 per bushel, for example, had a market value on the following August 31 of only $.90, then the company's earnings for the fiscal year would be charged with a ten-cent-per-bushel loss on all the wheat in store on August 31.

The policy of C. A. Pillsbury & Co. was to carry about two million bushels of wheat, a two-months' supply for the mills. This practice, according to Charles, had served the company well and helped produce profits in 19 of the company's 20 years. When Pillsbury-Washburn commenced business, its board of directors authorized Charles to follow the same policy. While this enabled the new company to achieve satisfactory results in 1890 and 1891, declining wheat prices in 1892 led Charles to write Glyn in June that "the bottom had dropped out of the wheat market again" with the average cost of the company's wheat at $.96 a bushel and the market at $.78. Charles continued, "We had better . . . carry no more heavy stocks of wheat and flour without hedging. This policy, while it will never pay big dividends, will pay fair dividends . . . and I think a conservative policy which would be sure to pay 5 to 6% on our stock for a series of years, ought eventually to bring our stock to par in your country.'' The price of wheat did not recover by the end of the fiscal year, and in 1892 the company was obliged to charge $418,841, the difference between the cost of the wheat and flour in store and its market value on August 31, 1892, against earnings. The directors voted not to pay a preference dividend for the year, barring declaration of an ordinary share dividend as well.[17]

For reasons not now apparent Charles's "conservative policy" of hedging was not adopted. Similar declines in the price of wheat in each of the next two years required earnings to be charged with $795,185 and $505,000, respectively, with the result that in 1893 and 1894 the directors again voted against payment of a dividend on the preference shares.

Finally, at the shareholders' meeting on November 22, 1894, Glyn announced that the board had "come to the conclusion that it will be better, for the present at any rate, instead of carrying, as we have been doing, two months' stocks, to carry a fortnight's stocks, which will only mean 500,000 to 600,000 bushels altogether." Charles, in attendance at the meeting, told shareholders that if the property were his own, he would continue the old policy until prices had attained a higher level and restored the losses of the past three years. But, he said, if the shareholders "want a policy which will insure you regular, fair dividends, instead of one which is bound to give irregular dividends, it will please me and the balance of the directors to have you so decide."[18]

Despite the heavy penalties of the preceding three years, two shareholders at the meeting questioned the wisdom of changing the policy. The chairman closed the meeting with this temporizing observation reported by the December 7, 1894, *Northwestern Miller*: "With regard to the change of policy, it might be well to give Mr. Pillsbury power to increase the period for carrying wheat, if he deemed it advisable. At any rate, the directors would bear in mind the opinions expressed, and he thought the shareholders might safely leave the matter with them, to do what they considered in the best interests of the company. (Hear! hear!)''

Pillsbury-Washburn's difficulties were compounded by the deteriorating state of the national economy. The Panic of 1893 led to a depression that continued into the second half of the decade. Commerce and industry stood still while Congress debated such crucial economic issues as a new tariff bill and the country's gold standard. The labor union movement was growing rapidly, and flour milling workers felt its effect. Prices were under heavy pressure, too. The company's average price for a barrel of flour fell from $4.12 in 1892 to $2.83 in 1896, and farmers were obliged to sell their wheat at low prices for most of the decade. The company's depressed earnings necessitated a wage reduction early in 1895, and the old rates were not restored until November 1.[19]

Vitos (above 1897), Flaked Oat Food (right, top 1898), and Germos (bottom 1897) were the first new consumer products introduced by Pillsbury-Washburn. The products were advertised with die-cut folders, cards, and magazine ads, respectively.

Meanwhile, the waterpower companies, unlike the flour milling operations, were providing dependable, consistent profits. As soon as Pillsbury-Washburn commenced business, it placed both the east-side and the west-side waterpower companies under a single management. William de la Barre, the highly respected Austrian engineer who had been manager of the Minneapolis Mill Company, was placed in charge of both power companies, reporting to Charles. From the outset, the board provided de la Barre with ample funds for maintenance, enabling him to keep the dam and falls in excellent repair.

Charles had declared before the acquisition that waterpower at the falls was not being fully exploited. Accordingly, he and de la Barre began to study the long-distance transmission of electricity, an emerging concept nationwide. As a result of their studies, they were able to develop plans for construction of a new dam about 2,200 feet downstream from the old one. The new structure would incorporate a power plant, which would utilize 44 waterwheels to drive ten dynamos, each capable of generating 1,000 horsepower. Planning accelerated when the Twin City Rapid Transit Company, in the process of converting from horse-drawn to electrically operated streetcars, expressed interest in buying power from the proposed plant.[20]

Thomas Lowry, president of the streetcar company, accompanied Charles to London, where they presented plans for the new dam and power plant to the Pillsbury-Washburn shareholders at their annual meeting in 1894. The shareholders approved the project, authorizing issuance of $955,450 in debentures to meet its costs. Construction began in May 1895, the dam was completed on March 20, 1897, and the streetcar company took a 40-year lease on the power.[21]

In the same year the new dam was dedicated, the company introduced its first new consumer product. With Pillsbury's Best® Family Flour an established household staple, the company began in 1897 to manufacture ready-to-cook breakfast cereal at the A mill. The first product to reach the market was Vitos, a packaged, wheat breakfast food so successful that it led Washburn Crosby Company to enter the breakfast food business. According to an 1899 letter written by an owner of the competing firm, ''Pillsbury has been putting up and selling Vitos for two years and is doing such a large business in it, that we have been compelled to take up this line ourselves. We are told that his profits from the sale of this article are large. This will give him money to advertise his flour with and we cannot afford to leave the field free to them.''[22]

Vitos was joined shortly by Pillsbury's Flaked Oat Food, a packaged oatmeal product, and Germos, a special dietetic flour. Encouraged by these early successes, the company purchased an abandoned paper mill, and de la Barre designed plans for construction of ''the finest cereal mill in the country'' on its site. The five-story mill, adjacent to the Excelsior and christened the Pillsbury C, was designed to turn out 500 barrels of oatmeal and 500 cases of Vitos per day.

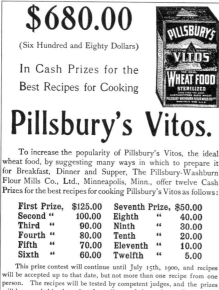

The new C mill (top 1900) was built to produce flaked oat food, which did not succeed. On the other hand, Vitos, which advertised in the *Cosmopolitan*, did well. This 1900 recipe contest (bottom) was the earliest precursor of the Pillsbury Bake-Off® contest.

When the mill was completed in the fall of 1900, the company decided to leave production of Vitos at the A mill, and the new C mill began to produce oatmeal in small packages, sacks, and barrels. The oatmeal business did not flourish, however, and early the next summer the company sold the milling and packaging machinery. Vitos continued to be sold for some years, however, and it was fondly remembered by a consumer who wrote the company in 1966: "I recall my Dad and Mother, poor immigrants from Sweden . . . debating whether or not they could afford a box of this wonderful breakfast food, and how eagerly we awaited as Mother prepared the nourishing, health giving, body building, sterilized . . . breakfast food. And, as I recall, it was smacking good." [23]

Introduction of the new cereal products helped focus attention on the company's marketing system. Originally, flour milling companies had relied on commission merchants to sell their flour outside the state. Even before 1889, however, the company and its larger competitors were moving away from sole dependence on commission merchants. Instead they were selling through brokers, making direct sales to jobbers and wholesale grocers, and even employing their own salesmen. In answering the 1889 *Northwestern Miller* survey, the company said it preferred direct sales by its own salaried agents, and in 1894 Charles reported that the company had agents in New York City, Albany, Buffalo, Portland, Pittsburgh, Chicago, and other large cities. A few agents, he said, were on salaries, some sold on commission, and others bought directly for resale. In succeeding years, the company continued to open sales offices in outlying cities and to build up its force of salaried salesmen. [24]

Trade regulation legislation was virtually nonexistent, and Pillsbury-Washburn followed competitive practices common to the day. It parceled out specific territories for its brokers and jobbers and made certain that no one else sold Pillsbury products there. The company was also watchful of the prices at which grocery stores sold its products, and it protected prices by threatening to deny its products to offending merchants. [25]

Probably no practice of the 1890s illustrated the magnitude of Pillsbury-Washburn's flour business more vividly than the so-called flour trains. For many years Minneapolis millers had accumulated large stores of flour in Buffalo warehouses, from which they could quickly fill carload orders for the eastern trade. A transit privilege granted by the railroads permitted flour to move to customers at the railroad's through-rate, rather than at the more expensive combination rates from Minneapolis to Buffalo and from Buffalo to the final destination. When the railroads withdrew the privilege of breaking shipments at Buffalo, the mills began to send special trains, made up of as many as 36 cars carrying 7,200 barrels of flour, to Buffalo. From Buffalo the flour continued without transfer from the cars, at the through-rates, to carload customers at various cities throughout the eastern United States. [26]

Pillsbury-Washburn used incentive programs for its sales force. This 1903 catalog (above) encouraged salesmen with an array of traveling trunks and other personal items.

"Flour Flyers" left the mill district each day for cities in the eastern United States. The train was featured on a postcard (right) written in 1907.

Trade cards (above, 1895) and ads (right, 1904) emphasized the company's role as an exporter.

Henry L. Little, a protégé of Charles A. Pillsbury, became the manager of Pillsbury-Washburn in 1897 and general manager when Charles died. His dealings in the wheat market were to become well known.

In 1895 the company posted its best earnings in four years. Dividends on the preference shares resumed, and the three years' accumulation of unpaid preference dividends was paid off by the sale of $679,000 in 7-percent income certificates. The improvement came in the face of Charles's report to the shareholders that 1895 was "the worst yet," with overproduction and excessive competition causing millers to sell flour "at any price." Glyn reminded shareholders at the November 26 meeting of the preceding year's decision to carry reduced wheat stocks, saying, "If we had been obliged to take over on August 31 as large a stock of wheat as we took over last year, there would have been no dividend at all. In view of this, I think you will agree that the policy has been a successful one." He was rewarded with an approving chorus of "Hear, hear!"[27]

Profits in 1896 showed continued improvement, reaching $518,848, but in 1897 earnings fell about 10 percent. The company had correctly anticipated a wheat shortage and bought more wheat than had been its recent custom; concurrently it introduced a policy of hedging. Flour price margins were low during the year, however, and flour milling profits suffered. The company's annual earnings were far below the $900,000 potential detailed in the 1889 prospectus, and on December 1, 1897, a seemingly dispirited Charles wrote Charles D. Rose, one of the company's large shareholders in London, that "The milling business was very poor the last six months of last year. We were barely able to hold our own. The advance in wheat did not help us any, because we are forced to the policy of carrying no stocks of wheat, but keeping hedges out against all stocks. So that we lost on the hedges, as much, or more, money than we made on the actual advance in wheat . . . The policy we are compelled to adopt (by vote of the directors) does not give us any benefit of the rise in markets, and prevents our losing much, if anything, on falling markets."

After 28 years of constant, close attention to the affairs of the company, Charles was ready for a rest. Sir William Forwood, one of the company's directors, visited Minneapolis for a few days in October to observe the company and acquaint himself with the workings of the business. He reported to the board that "Mr. Pillsbury goes down to the office at 8 o'clock and seldom leaves before 7," and concluded that it would be to the interest of the business to relieve him a little by appointing Henry L. Little manager. Charles agreed, and on November 12, 1897, the board voted Little's appointment, with the understanding that he would report to Charles, the general manager.[28]

Little, 40 years old and another native of New Hampshire, was a protégé of Charles, who hired him as an office boy in 1879. He worked for three years in the shipping department before going into the field as a traveling salesman for the company. In 1889 he returned to Minneapolis as sales manager and assistant to Charles, the position he held at the time of his appointment.

For some time Charles had planned a Pacific Coast vacation with his family, possibly to be followed by a trip to China and Japan. After writing Forwood on December 1 that "Mr. Little is taking hold, first rate," Charles left early in 1898 for California. Rather than continue to the Orient, however, he returned to Minneapolis after several weeks and resumed his duties with the company.[29]

Shortly after Charles returned from the West Coast, the first of two developments placing heavy strain on the company's Anglo-American rapport occurred. Early in 1898 a Chicago grain trader, Joseph Leiter, had set out to corner the Chicago May wheat market. Charles was celebrated in the Minneapolis milling community as its leading bull. He never overlooked an opportunity to advocate high wheat prices for the farmer and believed that, as he once wrote a London correspondent, "The simple fact is that it is easier to make twenty cents a barrel profit on flour when wheat is high, than it is to make five or ten cents with wheat at lower prices." Charles undoubtedly was impatient over the low wheat and flour prices that had prevailed for most of the decade. He saw in Leiter's undertaking a means to send the price of wheat up and, with it, the price of flour. Leiter was purchasing huge quantities of wheat on contracts calling for May delivery, indeed forcing the price of wheat to as high as $1.75 per bushel. Most of those selling to Leiter were selling "short," relying on their ability to buy wheat in the market for cash in time to fulfill their sales contracts with Leiter.[30]

On May 4, 1898, Charles wrote Glyn, advising him of Leiter's attempted corner and reporting that Peavey (a Minneapolis grain firm) and Charles had agreed with Leiter to keep their substantial stocks of wheat off the market so they could not be purchased by the "shorts." "I write you this," said Charles, "so that, in case Mr. Leiter should, some fine day, put the price of Chicago May to $1.75 or $2, you will not wonder why we do not sell our wheat. In good faith, we cannot do it, no matter how high that he may put the price." It is clear from other correspondence that Pillsbury-Washburn's stores of wheat substantially exceeded policy limits set by the English directors, and that the wheat purchases were not hedged.

The Leiter attempt to corner the market failed, and the price of wheat dropped sharply, as Leiter's sellers moved train- and barge-loads of wheat into Chicago to fulfill their contracts with Leiter. Leiter, who had contracted to buy at prices as high as $1.85 per bushel, lost between $10 and $12 million. In a civil suit in Chicago more than 15 years later, Leiter testified that he failed because the late F. H. Peavey and the late C. A. Pillsbury, who he declared were virtually his partners, released wheat on the Chicago market in late May.[31]

Sir William Forwood, one of the Pillsbury-Washburn directors in London, visited Minneapolis and recommended appointment of Henry Little as manager in 1897.

The company's earnings in 1898 matched the year before, but flour milling earnings had dropped from $251,909 to $24,474, the lowest on record. On the other hand, elevator earnings, principally derived from the Minneapolis and Northern Elevator Company, were excellent. On December 2, 1898, Glyn told shareholders that "The mills did very poorly. It was the old question that has happened to us so often, viz. loss on stocks of wheat . . . I am bound to tell you, however, that in spite of cables, letters, protestations of all sorts from the London board to the management at Minneapolis, we found ourselves landed with a much larger stock of flour [*sic*] than if our orders had in any way been attended to. The board, recognizing that this thing has happened very often before, that it has always been the same story, and that we were in a rather serious position, and also feeling that our business is not to hold large stocks, but to buy our wheat and make our flour, deputed me to go to Minneapolis and see what could be done to put the business on a more commercial scale."[32]

Charles told his side of the story in a long letter to Sir William Forwood on August 30, 1899. With respect to excessive purchases of wheat, he wrote, "I do not mean by this to defend myself or the Board of Directors [*sic*] in buying more wheat than we were authorized to buy; but the reports that were going over every week to Mr. Spencer (which were, presumably, given to the Directors) showed distinctly that we were doing it." In reference to the company's 1898 earnings, he said, "The wheat ground by the Pillsbury-Washburn Company last year stood on an average of 93½ cents per bushel, although the price during the season ran from 75 to 1.62 . . . This average of 93½ cents was more than two cents a bushel less than if we had bought our wheat on the market every day in the year; consequently the company never lost one cent on account of our carrying the unusually big stock of wheat . . .

"Now, as an actual fact, the wheat controlled by the Minneapolis & Northern Elevator Company, which was country wheat, was not mentioned in the talk between Mr. Leiter and myself; and when the market got away up to the top, I insisted on that wheat being sold, against the protests of some of the directors who had been doing the most kicking. And that is why the Minneapolis & Northern showed the profit it did. If we had not disobeyed your orders and bought and sold that Minneapolis & Northern wheat, we would not have paid the dividends on the Preferred Stock last year."

In the topsy-turvy market caused by the Leiter affair, Pillsbury-Washburn probably had a better year in 1898 than had Charles followed the well-understood policy of the board. It is certain, however, that during that year the relationship between the British chairman of the board and the American general manager of Pillsbury-Washburn reached its nadir. At the December 2 annual meeting, thanking two

Important to Flour Buyers.

CONSIDERABLE publicity has been given the past three months to the efforts made by certain parties to secure our mills for the purpose of forming a gigantic flour mill trust.

We want every buyer of flour the world over to thoroughly understand that the mills owned by this Company will at all times be operated strictly on a competing basis, and will never become part of any combination or trust.

No matter what course other millers may pursue, flour buyers can feel absolutely safe and secure in building up trade on

"Pillsbury's Best."

It is of the highest and most uniform quality, and will at all times be sold at **Anti=Trust** prices.

PILLSBURY-WASHBURN FLOUR MILLS CO., LTD.
MINNEAPOLIS, MINN., U. S. A.

★ MEMBER ANTI-ADULTERATION LEAGUE.

HENRY L. LITTLE,
MANAGER.

Sydney T. Klein, a British director, described Pillsbury-Washburn's chairmanship as "not a bed of roses." One reason was Thomas McIntyre's attempt to form a monopoly of flour milling concerns, which the company opposed publicly (left) in the *Northwestern Miller*.

of the co-directors for their remarks regarding his reelection as chairman, Glyn lamented piteously, "It is true, as Mr. Klein says, that my position is not a bed of roses, but you may take it that we do our best, though we have been a little handicapped by operations on the other side."

As Leiter's attempt at a corner ran its course, a second cause of discord developed. Thomas A. McIntyre, a New York promoter with substantial financial backing, sought in early 1898 to form a gigantic combination of some 15 flour milling companies in New York City, Syracuse, Buffalo, Milwaukee, Duluth and Superior, and Minneapolis. If he could bring all these companies under single management, he would have a near monopoly in the flour milling trade. The key to success, however, lay in his ability to gain control of either Pillsbury-Washburn or C. C. Washburn Flouring Mills Company, or both.

From the beginning, McIntyre was opposed by the Pillsburys and other Minneapolis shareholders of Pillsbury-Washburn, who saw major flaws in his business plan. But the English shareholders were another matter. Their expectations of large returns from Pillsbury-Washburn shares had not materialized. Would it not be a better bet to have their investment in an American trust, one enjoying a near monopoly in the field?

There was uncertainty in Minneapolis as to how the English shareholders would react to McIntyre's scheme, but it was clear that a vote of the shareholders would be necessary to adopt it. In his letter to Forwood on August 30, 1899, Charles recalled that when Glyn was in Minneapolis he told Charles he would not discuss the question of consolidation with McIntyre for at least another year. "Well," wrote Charles, "Mr. Glyn went east with Mr. McIntyre, and then crossed the ocean with him; and the conversion which took place was more miraculous than that of Saul of Tarsus. As soon as he got there, he began cabling me favoring the scheme." A number of major Pillsbury-Washburn share and debenture holders, including Charles Rose, were thought to be leaning toward the McIntyre plan. So the Minneapolis management quickly organized a team to go to England for two purposes: to prevail upon shareholders there to oppose the McIntyre plan, and to buy enough shares in England so that in any vote of the shareholders the McIntyre plan would be defeated. The team included Alfred F. Pillsbury, the son of Governor John S. Pillsbury, Arthur T. Safford, manager of the company's Buffalo office, and L. P. Hubbard, treasurer of the company.[33]

By January 1899 the Minneapolis group appeared to own or control enough shares to defeat any McIntyre sale. The London office cabled Minneapolis January 13 that "for the present" the English directors would have no further negotiations with McIntyre. On January 12, 1899, Little estimated that the Minneapolis investor group,

Charles M. Amsden, manager of the company's elevator operations, was appointed to the American management committee in December 1898.

headed by John S. Pillsbury and "our friends in Europe" held 8,228 ordinary shares and 22,484 preference shares. The group continued to acquire shares and on February 16, 1899, the American management committee (excepting Charles, who was vacationing in Europe) signed an open letter to shareholders informing them that the company would not be sold to McIntyre. The letter asserted that "a large majority of both classes of shares, ordinary and preference, are now owned by the original shareholders of this company, and by their friends . . . [and] a majority of all these shares are now owned and held by citizens of the United States."[34]

McIntyre was also thwarted in his attempts to acquire the C. C. Washburn Flouring Mills Company, but he did succeed in buying control of Consolidated Milling Company, the successor to Northwestern Consolidated Milling Company and the largest in Minneapolis. It was not enough. Although McIntyre's United States Flour Milling Company commenced business, it survived only briefly before going into receivership in February 1900.[35]

At the annual shareholders meeting on December 2, 1898, the directors announced the appointment that fall of Little and C. M. Amsden, manager of the elevator operations, to the American management committee. It also recorded with deep regret the death of George A. Pillsbury on July 17, 1898. After moving from Concord to Minneapolis in 1878, George had quickly won recognition in his new home, and he had served as president of the Minneapolis Chamber of Commerce, mayor of Minneapolis from 1884 to 1886, and president of the Northwestern National Bank of Minneapolis from 1880 until his death.

Charles, undoubtedly as disappointed as anyone in the results of the decade and wearied by the strain of the Leiter and McIntyre affairs, experienced a sharp decline in his own health late in 1898. In early December, shortly before the McIntyre affair was resolved, Charles left for Europe and Egypt on an extended vacation with his family. He did not return to Minneapolis until the following May. His health had measurably improved, but only to the point that his doctors allowed him to spend two or three hours a day at his office. On Saturday, September 16, he became ill, and on the following day he died in his home at age 57.[36]

Charles had, in his short lifetime, established himself as one of the greatest flour millers of all time. An entrepreneur of the same caliber as contemporaries Andrew Carnegie, Philip Armour, Cyrus McCormick, and James J. Hill, he helped revolutionize the industry's manufacturing and marketing systems, and he amassed a fortune in the process.

It is unfortunate that Pillsbury-Washburn, and particularly its flour milling operations, fared no better during Charles's lifetime. The *American Miller* quoted Charles as saying, with respect to Pills-

William de la Barre, an Austrian-born engineer, managed Pillsbury-Washburn's waterpower companies. He designed the company's C mill and was named to the American management committee in 1899.

bury-Washburn's flour milling profits during its first ten years, that "Had we made even the minimum profit that the closest and most calculating farmer in the state said we should make, namely 3 cents per bushel, it [the ten-year profit] would have been over $5,000,000. I am sorry to say that our profit has not come anywhere near this latter sum; sorry, because I believe that it has not been fairly remunerative to the millers." A detailed tabulation in the company's files reveals that for the nine years ending August 31, 1899, the company earned an average of only 1.42 cents on each bushel of wheat it milled.[37]

Responsibility for the poor results cannot be laid at the door of any one individual. In at least three of the nine years, heavy charges against profits were directly attributable to the carrying of excessively heavy stocks of unhedged wheat. This was not Charles's policy alone; the board of directors, and probably the American management committee, concurred in it. The nettlesome relationship between Charles and Glyn in the last few years was exacerbated by both the Leiter and McIntyre maneuvers, but they were hardly the cause of the anemic flour milling earnings. More probably, two outside factors prevented better results. The first was the long period of economic turmoil in the United States, and the second was the turbulent condition of the flour milling business itself, as the century's final decade witnessed the emergence of a very few large companies struggling for primacy.

It was to Charles's great credit that the famed company he had managed for more than 30 years continued to reflect his insistence on what had made Pillsbury best—high-quality products and first-class manufacturing facilities. As he wrote the secretary of the company on December 24, 1897, "Whatever else can be said about our business, one thing is sure, and that is that we have maintained the high standard of our flour, and have retained the confidence of all our customers."[38]

On October 13, 1899, a month after Charles's death, Glyn cabled Little with the "board's unanimous request" that John S. Pillsbury accept chairmanship of the American management committee and its announcement that de la Barre had been appointed to the committee. Little became general manager of the company and continued as a member of the American committee along with John Pillsbury, Washburn, Amsden, and de la Barre. Two years later, on October 18, 1901, John S. Pillsbury died at age 73. The first Pillsbury to settle in Minnesota, he was the last surviving partner of C. A. Pillsbury & Co. During his lifetime, he was heralded as one of Minnesota's foremost citizens, honored for his great service to the state as governor and as "Father of the University of Minnesota." Alfred F. Pillsbury took his father's place on the American committee, and Washburn succeeded him as committee chairman.

The company's earnings in 1900, Little's first year as general manager, held about even with those of the preceding year. That May the company's ordinary shares were quoted on the London Stock Exchange at £5½ to £6½, and its preference shares at £10½ to £11½. After having paid in 1899 the first ordinary share dividend since 1891, the directors omitted a common stock dividend in 1900. Still their hopes rose that regular dividends on the stock would be possible. Frank Spencer, secretary of the company, wrote Little on August 9, 1901, that "The majority of the ordinary shareholders on our registers bought their shares at an average of considerably under £5 per share, and if they get a 4% dividend which they surely will with rare exceptions, under our present system of running the company, they really get a better return for their money than the preference holders, a great many of whom have paid a premium for their shares."

Although Spencer's letter did not explain "our present system of running the company," a 400,000-bushel limit apparently was placed on the company's wheat inventories, and Little was obliged to make weekly status reports to the board.[39]

As the country moved into a new century, Minneapolis mill-workers and their unions had begun to talk about shortening their 12-hour working day. Labor at first considered asking for a ten-hour day, but after about two years of meetings and negotiations, the Minneapolis mills adopted in 1902 a basic schedule of three eight-hour shifts, six days a week. Time-and-a-half was paid for Sunday work. The flour loaders and a few other craftsmen, however, accepted a ten-hour day.[40]

The following year, the Minneapolis flour loaders demanded an eight-hour day at the same $2-per-day wage they had been receiving for ten hours of work. The companies rejected both the demand and the unions' requests for arbitration, whereupon union leadership called a strike against Pillsbury-Washburn and the other two largest Minneapolis milling companies. The companies responded by operating the mills with office workers, college students, and other local and imported workers. When the possibility of violence threatened, the companies set up dormitories and dining facilities in the mills; at one point Pillsbury-Washburn served a total of 3,000 meals a day in a kitchen and dining room established in its new C mill. Gradually the mills returned to almost full production with nonstriking personnel. By late October only one of the 22 struck mills remained idle, and the strike was over.[41]

In 1905, the United States shareholders again attempted to change the company's domicile from England to the United States and to retire the 6-percent debentures by selling debentures with a lower rate. The United States shareholders, led by Washburn and the Pillsburys, had sought the domicile change as early as 1899 in order

Minneapolis flour mill workers (above at the A mill in 1902) negotiated an eight-hour work day, six days a week, that year.

Pillsbury-Washburn also advertised its animal feed business. This simple ad (right) ran in the December 1905 issue of *Flour & Feed*.

PILLSBURY'S BEST FLOUR

is the standard flour all over the world, and

PILLSBURY'S FEEDS

are also the best feeds.

PILLSBURY'S MILLS make the best food for man, and the best wheat feeds for live stock.

Please Mention FLOUR & FEED in Writing Advertisers.

The horse-drawn delivery wagon (top, left) was the standard until Pillsbury-Washburn bought its first electric truck in 1904 (bottom).

to lessen their taxes. The English government imposed a substantial tax on the transfer of deceased American shareholders' shares. In addition, unlike the United States, England had an income tax. English companies recouped themselves by deducting a proportionate part of the tax from interest and dividend payments to its debenture holders and shareholders. A change in domicile required an affirmative vote of three-fourths of both preference holders and ordinary shareholders. Although a simple majority of both preference and ordinary shares were in American hands in 1905, the proposal never reached a vote.[42]

To strengthen its performance in the export market, in 1904 and 1905 the company experimented with the grinding of Canadian wheat in bond, that is, segregating the Canadian wheat and the flour milled from it so that none of the flour was sold in the United States. The Tariff Act of 1897 permitted milling foreign wheat duty-free provided it was exported after milling. The November 16, 1904, *Northwestern Miller* reported that Pillsbury-Washburn took the initiative in this movement, which, because of the lower prices of Canadian wheat, was seen as enabling United States millers to retain their export market. Both the Palisade and Lincoln mills ground the Canadian wheat. The *Northwestern Miller* reported on April 19, 1905, that exports of flour by the large mills of the Northwest showed a decrease in the present crop year of over a million barrels and said, "Had it not been for the operation by the Pillsbury company of two of its mills for about three months on Canadian wheat, the showing would have been even more unfavorable."[43]

In 1904, the company purchased a 21,000-pound electric truck, the "first of its kind ever used in the west." It was guaranteed to operate under full load at six miles per hour for 25 miles, powered by a single charge to its 44 storage batteries. The truck delivered flour to the Minneapolis trade, and soon after its arrival was said to convey in 2½ hours more than three teams could deliver in half a day.[44]

The company continued to expand its steady and dependable waterpower operations. When the demand for electrical power began to exceed Pillsbury-Washburn's production capacity in 1906, the board authorized construction of a second hydroelectric plant. Located on Hennepin Island just below the old dam, it drew water from the St. Anthony millpond through a 350-foot canal, returning it to the river below the falls via a long tailrace. Completed on December 1, 1907, at a cost of over $300,000 financed in part by a £43,000 debenture issue at 6-percent interest, it added 12,000 horsepower to the 10,000 produced at the original plant. It was leased for 25 years to the Minneapolis General Electric Company, which subleased it to the Twin City Rapid Transit Company. Charles's early decision to exploit the waterpower of the falls, together with his entrustment of the waterpower operations to de la Barre, had been of great benefit to the company. Spencer, writing de la Barre on May 7, 1907, observed, "We

Once tasted – Never wasted

The New Food

PILLSBURY'S BEST CEREAL

MADE BY THE PILLSBURY WHO MAKES "THE FLOUR"

Your Grocer Has it Now

One two-pound package makes 12 lbs. of delicious, creamy white food—always granular in form, even after cooking.

The cereal success of the day—just "The White Heart of the Wheat" sterilized. If you have not tried it do so to-day.

PILLSBURY'S BEST CEREAL STERILIZED
THE WHITE HEART OF THE WHEAT KERNEL
PILLSBURY WASHBURN FLOUR MILLS CO LTD
MINNEAPOLIS, MINN, U.S.A.

FOR BREAKFAST

Stir slowly one half cup into two and one half cups of boiling water, salt to taste and boil 1½ minutes. If too thick add boiling water. Serve hot with cream and sugar. When cold it makes a delicious luncheon dish, fried and served with syrup. Numerous dainty dinner desserts can be prepared with fruit and jelly.

"PILLSBURY'S BEST" TOOK THREE GRAND PRIZES

AT THE ST. LOUIS WORLD'S FAIR.

Quality recognized,—the famous Pillsbury's Best Flour received

↷ GRAND PRIZE for the HIGHEST GRADE of FLOUR
↷ GRAND PRIZE for the FINEST EXHIBIT
↷ GRAND PRIZE for the BEST LOAF of BREAD.

This Book Free

if you send coupon below and six cents in stamps for postage and wrapping.

The wonderful loaf of bread that took the GRAND PRIZE at the St. Louis World's Fair was baked by a woman using Pillsbury's Best Flour. The remarkable simplicity and effectiveness of her methods, induced us to have her Recipes made up in the form of a handsome 128 page book.

The Recipes are for all kinds of plain and fancy cooking and they all are what a woman calls practical and economical.

They give stylish appearance as well as delicious flavor to home cooking without extra work or expense.

We know of no cook book like this one.

Address PILLSBURY
MINNEAPOLIS
MINNESOTA

COUPON
Cut this out and mail with 6 cents in stamps for postage and wrapping to PILLSBURY, MINNEAPOLIS, MINNESOTA.

Name
Street and Number
City and State
My Grocer's Name (This line must be filled out.)
If the book please me I will try Pillsbury's Best Flour.

This "Book for a Cook" is 5½ x 9 inches and contains 128 uniquely illustrated pages. A practical book for practical home-makers.

A BOOK for a Cook

Always use Pillsbury's Best Flour

A Little Book for A Little Cook

Always use Pillsbury's Best Flour

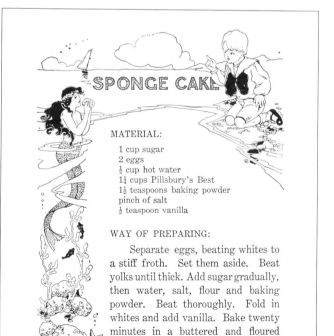

SPONGE CAKE

MATERIAL:

1 cup sugar
2 eggs
½ cup hot water
1¼ cups Pillsbury's Best
1½ teaspoons baking powder
pinch of salt
½ teaspoon vanilla

WAY OF PREPARING:

Separate eggs, beating whites to a stiff froth. Set them aside. Beat yolks until thick. Add sugar gradually, then water, salt, flour and baking powder. Beat thoroughly. Fold in whites and add vanilla. Bake twenty minutes in a buttered and floured shallow pan in moderate oven.

Pillsbury's
BEST

Sets the Pace
for Flour Excellence
the World over

In 1904, 1905, and 1906, Pillsbury-Washburn promoted its products in magazine ads (top, far left), in its first cookbook promotion (top, left), in a children's cookbook (bottom, far left and left) and with a needle case give-away (above) at the Louisiana Purchase Exposition in St. Louis.

all wish that the other branches of our business were as remunerative as the water power, for had it not been for the revenue received from this source our company would have ceased to exist many years ago.''[45]

The directors' reports to the shareholders for the years 1900 through 1906 referred frequently to the difficulty of making money in the milling business. The reports blamed recurring poor performances and unsatisfactory earnings for every year but 1904, when the company earned an all-time high of $734,785, on such catastrophes as poor-quality wheat, high cost of wheat, declines in prices of millfeed, absence of foreign trade, and excessively keen competition. Spencer wrote to de la Barre on May 7, 1907, that ''The flour business seems to be under one continual cloud . . . Just think what it would mean to us if we could only make three pence a barrel on all the flour we sold.'' Three pence per barrel was equal to about six cents in United States money, the average per barrel earnings during Charles's tenure as general manager.

In the year following John S. Pillsbury's death, Henry Little began to establish a reputation for skillful operations in the wheat market. One 1902 newspaper carried the headline ''How Henry Little Captured for his Company's Mills about all the Good Milling Wheat in Sight.'' It related Little's success in obtaining all wheat remaining from the 1901 crop, ''taking it from men who did not want to part with it and securing it at the lowest prices of the season.'' On May 17, 1905, a *Minneapolis Times* headline proclaimed ''Henry L. Little Running Corner in May Wheat.'' The story reported Little's heavy purchases in the Minneapolis wheat market, and suggested that he was involved earlier in an abortive attempt by the famous John Warne ''Bet-you-a-Million'' Gates to corner the Chicago May wheat market.[46]

At the eighteenth annual general meeting of the shareholders in London on December 13, 1907, the directors announced earnings of less than $450,000 in fiscal 1907. Their report stated that ''In the early spring of this year, reports of extensive damage having been done to the growing crops resulted in great speculation, and an important rise in the price of all grain. The price of wheat was forced up 30 to 40 percent, and was kept up by speculators considerably above the relative price of flour, making profitable milling impossible for several months.''

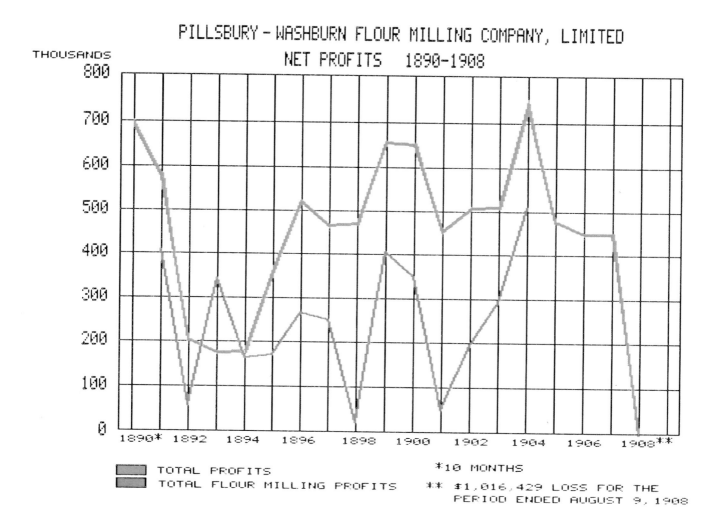

PILLSBURY – WASHBURN FLOUR MILLING COMPANY, LIMITED
NET PROFITS   1890-1908

TOTAL PROFITS
TOTAL FLOUR MILLING PROFITS

*10 MONTHS
** $1,016,429 LOSS FOR THE
    PERIOD ENDED AUGUST 9, 1908

The United States was in the throes of a currency panic at the time, and ordinary banking facilities across the country had been largely suspended. The directors reported that because "all the available funds of the company are at the moment required to carry on current business," they would recommend that the shareholders declare a preference dividend but postpone its payment until, in the opinion of the board, the company's cash position warranted such payment.

By May 16, 1908, the currency panic had ended, but that day the company's secretary wrote preference shareholders that "The Directors regret that their advices from Minneapolis . . . show that the conditions of business continue to be so difficult and unsatisfactory that the payment of the dividend is not practicable, and consequently I am instructed to inform you that it must be treated as indefinitely postponed."

As the company neared the end of the 1908 fiscal year, postponed dividends remained unpaid. Then on August 9 a Reuters cablegram appeared in the British press reporting that, with the concurrence of the company, Pillsbury-Washburn's general assets had passed into the hands of American receivers. Official confirmation reached the stunned stockholders in a letter dated August 12 from the Pillsbury-Washburn directors: "This company, which has always enjoyed a reputation second to none, has found it necessary to the conservation of the interests of its creditors and shareholders, to place its property temporarily in the hands of the court in order that the rights and interests of all parties in any way concerned may be fairly and effectually preserved."

Mills in Operation

Business Resumed

BY THE

Pillsbury - Washburn Flour Mills Co., Ltd.,

Minneapolis, Minn., U. S. A.

All Contracts to Be Filled.

No flour like "PILLSBURY'S BEST"

Under Management of

Albert C. Loring	
Charles S. Pillsbury	Receivers
Albert C. Cobb	

3 A Nice Mess
1908–1911

The August 9 announcement of Pillsbury-Washburn's receivership came with "dramatic suddenness," completely surprising the general body of its security holders. Pillsbury-Washburn's board of directors and two members of the American management committee had been just as surprised, a few days earlier, to learn that collapse of the company was imminent.[1]

Anyone close to the company in the summer of 1908 was aware that its weak cash position would not allow payment of the preference dividend declared the preceding December. And on July 1, 1908, Frank Spencer, managing director of the company, questioned a proposed land acquisition because "our present working capital is too small." But despite such signs of malaise, it seems generally to have been accepted that the prevailing economy was the cause of the company's problems. Once the economy straightened around, surely the milling business would return to normal, too.

As the month of July wore on, however, the company's cash position became serious enough that de la Barre cabled his concern to Spencer. Acknowledging the cable on Wednesday, July 22, Spencer thanked de la Barre and wrote: "The news contained in your cable came as a surprise and also as a shock for we have not received one word of warning from either the Committee, or Treasurer, that any danger existed and for anything we could tell in the absence of explanation, we could only surmise that the lowness of cash was accounted for by careful finance." Spencer informed de la Barre that Glyn had written Alfred Pillsbury, who represented the Pillsbury family on the American management committee. Alfred was planning a European vacation and Glyn, according to Spencer, had requested that Alfred meet with the English directors as soon as he arrived in London.[2]

At about the same time, Alfred was learning about the company's cash difficulties from quite another quarter—three of the company's principal bankers. Their message was that Pillsbury-Washburn's credit had fallen so low as to threaten the company's survival unless additional capital could be provided. Clive T. Jaffray, who in 1908 was a vice-president of the First National Bank of Minneapolis, later recalled: "While playing golf one day in the year 1908

A Pillsbury-Washburn ad in the *Northwestern Miller* on August 19, 1908, reflected the seriousness of the company's condition but let everyone know it was still in business.

with a prominent grainman, I was informed by him that he thought the Pillsbury-Washburn Milling Company was in trouble because of the speculation of its President, who sold wheat which he did not own. He bought a great deal of wheat at high prices, not paying for it at the time. It then dropped in price but he still had to pay the original cost.

"The next day I had a meeting with Mr. Decker of the Northwestern National Bank and Mr. Chamberlain of the Security National Bank to tell them what I had heard, inferring however, that it had been merely a matter of common gossip. Nevertheless, we decided to call in the three Pillsbury boys, Alfred, Charlie and John, to discuss the situation which we felt the company was in. This apparently came as quite a surprise to them."[3]

The meeting of the bankers with Alfred, 38, the son of the late Governor John S. Pillsbury, and with Charles S. Pillsbury and John S. Pillsbury, the 30-year-old twin sons of Charles A. Pillsbury, led to a decision by the Pillsburys to advance $1 million to the company on the security of a second mortgage. But while arrangements for the financing were being made, the Pillsburys were brought up short by an alarming discovery. Not only was the company almost out of cash, it also owed approximately $1 million on notes issued in the company's name but not recorded on its books! This development ended any thought of Alfred, Charles, and John to lend funds to the company. It also ended the prospect of any further bank credit.[4]

There is no record of the date on which William D. Washburn, chairman of the American management committee, learned of the crisis, although his first awareness of the situation must have corresponded closely with Alfred's. In 1908 Washburn was 76 years old, largely retired from business, and absent from Minneapolis a good share of the time. The remaining members of the American management committee—Henry Little, William de la Barre, and Charles Amsden—were involved in the company's day-to-day operations, and both Little and Amsden were signers on the unrecorded notes.

On Monday, July 27, Alfred cabled the board of directors to report "discovery of over $1,000,000 Company's indebtedness greater than supposed or Auditor's statement shows" and to advise of his immediate departure for London to lay the facts before the board. He arrived in London on Tuesday, August 4, accompanied by Ralph Whelan, a member of the Minneapolis law firm employed as the company's local counsel. The board members and Alfred joined efforts to raise more capital, but they were unable to interest lenders in either the United States or Europe.[5]

This serene view of the Pillsbury A mill
around the turn of the century gave no hint of
what was in store in 1908.

UNITED STATES CIRCUIT COURT,

DISTRICT OF MINNESOTA,

FOURTH DIVISION

THE SECOND NATIONAL BANK OF ST. PAUL,
NORTHWESTERN NATIONAL BANK OF MINNEAPOLIS,
FIRST NATIONAL BANK OF MINNEAPOLIS,
SECURITY NATIONAL BANK OF MINNEAPOLIS,
SWEDISH-AMERICAN NATIONAL BANK OF MINNEAPOLIS,
and JOHN S. PILLSBURY,

Complainants,

IN EQUITY.

against

PILLSBURY-WASHBURN FLOUR MILLS COMPANY, Limited,

Defendant.

TO THE HONORABLE JUDGES OF THE CIRCUIT COURT OF THE UNITED STATES, FOR THE DISTRICT OF MINNESOTA, FOURTH DIVISION.

The Second National Bank of St. Paul, The Northwestern National Bank of Minneapolis, Minnesota, The First National Bank of Minneapolis, The Security National Bank of Minneapolis, The Swedish American National Bank of Minneapolis, and John S. Pillsbury bring this their bill of complaint against Pillsbury-Washburn Flour Mills Company, Limited, and thereupon your orators state and represent to the Court as follows:

1. That The Second National Bank of St. Paul, one of your orators, is a national banking corporation created, organized and existing under and by virtue of the several Acts of Congress relating to national banks, having its office and principal place of business in the City of St. Paul, in the State of Minnesota, and that it is and always has been a citizen of the State of Minnesota.

2. That each of your orators, The Northwestern National Bank of Minneapolis, The First National Bank of Minneapolis, The Security National Bank of Minneapolis and The Swedish American National Bank of Minneapolis is a national banking corporation created, organized and existing under and by virtue of the several Acts of Congress relating to national banks, and that each of them has its office and principal place of business in the City of Minneapolis, in the State of Minnesota, and that each of them is and always has been a citizen of the State of Minnesota.

3. That John S. Pillsbury, one of your orators, is a resident of the City of Minneapolis, in the State of Minnesota, and is and always has been a citizen of the State of Minnesota.

4. That the defendant, Pillsbury-Washburn Flour Mills Company, Limited, is a foreign corporation created, organized and existing under and by virtue of the laws of the United Kingdom of Great Britain and Ireland, and that the defendant was at the time of its organization, and ever since has been and now is a foreign corporation and a citizen and subject of the United Kingdom of Great Britian and Ireland

5. That the defendant, Pillsbury-Washburn Flour Mills Company, Limited, is now indebted to your orator, The Second National Bank of St. Paul, in the sum of fifteen thousand dollars ($15,000.00), evidenced by a promissory note made and executed by the defendant in said sum of fifteen thousand dollars ($15,000.00), and which matured on the 6th day of August, 1908; that at the maturity of said note payment thereof was duly de-

[1]

The bill of complaint against Pillsbury-Washburn Flour Mills Company, Limited (the first page of which is shown above), asked for the appointment of receivers to take possession and to manage the properties of the company.

On the day the complaint was filed, these three men were named receivers: Albert C. Cobb (left, top), a Minneapolis attorney, represented the banking interests. Charles S. Pillsbury (left, bottom), the son of Charles A. Pillsbury, represented American interests in Pillsbury-Washburn. Albert C. Loring (above), the highly respected president of Consolidated Milling Company, was according to Charles "the one man we all had to have."

Meanwhile in the United States, Charles S. Pillsbury, John S. Pillsbury, and the banks and their attorneys were considering their next step. Although the mills were still operating, cash was virtually depleted, further credit was unobtainable, and an average $900,000 in notes was scheduled to mature in each of the months from August through December. Under these circumstances, the only choice lay between bankruptcy and receivership proceedings. Bankruptcy would mean an immediate forced sale of the company's assets to satisfy creditors and the end of Pillsbury-Washburn as a going concern. A receivership would allow the company to continue operations under a receiver until it could be either reorganized or sold, preferably as a single unit. If successful, the receivership might result in full payment to creditors as well as some return to shareholders. But a receivership would almost certainly take longer than a bankruptcy proceeding.

The decision by the banks and other major creditors in favor of receivership was supported strongly by the Pillsburys and apparently by Washburn as well. In England Pillsbury-Washburn's counsel, W. W. Paine, advised the board of the possible shareholder benefits from a receivership, and the board voted not to oppose the proceedings.[6]

A St. Paul bank, four Minneapolis banks, and John S. Pillsbury filed a bill of complaint in the United States Circuit Court, and it was presented to Judge Myron Purdy in Minneapolis on Saturday, August 8, 1908. The banks claimed a total of $340,000 in unpaid notes, and John S. Pillsbury was described as owning 1,894 shares of the company's preference stock and 1,978 of its ordinary shares. That same day the court ordered a receivership and appointed Albert C. Loring, Charles S. Pillsbury, and Albert C. Cobb, a Minneapolis attorney, as receivers.

Loring was essential to the receivership as far as the Pillsburys were concerned. Before Alfred left for London, the three Pillsburys had talked with Loring, the highly regarded president of Consolidated Milling Company, about his becoming a receiver. As Charles wrote Alfred in England on August 20: "I had a great many talks with Mr. Loring, and he finally said he would come down as receiver, if we three would agree on practically the terms we talked before you went away. That is, we would use our best efforts to reorganize and continue the Company, and give him the agreed salary with the percentage we talked of before. Of course, he was the one man of all we had to have, and I finally convinced him to accept the receivership. The banks original proposal was for the representatives of the three banks to be the three receivers. Of course, this was impossible, and they finally agreed upon Mr. Cobb as their representative, and they wished me to be the one representing the Pillsbury interests. So after much delay on this question, the present three were agreed upon."

This caricature of unknown origin is labeled

"Henry L. Little of Minneapolis."

The Pillsbury-Washburn receivership was reported on the front pages of Twin Cities newspapers on Sunday, August 9. The stories reported verbatim the language of the complaint, which alleged that "the business of the defending company was for many years a very successful and profitable business and would have so continued had it not been for the bad management of the same during the past few years under which management large losses have been made."

The *American Banker,* published in New York City, commented on August 22, that "The receivership of the parent company has developed a lot of information as to conditions which it is difficult to either diminish or refute. The various partisans affirm or deny that there has been speculation which would account for the stress of the company; also that there has been faulty methods of bookkeeping which tended to establish a false supposition of security; also that there has been an excessive amount of deadwood in the organization which consumed profits without giving any adequate service in return."

No one in the company undertook to elaborate upon the complaint's allegation of "bad management." Little, denying "emphatically" that his speculation in the wheat market on behalf of Pillsbury-Washburn had contributed to the company's downfall, resigned on August 10. By the end of the week he had moved his family east. L. P. Hubbard, the company's treasurer, who with Little had signed the unrecorded notes on behalf of Pillsbury-Washburn, retired on August 19. Amsden, who endorsed the notes as treasurer of the Minneapolis and Northern Elevator Company, remained in the company's employ and, like the others, maintained silence.[7]

William H. Dunwoody had no doubts about the genesis of Pillsbury-Washburn's difficulties. A contemporary of Charles, he had been an officer of Washburn Crosby Company and its predecessors since 1877, and in 1908 he was its vice-president. In a letter dated August 19, 1908, he wrote: "The P/W failure was a very bad one. Henry Little and his associates followed out the plan that was in use by their predecessor, by looking to speculation in wheat to make a considerable part of their profits. The usual result followed. While at times they made money, in the long run they lost very heavily in their speculative deals. Somehow or other they were able to conceal their losses from the auditors, who went through the accounts once a year, but is now said that the losses amount to over two million dollars. One defense that Henry Little makes is that he carried a large loss that C. A. had incurred in one of his deals, I suppose during the Leiter speculations which occurred a year before C. A.'s death, and he had been trying to make money enough to cover this up. This was a very poor excuse. I think the whole of their organization was demoralized by the speculative disposition of their predecessor."[8]

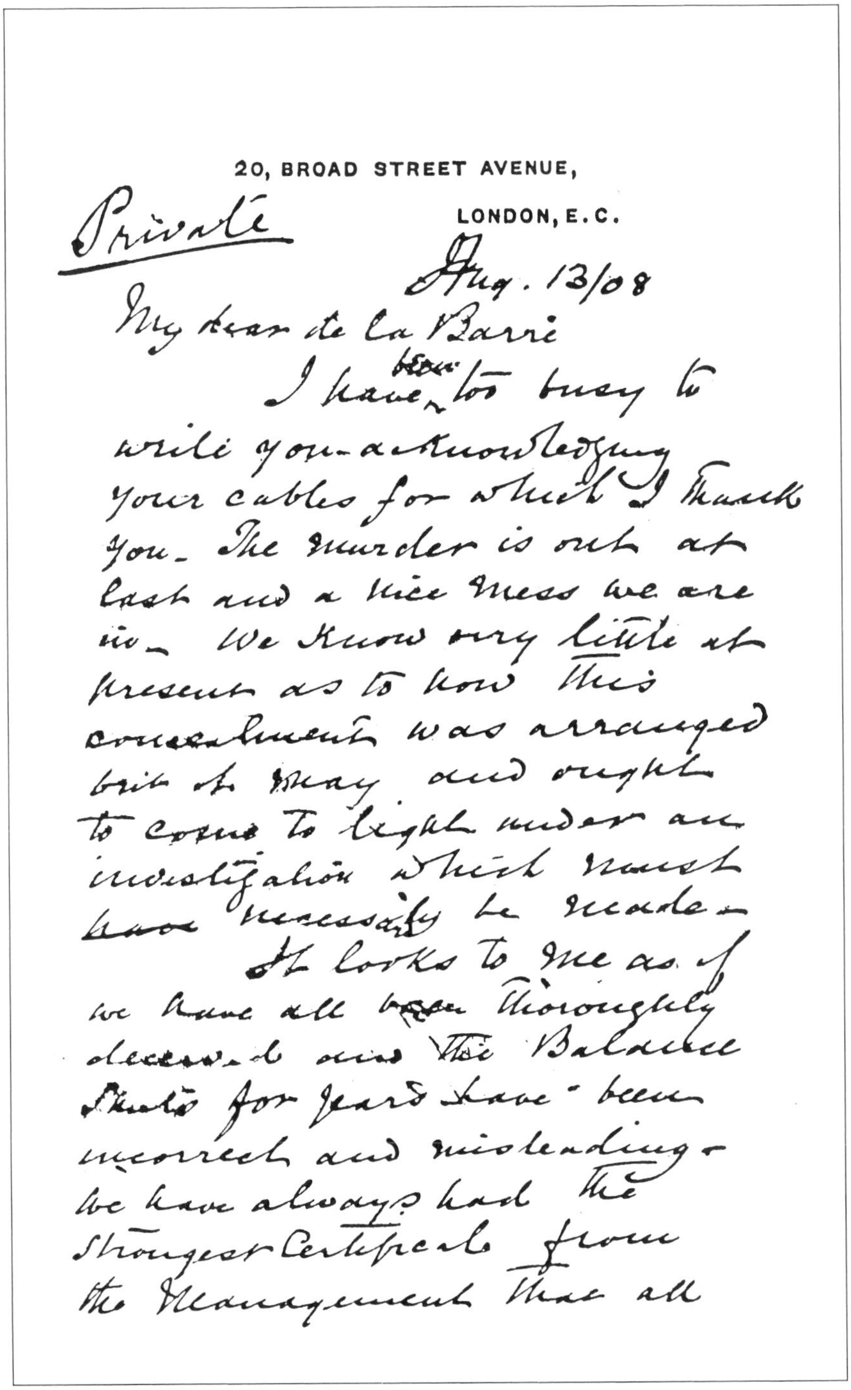

20, BROAD STREET AVENUE,

Private

LONDON, E.C.

Aug. 13/08

My dear de la Barre

I have been too busy to
write you—acknowledging
your cables for which I thank
you. The murder is out at
last and a nice mess we are
in— We know very _little_ at
present as to how this
concealment was arranged
but it may and ought
to come to light under an
investigation which must
have necessarily be made—
It looks to me as if
we have all been thoroughly
deceived and the Balance
Sheets for years have been
incorrect and misleading—
we have always had the
strongest Certificate from
the Management that all

Frank Spencer wrote William de la Barre on
August 13, 1908, that ''the murder is out at
last and a nice mess we are in.''

Meanwhile, the receivers lost no time in restoring the company's operations. The mills had closed down on Saturday afternoon, the day the court signed the receivership order, but the A mill reopened the following Tuesday at full capacity. The other four mills remained closed pending a full inventory. Ancillary receivers were appointed to protect assets from suits by creditors in other states where the company had property. A creditors' committee, chaired by Gilbert G. Thorne, a New York banker, was formed to represent the unsecured creditors and to work with the receivers. Marwick, Mitchell & Co., chartered accountants, were employed to make a full report on the company's assets and liabilities as of August 8, 1908. Substantial reductions were made in the number of office personnel.

In England the board of directors notified the shareholders and debenture holders of the receivership on August 12, informing them of the discovery in Minneapolis of large liabilities concealed from the board, the American management committee, and the company's auditors. The shareholders in England and the debenture holders proceeded to establish protective committees. Both groups pressed for appointment of a receiver to represent the English interests, and as a result, on October 8, John B. Niven of the New York and London accounting firm of Touche, Niven & Co. became the fourth receiver.[9]

The two waterpower companies, both in sound condition and generating strong profits, were left out of the receivership; they were the English company's principal source of revenue during the period. A separate receivership was ordered for the subsidiary Minneapolis and Northern Elevator Company, so that the court could supervise the total milling operation. Amsden and Henry F. Douglas were appointed co-receivers. Amsden resigned a few weeks later when the receivers, in order to conserve cash, leased the elevators to him and a partner for a term ending September 30, 1909. In addition to paying taxes, insurance, and maintenance, the lessees paid an annual cash rent of $25,000 plus a half-cent per bushel of grain put through the elevators.[10]

The Marwick, Mitchell & Co. report on the company's assets and liabilities was completed September 30. The accountants determined that on August 8, 1908, the company's assets exceeded its liabilities by $1,145,637, excluding the waterpower assets and the debentures, deemed to offset each other. But the company was out of cash. Its liquid assets were only $2,358,090, and its general liabilities were $5,203,547.[11]

Also, on September 30, a committee of American shareholders formed, with John S. Pillsbury as secretary. Of the 50,000 preference shares and 50,000 ordinary shares outstanding, the American committee held proxies for more than 21,000 and 31,000 shares, about 85 and 87 percent, respectively, of those held in the United States.[12]

John B. Niven, of the New York and London accounting firm of Touche, Niven & Co., was named the fourth receiver on October 8, 1908, representing English interests in Pillsbury-Washburn. His father was one of the founders of the world's first society of public accountants, in Edinburgh in 1854.

On October 3 the creditors' committee wrote the creditors that the receivers were carrying on the business at a substantial profit, and that they expected the operations to show satisfactory earnings during the succeeding months. The committee also expressed its confidence in the values placed on the company's assets by Marwick, Mitchell & Co. The letter added, ''Investigation has disclosed that about $1,758,000 of the indebtedness shown in the Accountants' report was kept in a secret private ledger, was not placed upon the general books until shortly before the receivership and had been omitted from the general financial statements issued by the Company, and that these irregular methods appear to have been commenced about May, 1905.'' This date corresponds to the period when Henry Little reportedly was attempting to corner the Minneapolis May wheat market. The letter concluded by reporting that the committee was considering various plans of reorganization designed to protect the creditors.

The receivership permitted two alternative solutions to the company's problems. The first was to negotiate an outright sale of the company, preferably as a single, going concern. The other solution, which gained immediate support from the American shareholders and the creditors committee, was to work out a plan of reorganization that would enable the company to continue.

One month after the commencement of the receivership, the board sent two of its members, Frank Spencer and George Cloutte, to the United States to do whatever was necessary to protect the company's interests. They met in Minneapolis with the receivers, the creditors' committee, and the major American shareholders, reaching broad agreement on the desirability of a reorganization.[13]

Once the objective was agreed upon, the scene shifted to London, where the work of formulating a specific plan began. The interests of five separate constituencies were involved. John S. Pillsbury and Ralph Whelan represented the American shareholders. The creditors' committee sent three of its members, who engaged Sir Frank Crisp to assist them. The company's board of directors was represented by its counsel, W. W. Paine; the English shareholders, by a committee headed by Sir William Crump; and the holders of debentures, by a committee chaired by George A. Touche.

With such a prominent array of participants representing often-conflicting positions, prompt agreement on a plan of reorganization probably was too much to expect. But the parties also differed in their views about the pace of the negotiations. The American shareholders, the board, and the creditors wanted to reach early agreement, fearing that delay might encourage impatient creditors to initiate bankruptcy proceedings and terminate the receivership. They believed also that the longer the receivership, the greater the company's loss of competitive position, both because of damage to its reputation

Capacity, 32,000 Bbls. Daily

THE FAMOUS PILLSBURY MARK

Under Management of

Albert C. Loring
Charles S. Pillsbury   Receivers
Albert C. Cobb

and because of the all-out efforts of competitors to profit from the situation. The English shareholders were divided, many of them wanting the company to make its first order of business an investigation of the irregular transactions that had produced the receivership. The debenture holders, on the other hand, deemed their security adequate and felt no need for an early resolution.[14]

Finally, however, the negotiators reached agreement on a plan of reorganization. The plan provided in substance for an operating company with a capital of not less than $2 million, to be subscribed in cash. This idea originated with the Pillsburys, according to Paine, who told shareholders at a meeting in November, 1908: ''Messrs. Pillsbury, apart from the association of their name, were the largest stockholders in the company, and when they realized the position into which the company had drifted . . . they were naturally anxious to do what they could to assist the company out of its difficulties.''[15]

The operating company would purchase Pillsbury-Washburn's liquid assets for about $2,250,000 and lend Pillsbury-Washburn $500,000 secured by its elevator properties and other collateral. Pillsbury-Washburn would use these funds to pay the costs of the receivership and about 50 cents on the dollar to creditors. It would then create a new issue of 20-year 5-percent second mortgage bonds that creditors would take at par for the unpaid balance of their claims. The operating company would lease the mills and milling properties for 20 years from August 8, 1908, at an annual rental of $100,000 plus one-half of all profits over $150,000. The lease could be renewed for an additional 20 years at the option of the operating company. Pillsbury-Washburn would continue to own and operate the two waterpower companies, and as soon as practicable Pillsbury-Washburn would sell the elevator properties and other collateral to repay the $500,000 loan from the operating company.

The board submitted the plan to the shareholders for approval at a meeting on November 26. One member of the shareholders' committee argued that a plan of reorganization should not be considered without restitution for the defalcations, ignoring chairman Glyn's earlier assertion that such a course would end ''all hope of reorganization or of saving anything for the shareholders.'' Another shareholder questioned paragraphs of the plan, suggesting that consideration be adjourned to a future date. Both Paine and Crisp responded that unless immediate action were taken, the shareholders would be in grave peril of bankruptcy proceedings by the firm's creditors. The meeting was adjourned for five days until December 1, and when the parties reconvened that day, the shareholders quickly approved the reorganization plan.[16]

Work started immediately to draft the lease, mortgage, and various other plan documents. But progress soon slowed as opposing interests of the parties became more difficult to resolve. The English board members began to chafe over the receivers' decision not to investigate the company's right to restitution. In fact, the receivers never did investigate possible restitution proceedings, perhaps viewing them as detrimental to the company's business or as a remedy the shareholders could pursue for themselves. At the request of the English board, however, in December 1908 the receivers notified the Swedish-American Bank of Minneapolis of their right to claim damages from the bank, which reportedly had been a depository for proceeds from the "B notes" (the name given to the unrecorded notes).[17]

At any rate, negotiations in London became unusually protracted and contentious and on at least two occasions threatened to break down completely. Finally in March the English interests agreed to send attorney Paine to represent them all in the United States. Paine met with representatives of the creditors and major American shareholders in New York, Chicago, and Minneapolis. In three weeks he obtained agreement on the terms of the various documents and returned to England. On June 2 and 7, 1909, the debenture holders and the shareholders met and gave final approval to the plan, lease, mortgage, and other documents.[18]

Meanwhile the operating company was incorporated in Minnesota in June 1909 as Pillsbury Flour Mills Company. The reorganization plan provided that Pillsbury-Washburn shareholders be entitled to proportionate ownership of the operating company. Despite a vigorous solicitation program, only 34 Pillsbury-Washburn shareholders responded positively, subscribing for operating company shares with a total par value of $125,400. The receivers reported to the court that "something over one hundred (100) letters had been received from shareholders (English and American) expressly stating that they do not care to become subscribers to stock in the proposed Operating Company." As a result, most of the $2,000,000 capital for Pillsbury Flour Mills Company was provided by the three Pillsburys and their friends in America.

In July of 1909, the court approved the plan of reorganization and ordered that all assets be turned over to the parent company. Pillsbury-Washburn appointed de la Barre as its agent to take delivery from the receivers of books and documents belonging to the company. Two months later the lease was signed, and the operating company purchased Pillsbury-Washburn's liquid assets, lending the company $500,000 as agreed. Creditors with claims under $350 were paid in cash. The others received 47 percent of their claims in cash and the balance in an equivalent amount of 5-percent bonds.

Pillsbury flour sacks sometimes served a secondary use. The dress shown in this unidentified 1910 photo could have been designed for a costume party, but innovative seamstresses in some of the company's markets put the cloth sacks to more utilitarian purposes.

The receivers formally transferred operation of the five mills to Pillsbury Flour Mills Company on September 7, 1909. Albert C. Loring, the only flour miller among the receivers, had been elected president July 30, 1909, under a five-year contract providing for a $25,000-per-year salary plus a share of the profits. He was 52 years old, already a veteran of 33 years in the flour milling business at Minneapolis.[19]

Loring found repairs to the mills were a pressing necessity. According to de la Barre, Little management had allowed the mills to "depreciate to such a degree . . . as to make it inexpedient to operate the mills in competition with other mills here in Minneapolis and elsewhere." Loring wrote Glyn on April 7, 1910, voicing his surprise "that the physical condition of your property, if possible, was more rotten than was the previous management, and that the mills were at least ten years behind the times and completely worn out."

Besides beginning a program of repairs, the new company made additions to the property. Construction of a 430,000-bushel brick and tile elevator next to the A mill was commenced in October, and in the following month work began on a new power plant to furnish electricity to all five mills.[20]

Early in 1910 the receivers filed their reports with the court and applied for discharge. The elevator receiver was discharged on February 16. Three days later the Pillsbury-Washburn receivers were discharged, on the condition that they obtain from the English board a resolution canceling $9,000 in bonds left in the receivers' hands after the creditors were paid. The required resolution was a mere formality. It appeared that after only slightly more than 18 months the receivership could be terminated.

But the accumulated strains and tensions of the last year and a half were taking their toll. The English board was disgruntled over its inability to examine the receivership expenses before they were submitted to the court. It also complained that there had been unnecessary delay in delivering to the board the account of receivership expenses and the operating company's statement for the period ending August 31, 1909. John S. Pillsbury and Whelan had come to London in May 1910 to complete a number of unfinished matters. When they requested that the board adopt the formal resolution required for the receivers' discharge, the board retaliated for its supposed slights by postponing action until after the annual shareholders meeting on July 21, 1910.[21]

The English board itself was riven by discord, divided down the middle with Glyn and Klein on one side and Cloutte and Spencer on the other. The latter two were strong advocates for instituting restitution proceedings, while Glyn and Klein were more ambivalent. Spencer wrote de la Barre on July 6 that he and Cloutte had been working hard for the shareholders, but "Glyn, Klein and Paine have been hanging together and we have been opposed at every turn . . . Glyn is not seeking re-election, so another Director will have to be appointed at the meeting. It is a jolly good job Glyn is doing for he has never taken much interest in things generally. Klein tries to run with the hare and hunt with the hounds and is not clever enough to keep up with either—he is all for keeping everything from the shareholders. How can he do them justice. He is a shareholder in the operating company—buys their flour and has a boy in the Minneapolis office so that his interest is easily traced."

As the day of the annual meeting approached, the board was down to three members. Spencer's contract as managing director had expired June 30, and it was not renewed. The directors' report sent to the shareholders on July 10 reported that the receivership expenses amounted to the "large sum" of more than $400,000 and expressed regret that the directors had had no way of controlling them. The report also presented the Pillsbury Flour Mills Company's operating statement, together with Pillsbury-Washburn's accounts for the period September 1, 1907, to August 31, 1909. The report informed shareholders that the question of obtaining restitution had been a matter of much anxiety to the board, which had recently placed the matter in the hands of lawyers in New York.

Cloutte, dissatisfied with the information conveyed by the board report, sent a separate letter to the shareholders on July 16. He attached a complete statement of the receivership expenses, implying that the directors should have done the same. He then set forth his own account of the "frauds in question" and noted: "It appears that in May, 1905, when the frauds in question commenced, and about the time the 'B notes' were first issued, Mr. Henry L. Little, the Manager, and member of the Local Committee of Management, opened a new or 'Special Account' in the Company's name at one of the Company's Bankers, and through this account the 'B' notes and fraudulent transactions were passed, the Bank honouring checques with one signature only, although they knew that, according to the Company's regulations, all cheques were to bear the signatures of two of the company's officials.

"In addition to this, when Messrs. Deloitte & Co., the Auditors, in the course of their work, called for a statement of all the balances from the Company's Bankers, this account, each year, was not disclosed, though all the others were duly certified. Had this account been disclosed in 1905 by the Bank, the frauds must have been discovered, and the Company would probably have been in a prosperous state at the present time."

As might be expected, the shareholders' meeting on July 21, 1910, was a tempestuous affair. The London reporter for the *Northwestern Miller* wrote that "The meeting had not proceeded far before one could see that many of the shareholders had come intent on relieving their pent-up feelings regarding the losses they had suffered." His account went on to say that in the general babble of dissatisfaction could be heard such complaints as "swindled," "robbed," "cheated," "fleeced," "outrageous conduct," "monstrous receivers' expense," "those responsible for gross frauds should be brought to justice," and many more.[22]

Although there was no provision on the meeting's agenda for action regarding restitution, that topic occupied much of the time of the meeting. The verbatim report included the following dialogue:

MR. CLOUTTE: The position we find ourselves in is one of the greatest Company scandals of modern times—(hear, hear)—to which the most publicity should be given. The concern was, and is, one of the best in the world if conducted as a legitimate milling business. It would seem that an undue thirst for dollars led H. L. Little, the Manager, to enter upon huge gambles in wheat at the risk of the Company, on the principle, I suspect, of "Heads I win, tails you lose." (Hear, hear.) The result you have before you . . . About the time that the frauds commenced, Little, who appears to have been allowed to become a sort of general Dictator, endeavoured to obtain the removal of Messrs. Deloitte & Co., the Auditors, on the ground that, instead of attending to audit simply, they were inclined to criticize the management, and their reports were, no doubt, considered too strong . . .

MR. HENDERSON: We had a bad time about two years after this Company was started; we had the very same thing happen in which one of the Pillsburys was mixed up—that is operating in the market—gambling on wheat. (Hear, hear.) We lost our interest for some time, and then when you were in the chair at the time, and my old friend, Mr. Jackson, was another Director, a firm determination was made to stop all gambling, and what I blame the Directors for is this, how is it that they did not make such a thing impossible in the future—I mean the Directors over there? . . . I cannot help thinking that the Directors both here and over there did not exercise the vigilance which, having had warning years ago, they ought to have exercised and thus made the thing impossible . . .

MR. JONES: This is, in my opinion, a huge conspiracy, and with your weakness, and Mr. Klein's weakness, you are unwittingly conniving at it.

THE CHAIRMAN [Richard H. Glyn]: What do you mean by saying that? All I told you was that if you open your mouth too much you are doing far more to assist people on the other side.

MR. JONES: We have lost all our money—this 800,000—and we have lost hundreds of thousands more in profits. I have lost 1,500 or 1,600, but I would willingly pay more to have the thing seen through . . .

MR. JACKSON: I will limit my enquiry. Would Mr. Pillsbury and his family join with us, should we decide to take proceedings?

MR. [John S.] PILLSBURY: All I have to say is that that is entirely a question for the Board of Directors to take up. It is just as much to my interest as to anyone's here, if there is any chance of getting the money back, but this is a question entirely for the Directors . . .

SIR WM. CRUMP: I hope you won't adjourn this meeting. I hope the business will be carried through to its proper conclusion, and that you will get a proper Board of Directors to act for you . . . I am informed that certain matters could be dealt with as between the Operating Company and our Board of Directors, so let us let [sic] the Board of Directors and let us have those conferences between the representatives of the Operating Company and the Board of Directors which are so absolutely necessary. I strongly deprecate any adjournment. (Applause).

The meeting finally turned to the approval of the directors' report and accounts. After defeat of a motion to adjourn for three months, the shareholders approved the accounts on a divided vote and proceeded to the election of directors. Glyn had announced he would not seek reelection. Sir William Crump proposed that Klein and Cloutte, whose terms had not expired, both resign so that a completely new set of directors could be elected. Klein expressed his willingness but declined when Cloutte refused. Shareholders then nominated Thomas Skinner, an English financial writer and director of several Canadian companies, and Charles Lock, a long-time member of the shareholders' committee. John S. Pillsbury seconded the nominations and acclaimed the nominees as "two able men who will be of the greatest value and assistance to the Company." And so they were elected new directors.

Within days the new board had organized, electing Skinner its new chairman. The board immediately passed the resolution that had been holding up discharge of the receivers, which became effective on August 3, 1910.

Around 1910, almost every small town could count on the company to help the local grocer provide a float for the Fourth of July parade.

Cloutte did not give up easily. On August 9, he sent another letter to the shareholders, criticizing Glyn's speech at the shareholders' meeting and taking issue with numerous other individuals. On August 20 the board called an extraordinary general meeting of shareholders to consider a resolution to remove Cloutte from the board. At the meeting on September 23 Cloutte was allowed to resign, despite the clear preference of the other directors to have the shareholders remove him.

In the meantime, the board had met on August 4 without Cloutte. It authorized Paine to write a letter to Whelan, offering to settle all outstanding issues between the two companies: "If this proposal be accepted the Board and the Company will, having regard to the strong view expressed by the Operating Company as to the effect on their credit of any such proceedings, bind themselves not to commence or to be associated directly or indirectly with or in any way to encourage the institution of criminal proceedings against any person in connection with these defalcations."

Paine's proposal was artfully designed to dispose of a number of subjects. One of these had its beginnings in November 1907, when Little sought to borrow money for the company on three notes totaling $500,000. Given to Pillsbury-Washburn by Watson & Co., a Minneapolis grain brokerage firm with which the company had been doing business, the notes, although secured, were of questionable value. To make the notes more palatable to prospective lenders, Little and Amsden pledged some of their own assets as further security. Pillsbury-Washburn then borrowed $100,000 from the Great Northern Railroad Company, pledging as collateral the Watson & Co. notes and their security. The security provided by Little was his one-half interest in a mining lease; Amsden pledged his 2,210 ordinary and 2,410 preference shares of Pillsbury-Washburn stock, worth about $35,000 in 1910.[23]

Paine proposed that in return for canceling the $500,000 note given by Pillsbury-Washburn to the operating company, Pillsbury-Washburn transfer to the operating company all the shares of stock in the Minneapolis and Northern Elevator Company, as well as the Watson & Co. notes and their security. Pillsbury-Washburn would also put an end to the still-simmering restitution agitation by releasing its claims against Little and Amsden in exchange for their surrender to Pillsbury-Washburn and the operating company of the security they had pledged in support of the Watson & Co. notes.

The operating company accepted the offer. There followed lengthy negotiations, conducted largely by Whelan and Paine, with Little, Amsden, the owners of the then-defunct Watson & Co., and the boards of the two companies. More than 18 months and almost 50 documents later, the complicated transaction was concluded. As part of the settlement, Pillsbury-Washburn and the operating company released any claims or rights that either of them had against Little and Amsden.

It should be noted that the packet of settlement documents included releases of claims for restitution by Pillsbury-Washburn of the Swedish-American Bank of Minneapolis and a long list of individuals and companies in Minneapolis and elsewhere. Although no explanation was given for these releases, they fuel speculation as to the confidential investigation conducted for Pillsbury-Washburn by its New York attorneys.

The settlement effectively closed off further discussion about possible criminal proceedings and restitution suits. Thus there was never a judicial determination of the responsibility for Pillsbury-Washburn's near failure. In a letter addressed on July 12, 1911, to Pillsbury Flour Mills Company, Whelan, referring solely to criminal liability, wrote, "We do not know whether any criminal offense was in fact committed by either Little or Amsden . . . Neither the noteholders of the British Co. nor the Company itself preferred criminal charges against them, and in the report of the Counsel of the British Co., employed to investigate the responsibility for the Company's losses, criminal prosecutions are advised against. Consequently the question whether any public offense was committed by either Little or Amsden is a doubtful one."

More than a year before Whelan's letter, de la Barre had summarized his views concerning restitution proceedings. Spencer had written de la Barre concerning the subject and de la Barre's reply posited the question of whom to sue. De la Barre concluded, "H.L.L. is in another state. W.D.W. has one foot in the grave and has no guilt. A.F.P. has his wealth tied up in the leasing co. and has no guilt. C.M.A. will make a strong fight. L.P.H. is on the Pacific Coast. Has no money. De la Barre? Bitter pill to swallow to have to prove he is honest. Who is next? I don't know! Do you?"[24]

Thomas Skinner, the new chairman of Pillsbury-Washburn, offered perhaps the most graceful requiem for the events of the period when, according to Whelan, he said that he had "observed a number of British Companies of the same nature as the P-W Co. and sooner or later they have all had to pull up stake, and move to the place of their operations in America in order to be made profitable."[25]

Pillsbury's
FAMILY OF FOODS

Light, tender pancakes, with a delicious flavor — bran muffins, healthful and appetizing — wheat cereal that makes breakfast an event — bread, cakes and pastry, which are real food treats — all are made best with The Pillsbury Family of Foods — a select family of selected foods.

Pillsbury's Best Flour — Health Bran — Wheat Cereal — Pancake Flour — rye, durum and graham flours — all are fully guaranteed. With satisfaction, *to you*, positively assured let Pillsbury be your guiding word to the best in foods. Your grocer carries Pillsbury Products.

PILLSBURY FLOUR MILLS COMPANY
Minneapolis, U. S. A.

4 A New Beginning
1909–1940

Twenty years passed between the sale of C. A. Pillsbury & Co. to Pillsbury-Washburn in 1889 and the lease of the mills to Pillsbury Flour Mills Company in 1909. At the beginning of the period Pillsbury-Washburn was the largest flour milling company in the world, in an industry that led all others in the United States in the value of its product. At the end of the 20-year period the company had slipped to second place; the industry itself had fallen to fifth place behind meat-packing, foundries and machine shops, lumber, and steel-rolling mills.[1]

Trends that emerged during the first 20 years of English ownership would cause major changes in the structure of the country's flour milling business. Two of these changes adversely affected mills in Minneapolis as well as in the rest of the Northwest hard spring wheat area.

The first development had its origin well before the turn of the century, when a hard winter wheat known as Turkey Red was introduced in Kansas. Brought to the United States from the Crimean Peninsula on the Black Sea, Turkey Red was well suited to southwestern growing conditions, producing a flour virtually equal in quality to the Northwest's hard spring wheat flour. The use of Turkey Red and related strains spread throughout the Southwest and first became an important factor in the market between 1905 and 1910. The new wheat was generally priced lower than hard spring wheat, and as Turkey Red production expanded, flour milled from Northwest wheat lost its competitive advantage and its profit margins narrowed.[2]

The second change related to flour exports, which had been so important in the rise of Minneapolis as a milling center and in the reputation and success of C.A. Pillsbury & Co. Flour exports from the Northwest area were a very satisfactory 4,847,000 barrels in 1900. Ten years later, however, export volume had dropped to about 1,800,000 barrels, as a result of changes in railroad rate structures that made it more economical to mill export flour closer to ocean ports. The level further declined to about 850,000 barrels in 1922, before beginning a precipitous descent that virtually eliminated the Northwest mills as flour exporters.[3]

The new beginning brought an expansion of the company's product line. This Pillsbury "Family of Foods" ad was in *The Ladies' Home Journal* in October 1919.

Albert C. Loring (left, top), "the quintessential miller," became president of the Pillsbury Flour Mills Company on September 7, 1909. At the same time, Alfred F. Pillsbury (above) and Charles S. Pillsbury (far left, bottom) became vice-presidents and John S. Pillsbury (Charles's twin, right, bottom) became secretary-treasurer.

A third development, the drop in the country's per capita use of flour, had a general effect not confined to Minneapolis milling. Changes in most Americans' lifestyles gave rise to new dietary habits and practices that resulted in a drop from 224 to 179 pounds annual per capita consumption of wheat flour between 1900 and 1920. Although this loss was largely offset by population increases, the trend reflected unfavorably on flour milling's prospects as a growth industry.

Such were the directions of the industry when Albert C. Loring became president of Pillsbury Flour Mills Company on September 7, 1909, under a five-year contract at an annual salary of $25,000 plus a share of the profits. Loring had spent his entire career in the milling business. In 1877 at the age of 19 he became secretary-treasurer of the Minnetonka Mill Company, a small country mill in which his father was a partner. When that mill was sold, he joined his father and others at the Galaxy mill in Minneapolis. Two years after the Pillsbury-Washburn consolidation, Loring spearheaded a merger of the Galaxy with five other mills to form Northwestern Consolidated Milling Company, then the city's second largest milling concern. He became its general manager in 1895.[4]

After the failure of Thomas McIntyre to acquire the Pillsbury-Washburn and Washburn Crosby companies for his milling trust, Loring helped McIntyre acquire control in 1899 of Consolidated Milling Company, Northwestern Consolidated's successor. Loring became a vice-president of the parent United States Flour Milling Company, managing Consolidated Milling until shortly after his appointment as a receiver of Pillsbury-Washburn in 1908.

When Loring became president, the three second-generation Pillsburys, who with Loring held a majority of the new company's shares, also became officers of Pillsbury Flour Mills Company; Alfred F. and Charles S. were its vice-presidents and John S. was secretary-treasurer. Of the three, John S. was the most active, and one writer described him as Loring's "chief lieutenant." He had a special interest in sales and for several years directed the company's sales department.[5]

Nevertheless, the operating head of the company was Loring, and the Pillsburys, all of whom had a number of outside interests, left its management to him. The three Pillsburys were determined, however, that the new company's credit be strong, and they personally guaranteed the firm's bank loans until 1923.[6]

The receivership and, in part, Little's past management, created numerous problems for the new company and its president. Foremost among these was the firm's damaged reputation, a vulnerability exploited effectively by its competitors. Employee morale was also a concern. Many of the company's top managers had either resigned or been replaced, and according to Loring, the receivers had found it extremely difficult to build and maintain the organization. Finally, the manufacturing facilities were badly run down.[7]

When the company built the new A mill elevator in 1910, Loring directed that sufficient space be left between the elevator and the A for another flour mill. Before a new mill could be built, however, Loring learned that the A mill itself needed rebuilding. Constructed entirely with wooden posts and girders in 1881, the structure was extensively damaged from dry rot and the constant vibration of the heavy machinery. The *Minneapolis Journal* in 1913 described the building as "twenty-two inches out of plumb, its rear wall convex to exterior view and its front wall concave as viewed from Main Street." Eight monolithic, reinforced-concrete buttresses were erected to support the rear wall; inside the building the wooden skeleton was totally replaced by steel, and the threatening bulges were eliminated. The company completed the work without shutting down the mill, and with buttresses in place the building remained structurally sound in 1984.[8]

Loring made sure that the quality of Pillsbury flour, reported to have deteriorated in the months before the receivership, met his high standards. In 1911 the company converted seven rooms on the top floor of its headquarters into a new, entirely modern laboratory. Along with state-of-the-art testing equipment, a small flour mill, capable of producing uniformly reliable samples of flour from only a bushel or two of wheat, was installed in the lab. The *Northwestern Miller* subsequently reported that "some of the Minneapolis mills have the finest laboratories in the world," and it illustrated the story with photographs of the new Pillsbury facilities.[9]

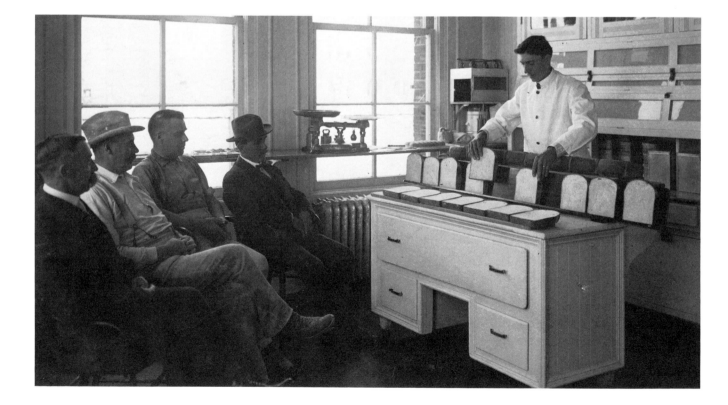

The Flour Question Settled

Because Pillsbury's Best

MINNEAPOLIS. MINN..U.S.A.

June 16th, 1916.

V. Hammes & Son,
Rossie, Iowa.

Gentlemen;-

    It is with pleasure that we announce to you the letting of contracts for the erection of a new mill, situated here in Minneapolis, which when completed this fall will add a few thousand extra barrels to our present capacity.

    The building of this mill we owe in a great measure to you and other loyal PILLSBURY customers, who have striven generously to place our product before the consuming public on the basis of its merits. We, too, have endeavored to manufacture a particularly high-grade flour of uniform quality in which you and other friends might well take pride.

    The new mill, we believe, has proven our mutual efforts not unsuccessful. We thank you and assure you our aims in the future will be governed along the lines on which we believe you would want us to progress.

        Respectfully yours,

    PILLSBURY FLOUR MILLS COMPANY.
RN:L

The A mill was reinforced with buttresses (top, right) in 1911. At the same time the company built a new flour laboratory, where the head millers of "the greatest flour mills of the world" (see advertisement bottom, right) viewed the bread made from their flour each day (left). The company let new contracts for further expansion of the A mill in 1916 (above).

THE "FATHER of WATERS"
Pauses at Minneapolis

To turn the wheels of the Greatest Flour Mills of the World

The Mark
Pillsbury's
BEST
XXXX
Minneapolis, Minn.

Pillsbury's

Daily Capacity 35000 Barrels.

In 1916, Pillsbury Flour Mills Company bought the old Phoenix mill and converted it to the Pillsbury Rye Mill (top), which continued operations into the 1950s. In 1917 and 1918 the company built a new supply house at the A mill. From there operated a fleet of new delivery trucks assigned to the sales department in the early 1920s (bottom).

With repair of the A mill complete in 1913, the company set out to enlarge its A mill operations. In 1914 it built a 2-million-bushel concrete elevator; the following year it constructed a new machine shop and began work on a million-bushel annex to the concrete elevator. In 1916 and 1917 the "South A," a 3,000-barrel capacity mill, was added to the complex along with a nine-story cleaning house (where wheat is prepared for milling) and a three-story flour warehouse. Removal of its cleaning machinery to the new building allowed the A mill to add another 1,000 barrels to its capacity. In 1917 and 1918, the two halves of a new supply house were built on Southeast Second Street, later providing garage facilities for a fleet of new delivery trucks. Finally, a four-story brick warehouse was built at the south end of the brick elevator in 1918. By 1915 the company had also sold the last of the former Minneapolis and Northern Elevator Company elevators it had reacquired from the English in 1912, and the elevator company was dissolved.

Construction of the A mill additions brought a temporary halt to rumors that Pillsbury would build a new mill at Buffalo, New York. These rumors had circulated intermittently since 1903, when Washburn Crosby built a 3,000-barrel mill in Buffalo. Because of more favorable freight rates for wheat than for flour, Washburn Crosby had perceived an advantage in having a mill located near the eastern trade. The *Northwestern Miller* quoted a Pillsbury spokesman as saying in 1917 that the addition to the A mill would take care of the company's growing trade and make the need for a new mill in Buffalo "less pressing."[10]

Along with upgrading the physical plant, Loring acted to broaden the line of Pillsbury flours. The company had milled durum wheat at the Lincoln mill in Anoka on and off since about 1905, supplying durum flour for the Baltic market and semolina for United States macaroni manufacturers. Beginning in 1910 the Lincoln milled durum exclusively, and in 1917 the Palisade also converted to durum. The company installed graham-flour milling equipment in the Anchor mill annex in 1915, and the following year it purchased and converted the 40-year-old Phoenix mill to a 1,200-barrel rye mill. Located at the corner of Main Street and Third Avenue Southeast, across the street from the A, the Phoenix had made extensive tongue-in-cheek use of the advertising slogan, "Next to the largest mill in the world."[11]

The steady growth of the United States baking industry was a motivating force for increasing mill capacity and adding other types of flour to existing lines. As the country grew, its towns and cities increased in size at the expense of its rural population, the practice of home baking declined, and the number of neighborhood bakeries increased. Commercial bakers in 1900 produced only 5 percent of the bread consumed in the United States. By the time the country entered World War I, this figure had risen to 30 percent, and bakeries were becoming sophisticated, highly mechanized operations. Pillsbury and the other milling companies competed vigorously to supply this large and growing industrial flour market.[12]

Simultaneously, Pillsbury was promoting its grocery store products to both the housewife and the grocer. The 196-pound family flour barrels had all but disappeared from the stores, and in their place were more manageable 100-, 50-, and 25-pound cotton or jute sacks.

The company's profits hovered around $150,000 annually until the outbreak of World War I in 1914. Profits then rose modestly until the United States entered the conflict on April 6, 1917. The market soon proved the axiom that, in time of war, wheat and its products are munitions to be acquired without regard to price.

German U-boat success in closing off shipments to Europe from other wheat-producing countries made the poor 1917 harvest in the United States more serious. The resulting uncontrolled, sometimes reckless, buying of wheat by representatives of allied and neutral countries brought about unprecedented high prices in the American wheat and flour markets. In April the cash price for wheat reached its highest point since the Civil War, and within a month the price had advanced by almost 50 percent again. Each successive increase in wheat prices brought a wave of hysterical buying, resulting in a flour panic. Speculation by flour jobbers and dealers, as well as by wheat traders, was rampant.[13]

Finally, on May 14, 1917, the Chicago Board of Trade voluntarily suspended trading in the futures market, and other important exchanges followed suit. Nevertheless, it was evident that some form of government control was necessary to prevent food prices from getting completely out of hand. In April, the Council of National Defense had called Herbert Hoover home from Belgium, where he had administered a successful food program when German invasion threatened the country with starvation. President Woodrow Wilson announced his intention to name Hoover the nation's food administrator as soon as Congress could enact legislation creating the U.S. Food Administration. Immediately Hoover began to formulate his program and to meet with leaders of the country's various food industries.[14]

The Food Control Act became law on August 10, 1917, and on August 29 rules and regulations for the milling trade were published. The country was divided into eight milling divisions, with a prominent miller named to head each division. These eight men, together with a chairman and secretary, constituted the U.S. Food Administration Millers' Committee, the governing body for the milling trade.

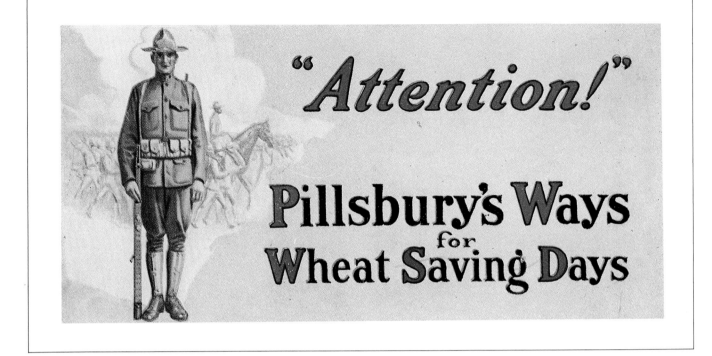

Pillsbury introduced a line of nonwheat baking flours in a World War I pamphlet in 1918 (above). Inside were described products including corn meal, rye, graham, barley, and buckwheat flours and rolled oats, shown again on the cover of *Carry-On* in 1920 (right).

Food he did not get
in France—

Pancakes

Form 751

National Guard troops patrolled the Minneapolis mill district during World War I (left, top). One soldier, in his spare time, built a model of the A mill, now on view at the Minnesota Historical Society in St. Paul. The company promised jobs to all its former employees returning from the war (above), and its postwar advertising focused on the returning veteran (bottom, left).

Loring headed the Northwest District, a group of 595 milling companies in the spring wheat area, consisting of 28 percent of the flour mills in the United States.[15]

The regulations were few in number. They established a maximum profit of 25 cents per barrel on flour and 50 cents per ton on feed and required monthly profit statements from each company. A government-owned grain corporation, authorized by Congress, made all wheat purchases and allocated the wheat among the mills on the basis of their flour production in the most recent three years. The regulations established procedures for millers to bid on government flour purchases and for the grain corporation to allot orders for export flour. To prevent hoarding and speculation, the law dictated that flour was not to be sold for delivery more than 30 days in advance; millers were to store no more than 30 days' supply of wheat.

Concurrently, a voluntary conservation program was put into place as the second great arm of Hoover's plan. Achieved mainly through the action of individual citizens, the program was stimulated and directed by influential women volunteers. The press cooperated in an intense educational and patriotic appeal for conservation. Some 14 million families, 7,000 hotels and restaurants, and 425,000 retail dealers pledged cooperation on wheatless and meatless days, among other methods of saving. Pillsbury's advertising encouraged these measures, publicizing the need to save on fats, sugar, and wheat and offering a free book of recipes for mixing wheat flour with wartime "wheat saving flours."[16]

In December of 1917 the Food Administration announced that all of the surplus wheat in the United States had been assigned. The ability of the country to meet allied demands for wheat now depended on savings that could be effected by substituting flour made from other grains. Pillsbury proceeded to change a part of its milling capacity to nonwheat flours, converting the Anchor mill to barley and the Lincoln to corn. Its ads pictured sacks of Pillsbury's Yellow Corn Meal, Buckwheat Flour, Rice Flour, Barley Flour, White Corn Flour, White Rye and Wheat Flour, and Pure White Rye Flour, all under the banner "Ways for Wheat Saving Days." Beginning February 1, 1918, bakers and wholesalers were required to purchase one pound of nonwheat flour for every four pounds of wheat flour; "Victory Bread" had to contain at least 20 percent flour from cereals other than wheat. Regulations governing the milling of wheat flour had gone into effect on Christmas Day of 1917; their adverse impact on flour quality led the company to terminate production of Pillsbury's Best® Flour for the duration of the war.[17]

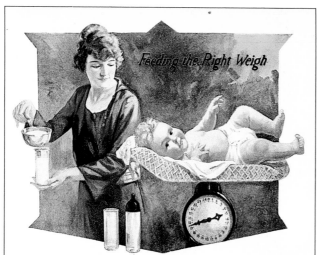

Feeding the Right Weigh

A Man's Food—

An Infant's Food—

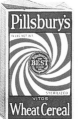

Creamy-white, granulated hearts of wheat—so easily digested that it forms the first and best food for infants, yet so nourishing and substantial that it sustains the hardest worker—such is—

Pillsbury's
FAMILY OF FOODS
Wheat Cereal

Here's Health!

Pillsbury's
FAMILY OF FOODS
Health Bran
Muffins

Results

More Milk
Better Milk
Healthier Cows
with
Pillsbury's Dairy Ration
(The feed without a filler)

Pillsbury Flour Mills Company
MINNEAPOLIS

In 1919, Pillbury introduced its "Family of Foods." Subsequent single-product ads like those done in 1921 (top, left and right) identified each product as one of the "family." Pillsbury Dairy Ration (bottom) was also new on the market in 1919.

On April 17, 1918, little more than a year after the United States entered the war, the *Northwestern Miller* proclaimed that the Food Administration had accomplished the impossible. With a wheat crop barely large enough to supply its own domestic needs, the United States had managed to feed itself and to supply the full requirements of the Allied troops.

After suffering through a period of extremely low wheat supplies before the 1918 crop reached the market, the country was rewarded by a bumper harvest. On July 1 the Food Administration released flour millers from all restrictions on wheat purchases, removed profit margin restrictions on flour, and substituted ceiling prices for flour and feed. The Armistice was signed November 11, 1918; on December 20 ceiling prices were canceled, and the milling industry began its return to normal conditions.[18]

The war ended as the company looked forward to its fiftieth anniversary in 1919. That year the company's magazine advertisements tempted grocery shoppers with pictures of Pillsbury's "Family of Foods," featuring a 25-pound sack of Pillsbury's Best® Flour as the centerpiece. The rest of the family consisted of Pillsbury Pancake Flour, Health Bran, and Vitos Wheat Cereal. Earnings were in a satisfactory range, furnishing a good return on the company's $2-million capital. Its profits hit $555,000 in the last year of the war, and in 1919 they reached a record $822,000. The directors responded by declaring a healthy 17-percent cash dividend on the company's shares.

The end of the war allowed millers to return to their endeavors to secure maximum returns from their by-products. Growth of the livestock and dairy industries resumed, resulting in greater use of commercial animal feeds and in increased demand for bran, middlings, and low-grade flours. In 1919 Pillsbury introduced Pillsbury's Dairy Ration, promising "more milk, better milk, healthier cows." A promotional booklet attested, "Pillsbury's Dairy Ration is extremely palatable. We have yet to see the cow that wouldn't clean up a full feeding of Pillsbury's Dairy Ration the first time it was offered."

In 1920, the directors of Pillsbury-Washburn and Pillsbury Flour Mills Company began to examine the future of their relationship. The lease of the flour mills was more than half over, and the American company's right to extend the lease for another 20 years was to expire on August 31, 1926. Nonetheless, as the 1920s began, no decision had been made upon whether to renew the lease. Pillsbury Flour Mills Company shareholders had received at least a 7-percent dividend each year from 1911. On the other hand, although Pillsbury-Washburn derived substantial revenues from its two waterpower companies and the lease of its flour mills, the high cost of servicing its debt had precluded Pillsbury-Washburn from paying dividends on

either its preference or ordinary shares since 1906. When Loring attended Pillsbury-Washburn's annual meeting in 1920, he warned the shareholders that he did not foresee much immediate improvement in the flour milling earnings, which had already begun to fall from their 1919 peak.

On October 13, 1921, the Pillsbury-Washburn shareholders, at their meeting in London, eliminated all preference shares and created a single class of 283,620 ordinary shares with a par value of £2 10s. Each preference share was exchanged for five shares of the new stock and each ordinary share for one. The reclassification eliminated all claims for unpaid dividends on the preference shares and reduced the par value of the company's shares to an amount not exceeding the fair value of its net assets. The ultimate purpose, however, was to arrange Pillsbury-Washburn affairs so that its properties might be sold to Pillsbury Flour Mills Company in exchange for an interest in that company. Loring attended the shareholders' meeting, and as proxy for a number of American shareholders, he voted for the reclassification.

While the two companies considered their futures, the heavy demand for flour extended well into 1921, when another intensive period of mill expansion and new construction began. By the end of 1923 wheat flour milling capacity had increased by almost 20 percent in the United States in a three-year period. The expanding demand for flour led to Pillsbury's first mill outside Minneapolis. Shareholders of a corporation formed to build a mill in Atchison, Kansas, ran into financial difficulties during construction. Pillsbury purchased the property in May 1922 for $170,000, immediately completed construction of the 2,300-barrel mill, and erected a 300,000-bushel elevator. Loring explained that "with the growth of its business, the company finds it desirable to operate flour mills at other points, in order that it may purchase wheat and distribute flour to the best advantage." [19]

At the same time Pillsbury made its long-anticipated move into Buffalo. Through its wholly owned subsidiary, the Island Warehouse Corporation, it took an option on land occupied by a large warehouse and by the modern, 2,600,000-bushel Mutual terminal elevator. In October 1922 the Island Warehouse Corporation purchased the property and entered into a construction contract for a $1-million, ten-story, 8,000-barrel mill with internal wheat storage for 325,000 bushels. Like the Minneapolis A mill, the Buffalo mill had two identical milling units. The first unit began milling on May 19, 1924, and the second unit went into production a few months later. Concurrently the company discontinued operations at its Minneapolis B and Anchor mills. [20]

Pillsbury Flour Mills Company acquired both the Atchison and Buffalo properties with its own funds. The 1909 lease with Pillsbury-Washburn had anticipated that competitive pressures over the life of the lease might necessitate new mill construction by the operating company. Accordingly, the lease permitted the operating company to buy or build new properties at its own expense. The earnings from the new facilities, after payment to the operating company of a specified return on its investment, went into the rent computations. Should the lease terminate, Pillsbury-Washburn had the option to purchase the added facilities from the operating company. Regardless of legalities, construction of the new mills at Atchison and Buffalo reflected a determination of Loring and the three Pillsburys to maintain Pillsbury Flour Mills Company as a competitive flour milling concern.

The boards of Pillsbury-Washburn and Pillsbury Flour Mills Company continued to discuss amalgamation. In early 1923 the Pillsbury-Washburn directors gave notice of an extraordinary shareholders' meeting to consider a plan of reorganization agreed to by the two boards. Pillsbury-Washburn's notice to its shareholders referred to the requirement of notice of renewal by September 1, 1926, and said, "At present the lessee company is not in position to say whether or not it will renew the lease, and as the uncertainty was felt to be greatly prejudicial to the business of the two companies it was considered desirable that some arrangement on the lines of combining and amalgamating [the two companies] should be made."

Start-up of the Buffalo mill (left) in 1924 led to consolidation in the A mill of the company's Minneapolis milling operations.

The arrangement worked out by the two boards provided for formation of Pillsbury Flour Mills, Inc., a holding company that would ultimately take title to all the shares of Pillsbury Flour Mills Company, the operating firm. The holding company would be incorporated in Delaware with an authorized capital of $12,500,000 divided into 250,000 shares of $50 par value each. As the first step, Pillsbury-Washburn would transfer all its assets to the operating company. In return, the operating company would assume all of Pillsbury-Washburn's debts except for debentures and second-mortgage bonds. The operating company would then deliver 35,453 shares of its stock to Pillsbury-Washburn, together with enough cash to retire the debentures and bonds.

In the second step, the holding company would allot 70,905 shares of its stock to Pillsbury-Washburn in exchange for the latter's 35,453 shares of the operating company, and 120,000 shares of stock to the other operating company shareholders in exchange for their operating company shares. Pillsbury-Washburn shareholders would then own 37.15 percent of Pillsbury Flour Mills, Inc., and the other group, which included Loring and the Pillsburys, would own 62.85 percent. Funds to pay Pillsbury-Washburn and to provide working capital would be raised through bonds issued by the two American companies.

The English company's board recommended the arrangement to its shareholders, who adopted it on June 27, 1923. After approval by the English court, its terms were carried out and the English company was liquidated. The result was that Pillsbury-Washburn ceased to exist, the American operating company succeeded to the ownership of all the English company's properties, and Pillsbury Flour Mills, Inc., the new holding company, owned all the shares of the operating company. A few former English shareholders in Pillsbury-Washburn owned shares in the holding company, but its controlling shares were in the hands of the Americans. The transaction was reported in the July 4, 1923, issue of the *Northwestern Miller*. With an excusable bit of patriotic overstatement, the story's boldface headline announced that the company was "Again Completely American."

The 1889 investors in Pillsbury-Washburn, if any still remained, fared variously, according to whether they had purchased preference or ordinary shares. Assuming that the $50.00 par value of Pillsbury Flour Mills, Inc., shares represented their market value, the preference shareholder would have recaptured his $48.50 investment, plus $14.00 for unpaid dividends. The ordinary shareholder would have received only $12.50 for his $48.50 investment.

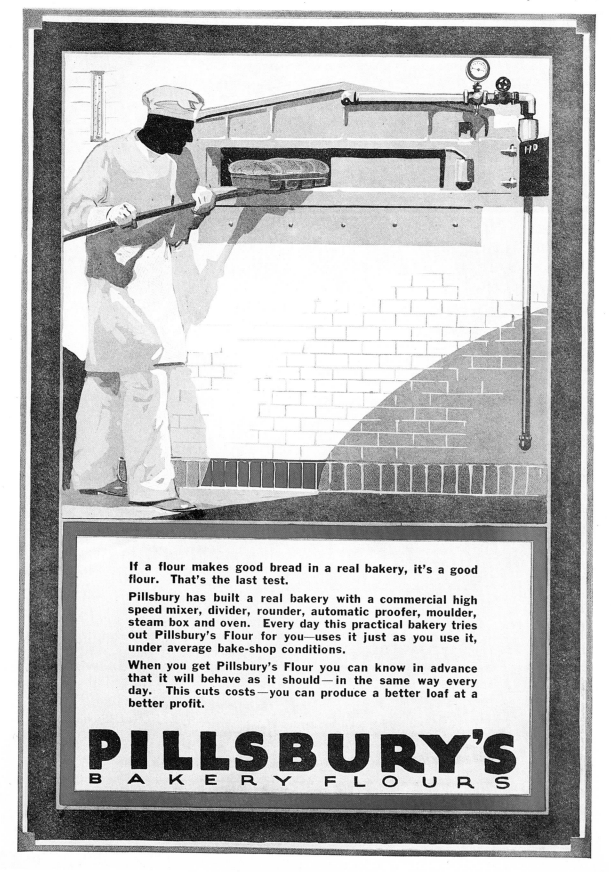

If a flour makes good bread in a real bakery, it's a good flour. That's the last test.

Pillsbury has built a real bakery with a commercial high speed mixer, divider, rounder, automatic proofer, moulder, steam box and oven. Every day this practical bakery tries out Pillsbury's Flour for you—uses it just as you use it, under average bake-shop conditions.

When you get Pillsbury's Flour you can know in advance that it will behave as it should—in the same way every day. This cuts costs—you can produce a better loaf at a better profit.

PILLSBURY'S
BAKERY FLOURS

Rapid expansion of the baking industry continued after the war. This ad for Pillsbury's bakery flours (left) appeared in the *Northwestern Miller* on September 18, 1929.

With the transaction complete, Pillsbury Flour Mills, Inc., still the country's second largest flour miller, owned mills in Minneapolis, Anoka, and Atchison, as well as the mill under construction in Buffalo. Pillsbury sold the two waterpower companies in October 1923 to H. M. Byllesby & Company, the parent of Northern States Power Company, for a combination of cash and physical property valued at between $4 and $5 million. In announcing the sale, Loring observed, "We are a milling company, not a waterpower company."[21]

When the Buffalo mill was completed in 1924, flour exports from the city of Buffalo were 3,023,000 barrels, as compared to 10,700 barrels exported that year from Minneapolis. Export shipments of flour from the Northwest had been declining for several years, and Pillsbury was no longer a major exporter of its own flour. Prior to its decision to build in Buffalo, however, the company had undertaken an ambitious export sales program, filling orders primarily with flour purchased from Canadian mills. As soon as the Buffalo mill began operations, Pillsbury was able to mill Canadian wheat in bond at Buffalo and again export its own product.[22]

After paying a dividend during its first fiscal year ending June 30, 1924, Pillsbury Flour Mills, Inc., omitted a dividend payment the next fiscal year in order to build its reserve. But net profits that year reached $1,087,000, and on September 1, 1925, the directors declared a 3-percent dividend. This payment began an unbroken series of dividend payment years, which at this writing has reached 60 consecutive years.

The baking industry continued to grow rapidly after the war. To meet baker requirements, flour millers produced a wide variety of flours specially formulated to produce bakery products such as breads, cakes, pastries, and doughnuts. Pillsbury's flour laboratories, renamed the "product control and bakery research department," devoted increasing hours to developing new bakery flour mixes for its salesmen.

A wave of major bakery mergers in the 1920s added materially to the concentrated buying power of the bakers. The customer had grown larger than the supplier by 1927, when the value of bread and bakery products first exceeded the value of flour milling products. Competition for the bakery business was intense, and millers constantly sought new ways to gain and hold business. Pillsbury's bakery service staff offered bakers production advice and assistance through booklets, technical publications, and seminars. Pillsbury advertising programs urged consumers to use more and more bakery products. Nonetheless, according to Herman Steen's *Flour Milling in America*, earnings from the bakery flour component of the industry were minimal: "Bakery flour margins for the miller have been narrow except for rather brief periods and on more than a few occasions have actually been non-existent . . . bakers [proved] to be better buyers than millers [were] sellers."[23]

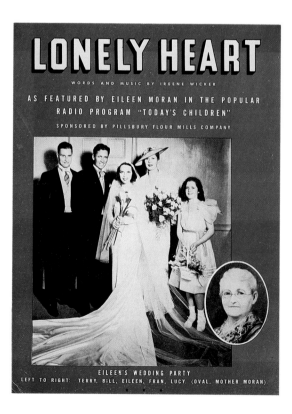

In the late 1920s Pillsbury promoted its sales of pancake flour with ads like this one in 1928 (far left). The next year it introduced its cake flour, shown in the 1931 ad (left, top). The company started advertising on radio in 1929. In 1935 Little Nick (above), a character introduced in Pillsbury advertising about 1910, announced the start of two programs, "Cooking Close-ups" and a soap opera, "Today's Children." The latter was popular enough to stimulate sales of sheet music (bottom, left).

The company met with only modest success in its attempts to gain a larger share of the highly competitive grocery market. In the last half of the 1920s it sought to improve its sales of pancake flour, a product field dominated by the well-entrenched Aunt Jemima brand. Then in 1929 it introduced Pillsbury Cake Flour, later called Sno Sheen®, an excellent product pitted against another well-established and heavily advertised product, General Foods' Swansdown® Flour. Pillsbury's Best® Flour, the crown jewel of the company's product line, had dropped to second place in the family flour market, probably during or soon after the receivership. Although it was not distributed nationally, Pillsbury's Best® Flour had a strong following in such principal markets as Minnesota, Wisconsin, Florida, Chicago, Pittsburgh, and part of Virginia.

In the 1880s and 1890s Loring had participated in the industry's conversion to large-capacity plants, designed to produce the highest volumes of flour at the lowest cost, and he displayed a seeming impatience with the consumer's growing preference for a smaller family flour package. Commenting on the "enormous" distribution cost increases involved in the change to small packages, he said in 1928, "To me we are moving too quickly. People are spending too much, and they are not really living. Thousands of young couples, beginning their married careers, are mortgaged to the hilt before they start. This fact is exceedingly disturbing to many business students today. Time only will prove whether the old virtues of industry and thrift are not after all the better way, not only for one's pocket book, but for one's piece of mind."[24]

Pillsbury was an early convert to the use of national radio advertising, both on the Columbia and National broadcasting networks. In 1929 it inaugurated on Columbia a series of programs conducted by a noted home economist and featuring Pillsbury products. Later, on the same network, it sponsored a second program, called "Cooking Close-ups from Pillsbury's Model Kitchen in Minneapolis." The company advertised on local radio as well, and its annals record the case of a prescient flour salesman who organized an orchestra in 1929 to entertain on Newark's local station. The orchestra was billed as the "Pillsbury Dough Boys."[25]

Along with producing top-quality products and advertising them, Loring believed in maintaining a strong sales force. In a 1928 interview with the North American Newspaper Alliance, he noted that the severe postwar competition had forced 2,000 small millers out of business. Attributing the downfall of these companies to their failure to build sales organizations, Loring said "they could make flour, but could not sell it."[26]

Pillsbury's sales offices in the late 1920s were located in approximately 25 offices around the country. Salesmen were responsible for both bakery flour and grocery sales and, in some cases, commercial feeds as well. Consequently they were obliged to deal not only with substantially different products but also with totally different buyers. It was not until the early 1940s that the company established separate sales forces for its bakery flour and grocery product lines.

Purchase of the Atchison mill in 1922 and completion of the Buffalo mill in 1924 enabled Pillsbury to maintain its competitive position. Because Southwest wheat cost less than Northwest wheat, Atchison and the other southwestern mills were able to obtain on the basis of price a large volume of business not available to other mills. At the same time, favorable freight rates for wheat compared to those for flour made it possible for Buffalo mills to buy spring wheat, mill it, and deliver the flour to eastern markets at a lower cost than could the Minneapolis mills.[27]

Minneapolis and the surrounding mills soon lost their place at the top of the industry ladder. For many years there had been talk in Minneapolis of overcapacity and of milling companies moving away. John S. Pillsbury testified at an Interstate Commerce Commission hearing in Minneapolis in 1927: "I simply want to call attention of the Commission to the tendency which has been going on here for the last ten or fifteen years to reduce the milling of the northwestern grain to a much smaller proportion than formerly existed. In spite of the growth of the population of the country, the milling of grain up here and merchandising it in the shape of flour has been steadily declining, due entirely to the fact that the grain from a great many sections of the country can be milled elsewhere to better advantage than it can be in Minneapolis." Buffalo became the country's largest flour manufacturing center in 1930. The Southwest had already replaced the Northwest as the nation's foremost milling region in 1925.[28]

Despite the decline in milling in the area, Pillsbury more than doubled its earnings in 1927, reaching a record high of $2,694,048. The next year's results were almost as good. Encouraged by the success of the Atchison and Buffalo investments and the strong economy of the late 1920s, the directors planned further geographical expansion. In July 1927 the company raised $6 million by sale of 60,000 shares of $100-par-value, 6.5-percent convertible preferred shares. At the same time it reclassified its common shares into 550,000 shares of no-par-value stock, reserving 150,000 shares for conversion of the new preferred shares.

Pillsbury built a mill in Enid, Oklahoma, in 1928. This photograph (above) was taken just prior to 1957.

In 1928 construction commenced on a 3,500-barrel mill at Enid, Oklahoma, the company's second mill in the Southwest. The company also built 2,500,000-bushel capacity elevators in both Enid and Wichita, Kansas. Early the next year the *Northwestern Miller* asked Loring about rumors that the company planned to build a mill in Springfield, Illinois, to establish a presence in the soft winter wheat belt. Loring, conscious of concerns that the flour milling industry might be overbuilding, replied that if another mill were built by the company, it would not increase total milling capacity. He said that the company was milling soft wheat flour and cereals at a disadvantage in Minneapolis; he added that any decision to build elsewhere would mean a realignment of capacity and the moving of idle or surplus equipment from Minneapolis.[29]

In 1928, the company constructed a family flour bag factory in Wellsburg, West Virginia, shown (above) in 1961. The next year it built a new milling complex in Springfield (top, right) and started acquisition of existing milling facilities in Astoria, Oregon (bottom, left).

The company made a non-flour-milling acquisition in November, 1928. Through a subsidiary, it acquired the Harvey Paper Company in Wellsburg, West Virginia, owner of a mill that specialized in paper suitable for flour containers. The next year the company built a warehouse at Wellsburg and acquired additional property on which it built its own family flour bag factory.

About the same time the company organized Unity Mills Distributing Company, a wholly owned subsidiary, to merchandise flour, feed, and other products such as paint, steel, and insecticides. By 1935 Unity Mills was operating distributing warehouses at 13 Minnesota cities outside Minneapolis and at three or four locations in both Iowa and Wisconsin. Never particularly profitable, the company was liquidated and its inventories disposed of in 1938. The Wellsburg bag factory, however, still operated in 1984.

In May 1929 Loring announced award of construction contracts for a new milling complex in Springfield. The mill, which commenced operating in 1930, was divided into A and B sections and had a total capacity of 3,800 barrels. The plant also included a 3,000-barrel cereal plant, a 1,300,000-bushel elevator, and a two-story warehouse. Machinery and equipment from the unused Minneapolis B mill were moved to Springfield.

In 1929 Pillsbury made its first acquisition of existing milling facilities since purchase of the old Phoenix mill in Minneapolis in 1916. The company and the owner of two flour mills in Astoria, Oregon, formed a new corporation, Pillsbury-Astoria Flour Milling Company, with Pillsbury the major shareholder. The new corporation then purchased the two Astoria mills. The mills produced flour under Pillsbury brands for export to the Philippines and the Orient, while continuing to export the former owners' brands. Two years later, in 1931, Pillsbury became sole owner of the mills.

While the front-page banner headline of the September 5, 1929, *Astoria Evening Budget* reported the Pillsbury purchase in Oregon, another story on the same page merited more attention than it probably received. Roger W. Babson, a noted statistician, predicted at a national business conference that a fall in the stock market would rival the collapse of the Florida land boom. He advised investors to pay their debts and avoid margin speculation. The following month the infamous Black Tuesday stock market crash set off the Great Depression.

Pillsbury reported record earnings of $2,814,564 for the fiscal year ending June 30, 1929, an earnings level it would not reach again for 18 years. During 1929 the preferred stock was retired by conversion to common. The authorized capital of the company was increased from 550,000 common shares to 1,000,000, of which 549,225 shares were outstanding. Previously listed on the New York Curb Ex-

Harrison H. Whiting was elected president of the company when Loring died. His four-year administration was fraught with complications brought on by the depression. Nevertheless, he prompted adoption of the company's first group plan for retirement benefits, life insurance, and accident and health insurance.

change, the company's common stock had first appeared on the New York Stock Exchange on August 25, 1927, opening at 37½ . On the day of Babson's speech the stock closed at 51¼, having ranged between 39⅛ and 63⅞ earlier in the year. On the last market day of 1929 the common shares closed at 34¾. In the years of the depression following they would close as low as 9⅜, on February 24, 1933.

In the early years of the depression the Pillsbury company made major changes in its Minneapolis facilities. The cereal plant at the A mill was discontinued and the east side of the mill was converted from spring wheat to durum. The Palisade mill building was torn down to the first story. The B mill elevator was sold, and the B and C mills were torn down to the first story and, along with the unused Anchor mill, converted to warehouse use. In Anoka the Lincoln mill was razed to its first story, and the "old mill" in Astoria was dismantled. Of the five mills acquired by Pillsbury-Washburn in 1889, only the historic Pillsbury A remained. In the language of the company's auditors, the reason for dismantling the Minneapolis mills was that their capacity "was in excess of the requirements for the milling of spring wheat in the Northwest area."

Although the Great Depression resulted in a downward trend in earnings, the company continued to pay its regular 50-cent quarterly dividends through fiscal 1932. In his letter to shareholders on August 20, 1932, Loring reported that "in view of the present economic conditions and the reduced earnings of the company," the directors had decided on August 3 to declare only a 30-cent dividend for that quarter. Loring added that salaries and wages of all employees had been reduced and economies effected "in many other ways."

Loring died December 11, 1932, after a brief illness. He had guided the company for 26 years as a receiver and as president, longer than any chief executive officer other than Charles A. Pillsbury. The dean of Minneapolis flour millers at the time of his death, Loring was the quintessential flour miller. His concept of the business was perhaps expressed best in his observation that the success of an individual producer of staples depended on his skill in buying and selling and on his ability to take advantage of savings and technical improvements. John S. Pillsbury, then a vice-president of the company, said, "We younger members of the firm find it almost impossible to express our admiration for him as to his personal consideration, kindliness and his remarkable judgment and business acumen."[30]

Three days after Loring's death the board of directors met and elected Harrison H. Whiting as president and chief executive officer of the company and John S. Pillsbury as chairman of the board. Whiting had joined the company in 1897, when he was 20 years old. Starting out as a stenographer in the traffic department, he moved to a similar job in the cereal department and soon was placed in charge of

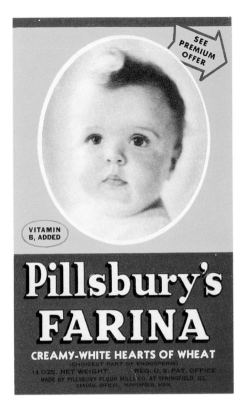

Pillsbury's Farina was the infants' version of
Vitos Wheat Cereal. A healthy baby was
pictured on the front of the box (above).

the company's advertising. His next assignment, responsibility for feed sales, launched him on a sales career. After the receivership he became manager of the company's Boston sales office and ultimately assumed responsibility for the whole New England territory. Returning to Minneapolis after the war, he was appointed general sales manager and was instrumental in improving the structure and manpower of the branch sales offices. Elected to the board in 1923, he was named vice-president in charge of sales on October 1, 1929.

The company was in strong financial condition when Whiting became president, and like most other milling companies, it was weathering the depression. Annual earnings from 1927 through 1931 had averaged a healthy $2,437,663, although in the last full year of Loring's presidency they had dipped to $829,642. In 1932 Pillsbury was predominantly a flour milling company rather than a grocery products company. Its principal internal records did not differentiate between bakery and family flour sales. The family flour sales policy was directed toward its 25-, 50-, and 100-pound sacks rather than its smaller sizes. While Pillsbury emphasized volume sales, its leading competitor had been building customer count with its strong promotion of the more convenient 5- and 10-pound packages.

The company had been accounting separately for its "specialty sales" since 1924. The products were Pillsbury Health Bran, Vitos Wheat Cereal, Pancake Flour, Dairy Ration, and Farina, to which Cake Flour had been added in 1929. Sales and profits of the specialty products line were not as high in 1932 as they had been in 1924. In fact, the specialties had been unprofitable since 1929, and selling and advertising expenses were cut back in 1931 and 1932.

Whiting's first year produced a modest turnaround, with earnings for the 11 months ended May 31, 1933, at $1,157,000. The company that year changed its fiscal year end from June 30 to May 31. Whiting explained in his letter to stockholders that the change was made "in order that the books may be closed before it is necessary to take into account any great amount of 'new crop' business or to buy any large amount of 'new crop' wheat."

Unfortunately Whiting's four years as president were mostly taken up with anticipation of and response to government efforts at ending the depression. In less than three months after Whiting took office, Franklin D. Roosevelt was inaugurated as president of the United States, ready and eager to carry out his promised "New Deal." Aid to agriculture was one of the administration's immediate concerns. Commodity prices, and particularly wheat prices, were at a dismal level in 1932 and 1933, the result of record domestic surpluses and a shrunken export market. Twelve days after he took office, President Roosevelt sent to Congress the Agricultural Adjustment Act, a measure he frankly described as a "new and untrod path."[31]

On May 12, 1933, the legislation, the consequences of which extended beyond Whiting's lifetime, was signed into law. Intended to raise agricultural prices, the act provided a means for farmers to reduce crop acreage in return for cash benefits financed by taxes on the same crop, which were collected at the point of processing. The tax on wheat processing was to be paid by the millers at the rate of 30 cents for each bushel of wheat ground after July 9, 1933.

The processing tax created major administrative problems for millers and customers alike, and these were exacerbated by early attempts to have the tax declared unconstitutional. The millers passed the tax on to their customers, causing a radical rise in flour prices. Many mills, including Pillsbury, inserted clauses in their sales contracts agreeing to refund the amount of taxes passed on if the act were found to be unconstitutional. In May 1935, the court enjoined collection of the tax by the millers until its constitutionality could be decided, and the tax payments were impounded pending the outcome of litigation. The following January the United States Supreme Court declared the act unconstitutional.

The decision by the Supreme Court led to refund claims and suits against the millers by bakers and other customers and, in 1936, to imposition of a windfall profits tax to recover the taxes passed on. In the end most millers refunded part of the tax to their customers, and both millers and customers paid large amounts of taxes for unjust enrichment. Pillsbury had set up a $6-million reserve, which cushioned financial impact on the company, but resolution of the problems caused by the processing tax went on for several years.[32]

Shortly after becoming president, Whiting prompted adoption of the company's first group plan for retirement benefits, life insurance, and accident and health insurance. The insured plan, effective in 1933, provided for regular contributions by both the company and the employees. The company paid $450,000 to the insurer to take care of all requirements for retirement benefits in respect of past services by employees, about half of this amount coming from proceeds of an insurance policy held by the company on Loring's life. The new program replaced Pillsbury's practice of using current earnings to pay benefits of up to $2,000 on the death of an employee, and retirement compensation "to deserving employees who have been retired."

The company effected a major reorganization in September 1935 in order to reduce expenses and avoid difficulties from proposed legislation to govern holding companies and tax intercompany dividends. A new corporation, Pillsbury Flour Mills Company, was incorporated in Delaware. (The original Pillsbury Flour Mills Company, incorporated in 1909, was a Minnesota corporation.) All of the properties of Pillsbury Flour Mills, Inc., and its subsidiaries were merged into

ADDRESS ALL COMMUNICATIONS TO THE COMPANY

PILLSBURY FLOUR MILLS COMPANY

OFFICERS & DIRECTORS
ALBERT C. LORING, President
CHARLES S. PILLSBURY, Vice Prest.
JOHN S. PILLSBURY, Vice Prest.
ALFRED F. PILLSBURY, Treas.
CLARK HEMPSTEAD, Secy.

DIRECTORS:
J. W. AVERY   HARRY C. PIPER
HENRY S. BOWERS H. H. WHITING
M. A. LEHMAN   DWIGHT K. YERXA
ROBERT LEHMAN   GEORGE A. ZABRISKIE

MINNEAPOLIS
U.S.A.

July 20, 1927

Mr. F. M. Overholt,

Pillsbury A Mill

3rd Ave. S. E. & Main St.,

Minneapolis, Minn.

Dear Sir:

Pursuant to your application for shares of Common Stock of Pillsbury Flour Mills, Incorporated, __50__ shares have been allotted to you. We have received $__250.00__ from you as down payment, leaving an unpaid balance of $__900.00__.

Please sign the enclosed installment note, the authorization for salary deductions and the stock power, and return the same immediately to us at the Minneapolis Office.

Very truly yours,

PILLSBURY FLOUR MILLS COMPANY

by___J. B. Beatty___

The company encouraged employee stock ownership, and this 1927 letter shows how employees could use salary deductions to purchase shares.

the new corporation, which exchanged $25 par value shares for the outstanding shares of Pillsbury Flour Mills, Inc. The only visible effect of the reorganization was to change the company's name.

Beginning in the summer of 1934 Minneapolis was the scene of a number of serious management-labor disputes, part of a nationwide drive for industrial unionization. In June a truck drivers' strike became so violent that the National Guard was called to maintain order. Settlement of that dispute was followed by a knitting mill strike, when again the National Guard was mobilized. By 1936 unrest extended to the flour mills, where some employees were members of the local Flour, Cereal and Elevator Workers Union. The local was one of about 75 in the United States and Canada that were affiliated with the newly formed National Council of Grain Processors and Allied Industries, a part of William Green's American Federation of Labor.

In late summer the local union forced the shut-down of two Minneapolis milling companies. The issue was not the usual one of wages or working conditions, but rather a demand for employer recognition of the union and collective bargaining. On September 3, 1936, pickets, believed to consist mostly of members of the truck drivers' union, surrounded the A mill and caused its closing. This was followed the next day by similar action at most other mills in the city.

Whiting was a member of a milling company delegation that met promptly with Governor Hjalmar Petersen to consider issues arising out of the strike. A representative of the National Labor Relations Board, a new federal agency created by the 1935 Wagner Act, came to Minneapolis to attempt conciliation and was joined there by a Department of Labor representative. The Pillsbury board, at two separate meetings in September, authorized payments to its idled millworkers, a practice adopted by most other milling companies as well. Perhaps prompted by the strike, the Pillsbury directors also adopted a vacation policy providing one week's vacation for persons employed from two to ten years, and two weeks for those employed more than ten years. The strike was still unsettled when tragedy struck. While horseback riding with his wife, Whiting was thrown from his horse, suffering serious injuries from which he died on October 3, 1936.[33]

Clark C. Hempstead succeeded Whiting as president and chief executive officer of the Pillsbury Flour Mills Company. Born in 1873 in Galena, a small town in northwestern Illinois, Hempstead came to Minneapolis with his parents in his early childhood. He graduated from the University of Minnesota and Harvard Law School. Returning to Minneapolis, he joined the firm of Koon, Whelan & Bennett where Ralph Whelan, Pillsbury's lead counsel during the receiver-

Clark C. Hempstead became Pillsbury's president in 1936, following the sudden death of his predecessor. He resigned as president in 1940 to resume his old position as general counsel, and he continued in the company's employ until he retired in 1946 at age 73.

ship, was a senior partner. Hempstead left the firm, which had become Koon, Whelan & Hempstead, to become secretary and general counsel of Pillsbury in 1921. He was elected a vice-president of the company in 1933.

A few days before Hempstead became president, Pillsbury and other Minneapolis milling companies involved in the labor conciliation proceedings had declared their willingness to negotiate with employees or their representatives; thereupon the Pillsbury mills and most of the others had reopened. Almost immediately however, Hempstead was confronted with another shut-down. The Northwest wheat crop in 1936 had been so sparse that the Pillsbury mills could not get enough wheat to operate their usual daily schedules, and employee checks became too small to provide a decent living. In order to distribute available work so that a living wage could be paid to the greatest number, Pillsbury laid off 71 employees and increased the workday for remaining employees from six to eight hours. Picketing by the union on November 2 led to another shut-down and submission of the issue to Governor Petersen. After hearing both sides he announced, ''I believe the employees now realize that the mill management was justified in laying off 71 workers because of decreased volume of business and that all of the 450 employees for whom work is still available will return to their jobs.'' After a few minor changes in the company's plan, the mills reopened November 11 with the lay-off still in effect.[34]

Negotiations for formal recognition of the union continued. On June 1, 1937, the company finally signed a contract with the American Federation of Labor, agreeing to recognize the union in all company plants where a majority of employees were members of affiliated unions. William Green personally signed the agreement on behalf of the American Federation of Labor. The same day the company and local union 19172 signed a supplemental agreement governing wages in Minneapolis; this was followed in due course by contracts between the company and local unions at the company's other mills.

Hempstead's first year was a successful one from an earnings standpoint. The company climbed back to the $1,518,000 level, prompting Chairman John S. Pillsbury to say, ''Despite constantly increasing expenses, including rapidly mounting taxes, we realized normal net earnings.'' The company constructed an additional flour milling unit at Springfield to produce 4,000 barrels daily. It transferred some of the equipment from the Minneapolis A mill there, since it still had more milling capacity in Minneapolis than it could operate advantageously. In the next year, 1937, Southwest wheat was in greater supply than Northwest wheat, and Minneapolis lost its second-place position among the nation's flour producers to Kansas City. Buffalo had taken first place from Minneapolis in 1930.[35]

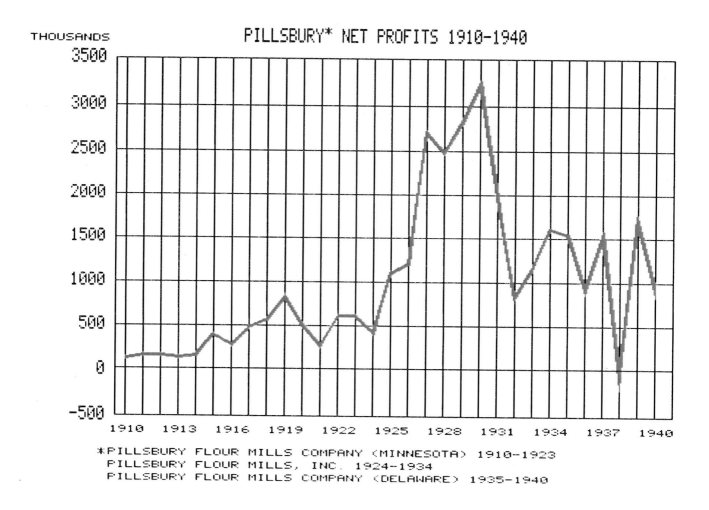

PILLSBURY* NET PROFITS 1910-1940

THOUSANDS

*PILLSBURY FLOUR MILLS COMPANY (MINNESOTA) 1910-1923
PILLSBURY FLOUR MILLS, INC. 1924-1934
PILLSBURY FLOUR MILLS COMPANY (DELAWARE) 1935-1940

Operations in fiscal year 1938 produced a $52,605 loss, the only loss year since Pillsbury Flour Mills Company began business in 1909. In his letter to shareholders on July 27, 1938, Hempstead reported that the loss resulted from severe competitive conditions in the flour market during the first quarter of the year. He wrote: "During June, July, and August, 1937, large quantities of flour were being booked by the trade, and competitive flour prices were much too low. The Company, faced with loss of valuable distribution unless it was reasonably competitive in price, decided that, even though the prices it might obtain would not be satisfactory, it was necessary to book, on a competitive basis, a fair share of the volume that was being sold. By this action the Company succeeded in maintaining its position in the trade, but a large portion of the flour booked by the Company during this period was sold at prices which resulted in severe loss." Despite the loss, the directors continued the payment of a $1.60 dividend, basing their action on the existence of undistributed earnings from previous years and an improvement in the flour market after the first quarter.

In 1939 the company's earnings reflected a continuing improved market with earnings of $1,692,318, the highest in several years. However, in 1940 earnings tumbled again, falling to $900,914. The company attributed the poor results to "unsatisfactory price conditions and the loss of the Company's export markets in Europe and in the Mediterranean countries."[36]

Hempstead resigned as president of the company on May 7, 1940. He was 67 years old, and he had accepted the position somewhat reluctantly to provide caretaker management following Whiting's death. He resumed his position as general counsel and was elected co-chairman of the board of directors. In 1946 he retired.

At the end of these middle years the company was still primarily a flour milling establishment. Year-to-year profit performances reflected prevailing conditions in the wheat and flour markets, commodities over which the company had no control. A small group of grocery products supplemented Pillsbury's Best® Flour, but the line was not growing and none of the products was in national distribution. The company had been guided over the last 10 years by three different chief executive officers, and it was about to get a fourth. According to the 1940 annual report, on May 14, 1940, there were 3,123 employees and 5,946 shareholders. The company's financial position was solid, its only funded debt consisting of a 3.75-percent mortgage in the principal amount of $5,600,000.

With the exception of two investment bankers, the 21-member board of directors was comprised entirely of current or retired company employees. Three of these were Pillsburys—John S., Alfred F., and Philip W. Philip was the grandson of Charles A. Pillsbury and son of Charles S. Pillsbury, who had died on May 29, 1939, after serving as a director from 1909 to 1939 and as vice-president from 1909 to 1932. Both John, who was chairman of the board, and Alfred, who had just retired as treasurer, had eschewed active management roles in the company in favor of devoting their principal energies to personal, civic, and charitable pursuits. Philip, on the other hand, had been a full-time employee of the company since graduating from college in 1924. He was to be Clark Hempstead's successor as chief executive officer. With 16 years of experience in almost all phases of the business, Philip was eager and determined to give a fresh purpose to the aging organization.

Winning Colors

WHITE · CHOCOLATE FUDGE · GOLDEN YELLOW

FRESH, MOIST AND BEAUTIFUL! Made with Pillsbury (the largest-selling cake mixes).
You get big, triumphant fresh cakes like these without cracking or separating a single egg.
The choice, wholesome country eggs are right in the mix. Milk is all you add.

Pillsbury
CAKE MIXES

WHITE · CHOCOLATE FUDGE · GOLDEN YELLOW

and the new Angel Food Cake Mix —

Pillsbury, the complete
Cake Mixes,
bought by more women than
any other brand—by far.

What goes into a Pillsbury Cake? All the good rich things it takes
to make a real quality cake, the finest ingredients money can buy.
Pillsbury spares nothing, cuts no corners. You get special shorten-
ings, specially granulated sugar, finest flavoring extracts, choice,
wholesome country eggs. And of course, Pillsbury's own wonderful
cake flour, sifted more than 40 times.

Milk is all you add

No eggs to buy. No flavorings or extras of any kind required. These
are the complete mixes, the quality mixes, the economical mixes.

5 Buckling Down
1940–1952

Philip W. Pillsbury was elected president and chief executive officer of the company on May 7, 1940. His path to the presidency traced back to 1923, the year his father, his uncle, and his cousin reacquired the family milling business from the English. That summer, before returning to Yale University for his senior year, Philip attended some of the negotiating sessions with the Pillsbury-Washburn representatives in London. His plans had been to pursue a medical career, but once the return of the properties was accomplished, his family persuaded him to cast his lot with the company.

Philip finished his final year at Yale, where he was named to the All-American water polo team and played guard on the school's undefeated, untied football team. Upon graduation in 1924, he set out on an eight-year program to instruct him thoroughly in every phase of the flour milling process. After all, the reputation and early success of the company had been built on the quality of its flour. C. A. Pillsbury and Loring had both been skilled flour millers, assuring that no flour would be better than Pillsbury's Best®. It was simple logic that this Pillsbury should also become firmly grounded in the art.

Starting as a clerk in the A mill wheat department, Philip worked at nearly every job in the mill. He stayed long enough in each to understand and perform all the tasks required from the receipt of the grain to shipment of the milled products. From time to time he was summoned from the mill by Loring to participate in a conference at the headquarters building or to spend a day in the president's office. In 1928 he joined the board of directors, at 25 years of age its youngest member in history. He moved to the Buffalo mill and then to Atchison, where for a number of months he worked as a ''trick'' miller, responsible for all milling operations during a shift. By the time Philip transferred to the sales department in 1932, he had attained active membership in the Association of Operative Millers, the millers' equivalent of the American Association of Cereal Chemists.

Philip's first sales assignment was in Chicago, where he ultimately became branch manager and for a time supervised the Kansas City and Denver offices as well. After three years in Chicago Philip returned to Minneapolis to assume responsibility for the company's sales in the eastern United States. Then, shortly after his seventieth

Under Philip Pillsbury's leadership the company shifted from its primary reliance on flour milling. Moving into the postwar period with a new line of consumer mix products including these three popular cake mixes, it quickly established a new image with the nation's grocers and homemakers.

Philip W. Pillsbury, the grandson of Charles A. Pillsbury, was elected president of the company in 1940. One of his first major decisions was to acquire Globe Grain and Milling Company, giving Pillsbury an important entry into the growing California and western states market. Globe's Los Angeles operations are shown in 1912 (left, top) and in the late 1950s (left, bottom).

birthday, Alfred Pillsbury retired as treasurer; in January 1940 Philip was named to the post. Alfred had one more step in mind for Philip. Both Alfred Pillsbury and Clive T. Jaffray, a Minneapolis banker and business leader who had been a friend and close adviser of the Pillsbury family for many years, were urging the board to make Philip president of the company.[1]

That opportunity came when Clark Hempstead tendered his resignation at the May 7, 1940, board meeting; the directors promptly elected Philip as Hempstead's successor. John S. Pillsbury continued as chairman of the board, a position to which he had been elected when Whiting became president in 1932. As had been the case since their adoption in 1923, the by-laws continued to provide for the president to be the chief executive officer of the company.

When the new president took office, the company's flour mills were running at capacity, and its two animal feed plants at Atchison and Minneapolis were competing successfully in their respective regional markets. The grocery products line—the other, never particularly successful, business of the company—was on a downhill slide. Over all, having recovered from the small loss experienced in 1937, Pillsbury's operations were in the black, and the stockholders were receiving regular dividends. But the company was locked firmly in the doldrums, badly in need of diversification, greater size, and more visibility in the grocery store.

In short, Pillsbury Flour Mills Company was neither a promising nor progressive organization, and its choice of the 37-year-old Philip as president did not give rise to great expectations. As he himself said, ''Several years ago . . . when I was asked to be president . . . there was a great deal of criticism from Wall Street, and other financial sections, as to 'Why are they picking a stockholder, a member of the family, to run this sleeping giant? Why haven't they got somebody in the corporation who can really buckle down and turn out bigger profits?'''[2]

By the time Philip turned over the chief executive reins 12 years later, the company was embarked on a new and exciting course, and the marketplace was viewing the company in a different light. People close to the situation in 1940 have attested that no one was as well equipped as Philip to revive the organization.[3]

Philip's first challenge as president and chief executive officer was to steer the company through a major decision that May—whether or not to pursue an opportunity to acquire Globe Grain and Milling Company, a large West Coast miller. Globe had begun business around 1890 as the McDonald Company, operating a small feed mill in Los Angeles County. By 1940 it owned flour mills in Los Angeles, San Francisco, and Sacramento and in Ogden, Utah; it owned feed mills in Ogden and several California locations, as well as a macaroni plant in Culver City, California. Its product line, distrib-

Pillsbury still operates the Globe flour and feed mills in Ogden, Utah, (left, top) today. One of its fleet of flour trucks is shown being loaded in the early 1940s at Los Angeles (left, bottom). A booklet (above) containing recipes for Globe products advertised Globe A 1 macaroni on its inside cover (right).

uted principally west of the Rockies, included bakery flour, family flour, pancake and waffle flour, biscuit mix and macaroni, all marketed under the Globe "A 1" label.[4]

General Mills, Inc., formed in 1928 by consolidation of Washburn Crosby and four other companies, had already expanded westward in 1929 by acquiring Sperry Flour Company, the West Coast's leader. Pillsbury's Best® Family Flour was still in second place, but its sales were lagging farther and farther behind General Mills' family flour. And a consumer research firm's report in May showed Sno Sheen®, Pillsbury's cake flour, in third place nationally, far behind its two principal rivals. It was evident that the company's business was slipping away, and so the board decided at the end of May to send representatives to California to conduct further studies of Globe. Finally, on June 24, the directors voted to make the acquisition. Alfred, who with John S. Pillsbury had previously been somewhat ambivalent in the matter, was quoted as concluding that he would rather "die from over-expansion and action than to suffocate from rotting."[5]

The $3.6 million purchase became effective July 16, 1940. The understanding with Globe's management was that Globe would operate as an autonomous division, with Minneapolis headquarters providing advice but keeping hands off the day-to-day operations. Globe immediately began to manufacture and distribute Pillsbury products along with its own "A 1" line, creating for Pillsbury its first effective outlet to the important West Coast market. Globe met a vital need, one that the Astoria acquisition 11 years earlier had not fulfilled. Globe's 4,000-barrel-per-day flour milling capacity brought Pillsbury's daily capacity to about 40,000 barrels, roughly half that of its principal competitor.

The company built its first foods research laboratory in 1941, locating it on the block behind the Minneapolis A mill (left, top). Concurrently it upgraded its consumer services, and in 1944 it established a new Home Service Department. In the early 1950s several members of the department, together with a young visitor, enjoyed a taste test (left, bottom).

Pillsbury had entered the 1940s without a plan for broadening its narrow product line and without any in-house capability for new-product development. Philip was eager to change this. For some time he had been studying product research programs in other United States food and nonfood companies, and three months after his election as president he secured board authority to construct and equip a foods research laboratory in Minneapolis. The new facility opened in early 1941. The next year a building was constructed adjacent to the A mill to house the wheat selection and the product control departments, reinforcing the entirely separate purpose of the company's new research organization.

The announcement of plans for the product research laboratory included the appointment of a director of research, to report directly to the president. Philip, meanwhile, kept himself current on corporate research practices by serving on the executive committee of the Industrial Research Institute, an affiliate of the National Research Council. The product development process was soon established as a key part of the company's operations, and in six years time the company's food research laboratories tripled in size.[6]

The first year under the new president was one of intense competition in the milling industry, and toward the end of the year it became apparent that earnings would fall below those of the previous year. At its meeting on April 30, 1941, the board of directors weighed carefully the dividend that would normally be payable about June 1. The board decided to reduce the quarterly dividend but not to break the company's string of 55 consecutive quarterly payments. Philip was a staunch shareholder advocate, sympathetic to their dividend expectations. Many years later he commented that the company had omitted to pay dividends in only one year since 1910, and that subsequently the omission proved to have been unnecessary.

For many years the company's feed mills at Minneapolis and Atchison had been producing animal feed for sale in neighboring cattle-raising and dairy areas. As was frequently the case in the industry, the two feed mills were constructed to add value to the by-products of the adjoining flour mills, and the feeds produced were essentially blends of these by-products. Vitamins and antibiotics were unknown when the two feed mills were built, and it was common practice for farmers to mix their own feeds. But in the 1930s a more sophisticated formula feed industry began to emerge, as scientists and feed technologists formulated new feeds and concentrates to increase livestock and poultry production. The nation's commercial feed business took on a new stature, and in the brief span between 1939 and 1947, the value of its product increased by more than 400 percent.[7]

In 1942 the company formed Pillsbury Feed Mills, a new division with headquarters in Clinton, Iowa (left, top). Inside, feedsacks are loaded onto pallets (left, bottom). A 1949 ad (above) featured one of the division's customers.

With five Globe feed mills added to those at Minneapolis and Atchison, the company decided to increase its stake in the promising business. In July 1942 it formed Pillsbury Feed Mills, a separate division, ranking in organizational structure with Pillsbury and Globe. Headquarters for the new division were established at Clinton, in northeastern Iowa, where that March the company had purchased an existing feed mill, modernized it, and added new feed laboratories. The feed mills at Minneapolis and Atchison became part of the new division, while the Globe plants remained a part of Globe.[8]

In the meantime soybeans, grown extensively throughout the Midwest, had become an important crop in the country's agricultural economy. Soybean meal, separated from the oil in the crushing process, was used principally as an animal feed ingredient, while the oil served many other food and nonfood uses. Continuing to reach out for ways to build its feed business, in 1943 the company purchased a soybean processing plant and elevators at Centerville in southeastern Iowa. The next year it constructed at Clinton, Iowa, one of the most modern soybean plants in the country. For several years the two plants were operated as a fourth division of the company, called Pillsbury Soy Mills. Later these operations became part of a combined feed and soy division.

When Philip became president of the company in May 1940, war in Europe was well under way, and it was clearly only a matter of time before the United States would be involved. Japan's surprise attack on Pearl Harbor came on December 7, 1941, and the United States was at war. It would be almost four years before Japan's surrender on August 14, 1945, following Germany's capitulation in May, would bring World War II to an end.

During World War II the flour milling industry escaped the severe regulation imposed during World War I. Instead of the short wheat supply and heavy Allied demand for flour that characterized 1917, the country's wheat stocks on April 1, 1942, were the highest on record for that date. Wheat production continued at a high level throughout the war years so that, except for the country's broadly imposed price controls, there was little government regulation of the industry.[9]

The major war effort of the flour milling industry was to publicize the nation's need for building strength through good nutritional practices and for avoiding waste. Pillsbury had pioneered in the enrichment of flour with vitamins and iron in 1941. Consequently its enriched flour had enabled bakers to anticipate a government order effective January 18, 1943. From that date all white bread, because it was consumed daily in significant amounts by practically everyone, was required to be enriched to prescribed nutritive standards.[10]

PILLSBURY FLOUR MILLS COMPANY

MILLS AT MINNEAPOLIS – BUFFALO – ATCHISON, KAN. – ENID, OKLA. – SPRINGFIELD, ILL. – ASTORIA, ORE.

GENERAL OFFICES   MINNEAPOLIS, MINN.

December 8, 1941

TO THE PILLSBURY FAMILY:

Our country has been attacked. All of us must join together as a unified nation. We must win to keep our markets, our jobs, and our American freedom.

Our work as producers of food is vital to our soldiers and sailors, to our factory workers, to the entire civilian population, to every mother and child.

For months Pillsbury Flour Mills Company has been helping build gun mounts. We have thrown our research facilities open to the government. To protect our mills from sabotage, keep outsiders out and take extra care of machinery and equipment.

We all have one goal -- to do everything we can to help win and end this War. Until called on by our government for additional services, do your own job well. Take extra care of your health. Be calm.

Respectfully,

Philip W. Pillsbury

President

PWP:EB

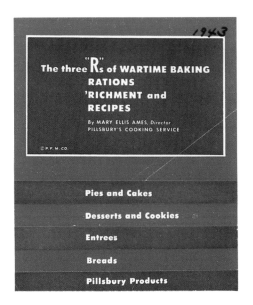

The three "R"s of WARTIME BAKING
RATIONS
'RICHMENT and
RECIPES

By MARY ELLIS AMES, Director
PILLSBURY'S COOKING SERVICE

© P. F. M. CO.

Pies and Cakes

Desserts and Cookies

Entrees

Breads

Pillsbury Products

Philip Pillsbury wrote this letter (left) to employees the day after Pearl Harbor was attacked. As part of the war effort the company encouraged food conservation and good nutritional practices through such means as special wartime baking recipes (above).

The armed forces needed special food products and new kinds of packaging during the war. Commenting on the packaging requirements years later, Philip reported that, ''Along with our good bag manufacturing friends, we developed sacks that could be dropped into the ocean out of Japanese artillery range and have the tide float them to our boys having a tenuous hold on the beachheads.''[11]

The foods research laboratory, acting through a specially constituted War Supply Department, developed a number of products for the U.S. Army Quartermaster Corps. For the army's K and C rations the company produced a premixed, precooked cereal of wheat flakes combined with puffed wheat. The cereal was compressed by outside contractors, including the Cambridge Tile Company in Ohio, into 1½-ounce oblong bars for the K ration and into discs for the C ration. Pillsbury also produced dehydrated bean soup and green pea soup mixes, and undertook some limited work on cake mixes for the quartermaster corps. In addition to supplying the armed forces, the company produced supplies to feed persons in liberated nations and to be included in cartons of food sent to prisoners of war by the American Red Cross. Even the A mill machine shop became a military supplier, producing gun mounts for the navy.[12]

The company's revitalization did not go unnoticed. *Business Week* reported in its February 5, 1944, issue that Pillsbury ''has launched an extensive program of diversification under the leadership of its youthful president,'' and it predicted that ''after the war, Pillsbury salesmen probably will be peddling dry cereal, dehydrated soups, and possibly some new baking mixes to grocers along with their standard lines of flour, pancake flour, cake flour, etc.'' Other articles in the press kept the public abreast of the company's broadened activity.

During the war years Philip devoted large amounts of his time to establishing a strong bond between the company and its employees. Visiting company facilities across the country, he renewed acquaintanceships and met personally with a large number of plant and office employees. At some locations he presented service pins to longtime employees. He awarded lapel pins to the Springfield mill employees, in recognition of its having been the first milling organization to receive the U.S. Army-Navy ''E'' Award for outstanding achievement in war work. During the war he wrote a monthly letter to all employees in service, wrote personal replies to all letters received from these employees and sent each of them his or her hometown Sunday newspaper. As a result, a high percentage of veterans returned to employment at Pillsbury, and a spirit of company loyalty developed that is still evident. As Philip once opined, ''There's more of a soul to the company when there's a family tinge to it.''[13]

ORANGE DESSERT PANCAKES

Makes 20 three-inch cakes

2 • cups unsifted PILLSBURY PANCAKE
    FLOUR (Plain or Buckwheat)
2 • teaspoons grated orange rind
2 • eggs, well beaten
1 • cup strained orange juice
⅔ • cup water
3 • tablespoons melted shortening
  • Sweetened orange sections
  • Whipped cream, if desired

1. Combine flour and orange rind. **2.** Combine eggs, orange juice, and water. Add slowly to dry mixture. Add shortening; beat until free from lumps. **3.** Bake on hot greased griddle, turning only once. **4.** Serve with sweetened orange sections and whipped cream, if desired.

The company moved its headquarters to the Metropolitan Building (above), later renamed the Pillsbury Building, at 608 Second Avenue South in 1942. The company celebrated its seventy-fifth anniversary with a special recipe book (left, top and bottom) and with activities at the A mill, where Philip Pillsbury personally bagged sacks of flour for visitors (far left).

Despite severe material and manpower shortages as well as other abnormalities brought on by war, there was a growing sense of optimism in the company. And as if to set the stage for a fresh start, the company on February 2, 1942, moved its headquarters from the Metropolitan Life Building, its home for 51 years. The new headquarters were three blocks away in the Metropolitan Building at 608 Second Avenue South, a building subsequently purchased by the company in 1946 for $355,000. Space was provided for an advertising department, as the company prepared to increase its expenditures in that area. Robert J. Keith, who later became Pillsbury's chief executive officer, was put in charge of the company's national advertising.

The year 1944 marked Pillsbury's seventy-fifth anniversary, and on June 5 it celebrated its founding in a ceremony at the A mill. That same day Allied forces made a triumphal entry into Rome; the next morning witnessed D-Day on the Normandy beaches. Minnesota's governor, Edward J. Thye, one of the speakers at the A mill celebration, praised the company's service to the country in two world wars. At the close of the program, Philip reverted to his days as a packer at the mill and packed small souvenir sacks of Pillsbury's Best® Flour for the guests.

While maintaining wartime production at capacity levels, the company's management was also looking ahead to the immediate postwar period. If the company were to enjoy substantial growth, it would have to establish an identity beyond that of a pioneer flour miller. In September 1944 the shareholders took a first step in this direction, changing the corporate name from Pillsbury Flour Mills Company to Pillsbury Mills, Inc. At the same meeting they authorized the issue of 100,000 shares of cumulative preferred stock, of which 75,000 were sold immediately. Part of the $7.3 million proceeds would retire an outstanding bond issue, freeing the company of all secured debt. The balance of the proceeds went into working capital.

Philip had appointed a postwar planning committee for the company a few days after the Pearl Harbor attack. Its April 25, 1944, report to the board listed the results of a questionnaire seeking recommendations of employees for postwar product lines. The responses showed an employee group intent on breaking away from the company's 75-year emphasis on traditional flour mill products. The committee reported that 76 employees favored dry cereals and 75 recommended convenience foods. Soups were recommended in 49 responses, and there was support (in declining order) for additional ready-to-cook cereals, expansion of hotel and restaurant products, dog food, macaroni, spaghetti and related products, and sale of patented doughnut machines.[14]

Americans who make you proud to be an American

YANKS CAPTURE HILL

Hill of Heroism

Summer, 1944. From their Normandy beachhead, the advancing Americans are closing in on the great port of Cherbourg. A strategic German-held hill overlooking the city belches death from five 105-millimeter guns, five 88's, and 16 other automatic weapons. Through fragrant meadow grass, up wooded slopes raked by deadly fire, a lieutenant from Minnesota leads 125 men toward the enemy positions. Three times, as death and wounds reduce his force, the lieutenant leaps atop a tank to rally the survivors and keep them moving forward. Sixty men—less than half the force that started the assault—are still in combat when the enemy guns cease firing and white flags appear. Behind those flags come 228 Germans, hands in air, leaving 70 dead comrades around the silent guns. . . . "Yanks Capture Hill," say the headlines.

How can any of us do enough to back up men like this?

TO HASTEN THE FINAL VICTORY...
BUY WAR BONDS!...BUY MORE BONDS!

PILLSBURY MILLS, INC.

[formerly named PILLSBURY FLOUR MILLS COMPANY]

1¼ lbs.   Prepared

Pillsbury's
GOLDEN
BAKE
MIX
WITH 20% SOY

MIXTURE OF WHEAT FLOUR, SOYA GRITS, RICE FLOUR, SALT,
SODA, MONOCALCIUM PHOSPHATE, AND POWDERED SKIM MILK

For PANCAKES
WAFFLES...MUFFINS

Manufactured by Pillsbury Flour Mills Company at Springfield, Illinois
General Offices: Minneapolis, Minnesota

Reg. U.S. Pat. Off.   © P. F. M. Co.

During the war, the company ran a series of
ads like the one (left) prepared for the *Northwestern Miller* in the fall of 1944. That year
it also introduced a new soy flour product,
Golden Bake Mix (above), formulated as a
response to wartime rationing of other
protein foods.

With Philip's firm encouragement, a commitment to improve the
company's standing in the consumer market was building. Although
significant expansion of Pillsbury's grocery product line would have
to await the end of the war, the company did expand its homemaker
services by upgrading the Pillsbury Cooking Service to a much
broader Home Service Department. Along with increasing its staff of
home economists, the department in 1944 created a fictitious Ann
Pillsbury to symbolize its services. As the *Northwestern Miller* wrote
on November 1, 1944, ''In keeping with customary trade practice,
the identity of Ann Pillsbury will be given to all activities by the department.'' In 1944 Ann Pillsbury signed all company advertisements
as well as a special anniversary cookbook published by the company.
The following year the department moved into a specially designed
Ann Pillsbury Home Service Center on the top floor of the headquarters building.

That year the company introduced its first new grocery product in
several years—Golden Bake Mix for pancakes, waffles, and biscuits.
Made with soy flour, a valuable source of protein, it was advertised
as helping the homemaker counter wartime rationing of meat and other
protein foods. Unfortunately, the product's taste did not equal its nutritional qualities, and it was not a success. Its early demise was has-
tened by a federal court decision in late 1945 enjoining the use of the
Golden Bake name, which was similar to that of a competing
product.[15]

Meanwhile the company had been working hard to improve its
share of the family flour market. In the early 1920s there emerged a
clear-cut consumer preference for small-size family flour packages.
The popularity of 5- and 10-pound packages rose with the advent of
chain stores when shoppers began to show a marked aversion to carrying 25- and 50-pound sacks home from the store. But even as late
as Whiting's presidency, Pillsbury's emphasis remained resolutely
on selling a high volume of flour by concentrating on the market for
100-, 50- and 25-pound sacks. In 1970 Philip recounted that, ''Railroads published daily figures of all flour mill loadings, and we were
all very happy that the sales department emphasized selling large
sacks. Let the competition have the 5 lb. and 12 [*sic*] lb. business!
This terrible mistake of emphasizing [large] sizes in the family business was later referred to as trying to stay in the buggy whip business.'' General Mills' winning strategy was just the opposite—to
concentrate on building the broadest possible customer base by vigorously promoting the smaller sizes, especially in large population
centers.[16]

Immediately after the end of the war the flour milling industry was called upon to help relieve the threat of famine in a number of the world's impoverished nations. Packers at the Buffalo mill (above) prepared double-strength sacks for export to west Africa.

Philip was acutely aware of Pillsbury's strategic mistake, and he instituted steps to correct it. In the early 1940s Philip established separate sales responsibilities for the company's sales forces, allowing grocery product salesmen to concentrate exclusively on the grocery trade while bakery flour and mix salesmen handled the bakery sales. He ordered improvements in the company's smaller-sized flour packages, and he sharply increased advertising expenditures for Pillsbury's Best® Flour and other Pillsbury grocery products. In addition, the protein content of family flour was decreased, creating an all-purpose flour equally successful for bread, cake, biscuits, or pie.

Significant strategy change during the war was ruled out by material and manpower shortages, coupled with a need for all-out production. But Philip nevertheless laid the groundwork to increase the company's chances for renewal and development after the war. One such undertaking was the refashioning of the company's board of directors to make it a greater source of leadership and direction for management. The board that elected Philip had 21 members, with two investment brokers its only "outside" board members. At the September 1941 annual meeting, the stockholders reduced the board to 13 members and elected Clive Jaffray a director. In 1944 the election of Edward B. Cosgrove, president of the Green Giant Company, brought vital marketing expertise to the board, and in 1946 James F. Brownlee, a New York executive with a distinguished record in sales, marketing, and advertising, added even more. In 1944 the company employed Samuel N. Stevens, president of Grinnell College in Iowa, to act as a consultant in personnel and organization matters; six years later he was elected to the board.[17]

Before resuming its normal peacetime activities the milling industry was called upon to answer one more urgent need. In 1946 various parts of the world faced serious danger of famine, brought on by severe drought and the inevitable dislocations of war. That February, to provide more wheat for the stricken nations, the United States government ordered millers to cut back domestic distribution of flour to 85 percent of the previous year and to change the normal extraction rate from 72 to 80 percent. The brown flour produced by using a greater part of the wheat berry led to a temporary disappearance from the marketplace of Pillsbury's Best® Family Flour and other premium brands. But when controls were lifted before the end of the year, the country had exported an additional 25 million bushels of wheat.[18]

At war's end the company consisted of four divisions—the Pillsbury division was the largest, followed by the Globe, feed, and soy divisions. As the company's focus sharpened, two reorganizations occurred. The first came on June 1, 1946, when the Pillsbury division was broken into flour and cereal, bulk premix, and overseas divisions. Concurrently the feed and soy divisions were combined,

Pillsbury's Pie Crust Mix, introduced in 1946 and shown in a 1948 ad (above), was practically unopposed in the market.

while the Globe division continued unchanged. The changes in organization were accompanied by introduction for the first time of a management incentive pay program for key employees, based upon performance of both the company and its separate divisions. Only a year before the company had adopted a budgeting system including procedures for annual planning, comparison of performance to plans, and approval and control of capital expenditures.

The second reorganization occurred on June 1, 1947. In the light of the company's growing emphasis on consumer foods, the flour and cereal division was further divided into grocery products, flour milling, and grain divisions. These new alignments, completed seven years after Philip became president, clearly signaled the company's future direction.[19]

Pillsbury made a conscious decision not to enter the dry breakfast cereal business after the war, even though the category had received the most "new-product" votes in the 1944 questionnaire to key employees. In response to shareholder inquiries as to why the company did not do so, the company wrote, "To enter this field would require a huge investment program because those companies now in the field have established strong brand franchises . . . They have invested many millions of dollars to gain their position in the market."[20]

Within six months after the Japanese surrender, however, the board of directors approved two new grocery products. The first approval, on December 18, 1945, authorized production of a packaged biscuit mix under the name Minitmix. The plan called for the product to be in national distribution by May 31, 1947, and to produce profits by 1950. While the product was a good one, General Mills' Bisquick had preceded it by several years and had gained a strong national market position. Minitmix's share of the market did not reach satisfactory levels, and the product was discontinued in 1952.[21]

It was a different story with the second product, the first of a new line of Pillsbury products that would show the company in a brand new light. Pillsbury's Pie Crust Mix, approved by the board on February 13, 1946, was practically unopposed in the market. A complete packaged mix, it enabled the homemaker to prepare a two-layer piecrust simply by adding water to the mix. Introduced in 1946, it was followed the next year by Pillsbury's Hot Roll Mix and in 1948 by Pillsbury's White Cake Mix and Pillsbury's Chocolate Fudge Cake Mix, the first chocolate cake mix to appear in the grocery store.

Paul S. Gerot, who at the beginning of 1946 was vice-president of sales and advertising in the Pillsbury division, recalled: "The company took the position that we ought to go where other people were not. We ought to be innovative enough and sensitive enough to the changes in life style that were occurring, to go into products that either were not available to consumers, or were very much in the embryo stage.

HOMEMADE
Hot Rolls!

EASY..QUICK with the new

Pillsbury HOT ROLL MIX

Now—every time you make them—perfect homemade raised rolls. Cinnamon rolls, coffee cake, too. So easy with the new Pillsbury Hot Roll Mix. Made by Pillsbury, so you know it's good. Easy-to use yeast included. Simple— you just add water to yeast, and mix. Ann Pillsbury's directions right on package.

You and Ann Pillsbury

CAN MAKE A GREAT TEAM Ann Pillsbury has developed a new Hot Roll Mix in *her* kitchen to save you time in *your* kitchen, and give you perfect results every time.

Pillsbury's Hot Roll Mix (above) was introduced in 1947.

"I recall we emphasized that we were capable of developing a pie crust mix, which at that time really had no market at all. But it had convenience and quality, and with a good product, a good label, a good name, and good advertising, we felt that we could move very effectively in that area. Well, there were those who argued we were spending a lot of time on minor items, but we took the position that a 35 or 40 per cent share in a minor category was far better from our point of view than a 5- or 10-per cent share in a bigger arena. So that's the philosophy on which we operated.

"We followed that with a hot roll mix, when there was only one regional brand on the market. We thought we had a better product, we knew we had a good label and a good name and we established a very dominant position in that area.

"That is about the time the trade began to realize that these people may know what they are doing. Our sales people became a little more confident of our direction and before we knew it we became known as 'mix headquarters.' It was a wonderful thing to have happen because it meant that when our salespeople approached our customers with a new product, they'd get an early and favorable customer reaction and we wouldn't run into the resistance that some products had because they were 'me too' products."[22]

The success of the new mixes cemented Pillsbury's consumer franchise. The Pillsbury name became much more important in the grocery store and in the home as its new mix products, supported by effective advertising, maintained their market leadership. Sales of Pillsbury's Best® Flour and the rest of the grocery product line, benefiting directly from the company's increased visibility, strengthened and took on new life.

It had not been an easy task to prod the organization of an old-line flour milling company into an aggressive, market-oriented, consumer-directed existence. In order to counteract persistent complaints from some of the old school that too much was being spent on consumer product marketing, the board began early in 1945 to allocate advertising and promotion funds to each grocery product on the basis of its projected sales volume. Even in 1946, Philip had been obliged to support the introduction of the new piecrust mix over the objection of one of his veteran officers, who asked, "Why not spend your time on important things!"[23]

The war had been a boon to the sale of bulk premixes, blends of flour, and other ingredients marketed to wholesale and retail bakers. Shortages of labor and irregular availability of critical ingredients produced a heavy demand by the country's bakeries, hotels, and restaurants for ready-made doughnut, cake, and pastry mixes. The convenience of the prepared mixes, together with savings in preparation time and ingredient cost, ensured their popularity after the war.

In 1946, the company completed construction of a new feed mill in Lima, Ohio (above, inside).

As a result, one of the company's postwar priorities was to add to its bulk premix capacity. The August 1946 issue of *Pillsbury People* announced that the company would build a new bakery mix plant in Springfield to meet increased demand. The new plant was the first in the country designed solely for manufacturing premix products for the bakery and institutional trade. It opened on July 20, 1949, when Illinois Governor Adlai Stevenson pushed a button activating the automated plant.[24]

While postwar expansion of the formula feed business had not generated within the company the level of enthusiasm accorded to the production of new grocery products, the feed division managers were pushing hard for more capital investment in their division. At an April 26, 1944, board meeting the division president recommended that new feed plants be built in Texas, in the Southeast, and in either eastern Illinois or Indiana. As soon as the war ended, the company announced that construction would commence on a new plant in Lima, Ohio, and that plant opened in 1946. The new location assured better service to customers east of the Mississippi, particularly the extensive broiler operations in Delaware and Maryland. In 1946 the company replaced the Los Angeles feed mill with a new plant in east Los Angeles, and in 1950 it made major improvements in the Minneapolis plant.[25]

By 1950 Pillsbury was a prominent factor in the formula feed industry, with ten feed plants supplying important livestock and poultry producing areas. In a 1952 magazine interview, Philip contrasted this with the company's insignificant feed operations before the war, noting: "Today our feed & soybean division accounts for a quarter of our volume which means it's bigger than total company sales were in 1941." Formula feeds, grocery products, and bakery flour and mix had arrived as the company's three major components.[26]

The decision to form a separate grain division as part of the June 1, 1947, reorganization reflected recognition of the grain merchandising business as a significant profit opportunity. For many years Pillsbury had bought and sold wheat beyond the requirements of its own mills, often storing the grain in its own mill elevators until it could be sold to third parties. After the war Allan Q. Moore, who was vice-president for grain in the old flour and cereal division before becoming a corporate vice-president in 1947, aggressively expanded grain merchandising operations until they were accorded divisional status.[27]

The new division, Philip announced, "will operate as a separate unit in the purchase, sale and handling of all grains other than in the procurement of grain to be processed by other divisions. The latter will continue to have their grain procurement departments." Edmund P. Pillsbury, Philip's cousin, who had worked for seven years in the company's Chicago and Minneapolis grain offices, was named to manage the new division. That July, purchase of a million-bushel el-

A new bakery mix plant (left, top) was opened in Springfield, Illinois, in 1949, and in 1952 the company purchased the Pool elevator in Buffalo (left, bottom) to provide additional storage for the grain merchandising division.

evator at Davenport, Iowa, provided additional storage. In 1950 the division purchased an elevator at Council Bluffs, Iowa, and in March 1952 it bought the two-million-bushel Pool elevator in Buffalo, New York.[28]

The grain division was expanded by creation of a feed ingredient merchandising business to buy and sell soybean meal, bran, and other ingredients used in feed manufacturing. Edmund was killed at age 37 in a private-plane crash on February 22, 1951, but that year the division produced about 18 percent of the company's profits. By the time Philip retired as president on May 31, 1952, the grain division was operating 11 leased or owned terminal elevators through some 16 grain merchandising offices, and it had several separate offices in various parts of the country engaged solely in merchandising feed ingredients.[29]

Perhaps no single event in the 1950s attracted more favorable attention than one first staged in 1949. The grocery products division's new mixes had scored a notable success by bringing a new era of baking convenience to the American homemaker. How could this momentum be maintained, and what further boost could be given to sales of Pillsbury's Best® Family Flour, the division's flagship product? Early in the year members of the division took the question to its advertising agency. Together they came up with a plan that would become an American institution—the Pillsbury Bake-Off® contest.

The group concluded that its purposes could be served in two steps. The first was to bring out the best flour-based recipes to be found in the kitchens of the nation's 39 million families. The second was to insert these recipes in packages of Pillsbury's Best® Flour. In order to find the recipes, they decided to conduct a contest, inviting homemakers to submit their best. From thousands of entries, a panel of home economists selected the 200 best recipes. These were kitchen-tested by another panel that selected a hundred finalists to bake their recipes at a judging in New York City. One of Minneapolis's favorite newspaper columnists described the event in his December 13, 1949, column: "I stood on one of the balconies of the grand ballroom of the Waldorf Astoria hotel Monday and looked down upon one of the strangest sights New York City has ever seen, and a Minneapolis firm was entirely responsible for it. Just six hours before the final couples of a dancing party were dragging their weary shapes off the floor to go home. In that brief space of time, from 1 a.m. to 8 a.m., the grand ballroom had been miraculously transposed into what might well be called a baking orgy—97 women and three men standing nervously over 100 ranges preparing their prize winning recipes ready to compete for $100,000 in cash prizes."[30]

The first Pillsbury Bake-Off® contest was held in 1949 in New York City. Celebrity participation was a prominent feature of the early contests, and in 1949 Philip Pillsbury, Eleanor Roosevelt, and Art Linkletter presented the awards to the winners (left, top). The event was still an important part of the American scene in the 1980s (above), and Philip Pillsbury led contestants to their cooking ranges every year from 1949 to 1984 (left, bottom), the year he died.

What had been intended as a single contest became a regular event continuing in much the same form in 1984. Responding to shareholders who questioned the cost of the first Bake-Off® contest, the company's director of advertising and public relations said, ''The pay-off is that the Grand National [Bake-Off], ably merchandised by our top-notch sales force, contributed its part to the 700,000 increase in the number of Pillsbury's Best customers during the year . . . The recipes we gathered gave us an exclusive selling feature, a service feature no other flour has, and added substance and strength to our advertising. And the good will we earned alone paid for the cost.''[31]

Although profits for the fiscal year 1950 were the lowest since the end of the war, an upswing in earnings seemed near when the board met the following December. The company's several divisions were well staffed, and the businesses were all operating on an even keel. The time seemed right for expansion, and at the meeting management presented ''the question of the possible expansion of company activities.'' Management recommended and the board agreed that any acquisition must meet the standards of ''adequate earnings, sufficient working capital, good management, and a business whose earnings will improve as a result of combination with our present activities.''

A golden opportunity for such an acquisition soon was presented in the Ballard company of Louisville, Kentucky. This milling firm had started in 1880 as Jones, Ballard & Ballard. It incorporated in 1909 as Ballard & Ballard Co., Inc., with Charles T. Ballard and his brother, S. Thruston Ballard, serving as presidents in the years 1909 to 1926. Dr. David C. Morton, son-in-law of Thruston Ballard, became president of the company in 1926, and in the years from 1944 to 1951 his two sons, Thruston B. and Rogers C. B. Morton, both of whom were to become active in national politics, served successively as president. Herman Steen wrote, ''Great prestige and trade standing were enjoyed by Ballard & Ballard Co., Inc., which for two generations had the largest flour mill in the South and the largest volume of household flour business in that area.''[32]

In early February 1951 Ballard's principal owners informed the Pillsbury company of their intention to sell; shortly thereafter, the company opened purchase negotiations. Years later Gerot described the acquisition: ''The Ballard company was involved in the formula feed business and its Obelisk brand family flour had a strong position in certain Southeastern cities such as Atlanta, New Orleans and Jacksonville, key markets where Pillsbury was not too strong. Where they were strong, we were weak; and where we were strong, they were weak.

''We saw that as a big opportunity to put the power of the two selling organizations together to develop both brands in a substantial way. Our commercial feed people thought the feed business would be

Ballard & Ballard Co., Inc., acquired in 1951, "for two generations had the largest flour mill in the South and the largest volume of household flour business in that area." Its Louisville, Kentucky, headquarters operations are shown (left, top) in pre-World War I days and (left, center) close to the time of acquisition. Less than a year later the company purchased the Duff Baking Mix Division in Hamilton, Ohio, from American Home Products Corporation (bottom).

a big advantage to them—the new plant in Louisville. That turned out to be a mistake . . . They had a semblance of a consumer mix business which we weren't interested in at all, but of course we had to take it . . .

"They had one interesting product, Ballard® OvenReady® Biscuits, and a good piece of their profit was coming from this product. We said, 'If we could build a mix business with a variety of product—pancake and pie crust and cake mix and hot roll mix, and so on—why can't we put research behind this refrigerated idea and develop a wide range of refrigerated products—cinnamon rolls and so on?'

"So we pushed through pretty hard, and the comptrollers who looked at it said, 'You're paying too much money.'

"And we said, 'Well, whether we pay half a million or a million too much is not important. It's a question whether the idea behind it is right, whether the philosophy is correct. If the philosophy is right, it will be the greatest bargain we've ever had. If the philosophy is wrong, it will be expensive at any price. We finally came to terms.' "[33]

The purchase was completed on June 12, 1951. Pillsbury acquired the Ballard assets for 115,000 shares of Pillsbury common stock, valued at about $3.85 million on that day's market. Ballard's family flour and mix business was assigned to the grocery products division, its feed business to the feed division, and the refrigerated biscuit business to a new OvenReady® Biscuit division. The company continued to use the Obelisk label on Ballard's family flour.

Less than a year later, with Pillsbury's grocery products sales beginning to outstrip its production capacity, the company purchased for about $2.25 million the plant and business of the Duff Baking Mix Division of American Home Products Corporation. A pioneer in the consumer mix business, Duff had a new plant at Hamilton, Ohio, completed in 1948 and built on a single level covering three acres of ground. It gave Pillsbury an excellent production facility for both Pillsbury and Duff consumer mixes. The purchase enabled the company to shelve earlier plans that had included possible construction of a new plant at Springfield or Buffalo.

The last acquisition approved during Philip's period as president was the purchase of two Canadian flour milling companies—Renown Mills, Limited, and Copeland Flour Mills, Limited. Renown had elevators and a large flour mill at Calgary, Alberta, and Copeland owned a flour mill at Midland, Ontario. Pillsbury's 1952 annual report explained the rationale for the purchase in these terms, "The price variation between Canadian and U.S. exported flour almost forces an exporter of Pillsbury's stature to obtain Canadian property to keep its foreign markets open. Furthermore Pillsbury's export market has increased over the past few years to require additional capacity."

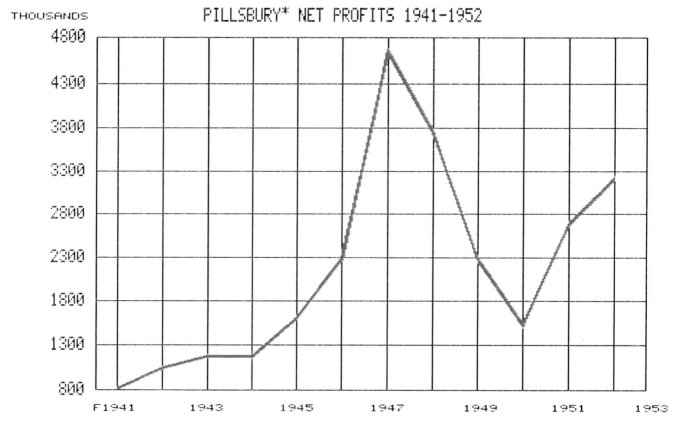

THOUSANDS

PILLSBURY* NET PROFITS 1941-1952

* PILLSBURY FLOUR MILLS COMPANY 1941-1944
  PILLSBURY MILLS, INC. 1945-1952

The last acquisition during Philip Pillsbury's tenure as chief executive officer consisted of two Canadian flour milling concerns— Renown Mills, Limited, at Calgary, Alberta (above), and Copeland Flour Mills, Limited, at Midland, Ontario (left, top). When Philip's period as chief executive officer ended, the company had begun to reverse a three-year downward trend in profits (left, bottom).

Pillsbury continued to be the country's largest exporter of flour. Prior to the Canadian acquisitions it accounted for more than 30 percent of American flour exports as well as 8 percent of Canadian flour exports. From its principal export office in New York City, the company also conducted an export feed business to Latin America. An office in Portland, Oregon, handled sales of flour to the Philippines and the Orient.[34]

In 1952, after almost 28 years with the company and 12 years as chief executive officer, Philip retired as president and became chairman of the board. He had been planning the transition for more than a year, and, in preparation for the move, on June 1, 1951, had named Paul Gerot executive vice-president, with operating responsibility for all the company's divisions. On May 31, 1952, confident of Gerot's ability to maintain the company's momentum, Philip moved to the board's chairmanship. Gerot succeeded him as president and chief executive officer. John S. Pillsbury, then 73, was elected honorary chairman of the board.

Philip's retirement left George S. Pillsbury, the youngest son of John S. Pillsbury, and John P. Snyder, Jr., a great-grandson of Governor Pillsbury, the only family members active in the business on a day-to-day basis. Various family members held substantial numbers of company shares, but their combined interest after the sale by the company of 160,000 shares in August 1952 probably was under 6 percent.

In 1940 Philip had assumed charge of a flour milling company that had undergone little change since its 1923 return from English ownership. When he concluded his stewardship, Pillsbury had been transformed into a formidable, multidivisional competitor in the food processing industry. The change is partly reflected in these figures:

	Year Ending May 31, 1940	Year Ending May 31, 1952
Net Sales	$ 47,235,669	$314,907,587
Net Profits	$ 900,914	$ 3,209,893
Net Current Assets	$ 14,966,579	$ 31,977,721
Number of Shareholders	3123	8098
Number of Employees	5946	8130

There was still work to be done, but during the 12 years of Philip's leadership, Pillsbury had found its direction and envisioned its future.

"Try my new Pillsbury Swirls."

"The prettiest hot rolls that ever came to dinner."

"Poppin' Fresh," the Pillsbury Dough Boy, has a fondness for fresh, hot, home-baked dinner rolls.

But (being notoriously softhearted) he doesn't think they should be a lot of bother for you.

That's why he's so tickled over his new Swirls.

All you do is: (1) Pop open the Poppin' Fresh Dough. (2) Bake.

You get eight light, tender, golden, flaky, perfectly lovely, swirly-peaked rolls. In minutes. Fresh and hot from the oven.

The Dough Boy isn't one for making outlandish claims. But he says new Swirls make fresh home baking prettier and easier than ever.

Being a Dough Boy, he ought to know.

Poppin' Fresh Dough. In the dairy case.

6 At the Threshold
1952–1972

In 1952 the company stood at the threshold of its greatest period of development since the days of Charles A. Pillsbury. Charles had started with a small flour mill in a pioneer community and gone on to fashion the greatest flour milling enterprise in the world. This time growth would take another form, as over the next 20 years the traditional flour milling company would be restructured into a broadly diversified food company. An increase in profitability, from $3.2 million in 1952 to $16.9 million in 1972, would accompany the change. But the central significance would be the new scope of Pillsbury's business operations.[1]

The 20-year period of growth occurred in three stages. During the first eight years the organization was fully absorbed in proving that the company could compete successfully in the consumer food products market. Then from 1960 until Paul Gerot's retirement on September 12, 1967, the company established major new dimensions with acquisitions in the United States and Europe. In the last stage, led by Robert J. Keith until his retirement in December 1972, Pillsbury reached out for even more diversity with a number of nonfood acquisitions.

When Paul Gerot assumed leadership of the company in 1952, the company was clearly embarked on a new course. But successful navigation of the course would require a strong, relentless, and skillful corporate performance. Despite Pillsbury's standing as a leading American flour miller, flour mills were closing in significant numbers, and Pillsbury had yet to prove it could be competitive in the fast-moving world of major food processors. In a list of prominent food companies to which the company compared itself in 1952, Pillsbury's earnings ranked at the very bottom:

	Pretax Profit in Millions
Procter & Gamble	$92.4
Campbell Soup	51.7
General Foods	51.0
Ralston-Purina	21.4
General Mills	21.1
Quaker Oats	16.0
Pillsbury	7.0

By 1952 the company was on its way to becoming a broadly diversified food company. One of its early and most rewarding additions was the refrigerated fresh dough business, which in 1965 introduced as its symbol Poppin' Fresh®, the now-famous Pillsbury Dough Boy.

Fortunately, the company's new chief executive officer was well equipped for the demanding task that would occupy the rest of the 1950s—that of building a strong and durable packaged food franchise.

Paul Gerot had joined Pillsbury in 1926, shortly after completing his studies at Northwestern University. He started work in Chicago, where one of his first assignments was to sell Pillsbury pancake mix to housewives in a predominantly Polish section of the city. It was the beginning of a rapid climb on the sales ladder. In 1932 he took charge of the company's St. Louis branch office, with orders to improve its performance or close it. Three years later, the St. Louis office topped all company branches in a consumer product sales contest, assuring its continued existence. Gerot returned to Chicago in 1938, first as branch manager and then as west central division manager. He came to Minneapolis in 1944 and served in several middle management sales and advertising positions before becoming president of the new grocery products division in 1947. He was elected to the company's board of directors in 1950.[2]

By the time he was appointed chief executive officer in 1952, Gerot had already played a major part in the introduction of the company's consumer mix products. His innate sales ability was complemented by a penchant for product research, market research, and innovative marketing and advertising. He was a stickler for fundamentals, and he demanded thoroughly prepared marketing plans followed by all-out execution. Of even more immediate value, he possessed a secret weapon acquired in the 1951 acquisition of Ballard & Ballard.

In 1931 Ballard had obtained a patented process for packaging refrigerated fresh dough. The invention provided for encasing fresh dough in a sealed package, where the dough could rise against the container walls. Kept under refrigeration, the dough was ready for baking when the package was opened. Ballard used the process to manufacture a refrigerated biscuit product, marketed as Ballard® OvenReady® Biscuits and distributed through the Kraft Foods division of what became Dart & Kraft, Inc.

By the time of the Pillsbury acquisition, Ballard was manufacturing the biscuits in two small plants in Louisville, Kentucky, and Denison, Texas, and in a rented building in Atlanta, Georgia. Kraft also produced the product for Ballard in another small plant in Los Angeles. OvenReady® Biscuits, with sales centered in the Southeast, were Ballard's single largest producer of profits. But according to Lowell Armstrong, a longtime Ballard and Pillsbury employee, the Morton family considered refrigerated dough as a ''sideline that would never pay the family bills.'' Flour, Armstrong said, was their first interest and formula feed was next. Moreover, the product still had major production problems in 1951—the biscuits had a short

Paul S. Gerot served for 15 years as the company's chief executive officer. After Pillsbury's position in the consumer food industry had become firmly established in the United States, he directed the company's expansion into consumer food markets abroad, and in 1967 he spearheaded the company's acquisition of Burger King Corporation.

shelf life and the containers sometimes exploded as the encased dough rose. To further complicate the issue, the original patent had expired, and several other manufacturers were trying to enter the biscuit market.[3]

Gerot was quick to see the possibilities of the refrigerated fresh dough process, especially when he learned that Ballard technicians were working on an automatic packer that would increase production to 160 packages per minute. (In 1984 Pillsbury's fastest automatic packaging machines produced 800 packages per minute.) In 1952 Gerot asked the Ballard people to list every single product they could think of that might be made through a similar process with refrigerated fresh dough. As Armstrong said later, ''I thought it was the craziest thing anybody could ever ask. But we sat down and worked up a list of some 30 to 50 products. So help me, a big share of those products are now on the market!''[4]

The ultimate fate of Pillsbury's refrigerated dough business was to hang not on containers or competition, but on the disposition of a complaint filed by the Federal Trade Commission on June 16, 1952, two weeks after Gerot's election as chief executive officer. When Pillsbury acquired Ballard & Ballard and Duff, all three companies were engaged in the home-mix business; both Pillsbury and Ballard were also flour millers and feed manufacturers. The complaint alleged that the acquisitions unlawfully injured competition and demanded that Pillsbury divest itself of all assets acquired from Ballard and Duff.[5]

The case plodded its way through the administrative and judicial systems for an incredible 14 years. First the Commission's hearing examiner dismissed the case in 1953, only to be overruled by the Commission. After reopening the hearings the examiner found in 1959 that both acquisitions violated the law. He recommended that Pillsbury be required to sell all the acquired assets except for the formula feed and refrigerated biscuit businesses acquired from Ballard. The Commission adopted the hearing examiner's findings in 1960, but it ordered that Pillsbury divest itself of *all* the acquired assets. The company appealed to the United States Circuit Court of Appeals for the Fifth Circuit. Finally, in 1966, the Court of Appeals decided that Pillsbury had been deprived of due process of law in the proceedings, and it ordered the case remanded to the Commission for whatever action it deemed appropriate ''in view of both the lapse of time and the present state of the case law applying Section 7.'' The Commission gave up at last and dismissed the case on April 4, 1966; but with a final thrust, it warned that ''Any further acquisition by (Pillsbury) will be given careful attention.''[6]

The uncertainties brought on by the case were even more serious than its great expense and the endless amount of executive time it consumed. Ordinary operating and capital expenditure decisions,

In September 1958, the company opened its new plant in East Greenville, Pennsylvania (left, top), and in less than a year, one in New Albany, Indiana (left, bottom). Both produced refrigerated fresh dough products (left, center).

particularly those related to the refrigerated business, had to take into account every possible permutation of ''the FTC case.'' Acquisition strategies took a conservative cast, and the controversy cast a disconcerting, often inhibiting shadow over the company for most of Gerot's administration.

Despite the threat of divestment, Gerot and the board elected to press ahead with the refrigerated dough business. Early in 1953 Pillsbury and Kraft amended their distribution contract, and Pillsbury took responsibility for West Coast biscuit manufacture. Construction of a new refrigerated dough plant in Los Angeles was the first step.

In April Gerot reported to the board that Ballard® OvenReady® Biscuit sales were about to outstrip production. Seven percent of the population, Gerot said, was buying refrigerated biscuits, and further volume increases were expected. The board authorized additional facilities, and biscuit manufacturing machinery was installed in a leased plant at Downington, Pennsylvania. That year OvenReady® Biscuit deliveries increased almost 60 percent, and the first Pillsbury brand refrigerated product, Pillsbury Buttermilk Biscuits, went into test market. Two years later, in 1955, Pillsbury Quick Cinnamon Rolls reached the market, the first fruit of Gerot's request of Lowell Armstrong to ''list every single product'' that could be made from refrigerated dough.

Demand for the new refrigerated products continued to grow. In August 1957 the company announced the Downington operation's move to a new plant under construction at East Greenville, Pennsylvania. The announcement added: ''When the Downington plant went into operation in January, 1954 . . . we were making only two items: Pillsbury Buttermilk Biscuits and Ballard® OvenReady® Biscuits. We are now making eight additional items, including Pillsbury Sweetmilk Biscuits, Ballard® Buttermilk Biscuits, Caramel Nut Rolls, Quick Cinnamon Rolls, three flavors of refrigerated ice box cookies, and Quick Cinnamon Rolls With Icing.''[7]

The East Greenville plant opened in September 1958. In less than a year the company opened a still larger plant in New Albany, Indiana, across the river from Louisville, where the whole operation had begun. Refrigerated research and development moved from Louisville to New Albany, where 33,000 square feet of new laboratories doubled the size of the old Louisville research facilities.

By the end of Gerot's first eight years as chief executive officer, the annual earnings of the refrigerated division had reached $5.6 million, several times those of Ballard & Ballard in 1951. Competition heated up, as Borden, Inc., General Mills with its 1956 acquisition of the Puffin brand, and a number of private label manufacturers all tried to gain a larger share of the growing market. Pillsbury continued to hold fast to its majority of the biscuit market, however, and in the so-called specialty area, Pillsbury had an even more commanding lead in the broad line of cookie, dinner roll, and sweet roll products.[8]

While the company was establishing leadership in the refrigerated dough market, there was no easing of the pressure to produce more dry grocery products, which Pillsbury had managed separately from the "refrigerated division" as the "grocery products division." The home-mix market had settled into a battle of competing lines, as distinguished from the earlier struggle to be first with a new kind of mix. Pillsbury held the lead in the piecrust, hot roll, and cake mix lines in 1952, but General Foods and General Mills were closing in, and several regional milling firms were trying to establish a market position as well.[9]

From a production standpoint the company was strong. The timely purchase of Duff's modern manufacturing plant at Hamilton, Ohio, met the need for additional production, and the plant was enlarged in 1953. The company already owned an excellent grocery products plant at Springfield, Illinois, an adequate plant in Los Angeles, and the Louisville plant acquired from Ballard.

The Duff line of home mixes was sold to a third party in 1953, but Pillsbury retained the right to use Duff's formulas, adding gingerbread and spice cake mix, two Duff favorites, to the Pillsbury line. At the same time Gerot continued to push hard for internal product development in order to lengthen the Pillsbury line. Pillsbury cookie mixes entered the market in 1954 and were followed in 1955 by brownie and frosting mixes. The next year a major addition doubled the size of the Minneapolis research and development laboratories, and the rush to market of new Pillsbury products accelerated. The 1959 annual report to shareholders listed nine new products introduced by the grocery products division. Seven more entered the market the following year, including instant mashed, quick hash brown, and scalloped potatoes, the division's first major departure from mix products. The company formed a potato manufacturing division in fiscal 1960, and in June 1960 it purchased a facility at Grand Forks, North Dakota, to process potato products for the grocery products and institutional foods divisions.[10]

The company's new product introductions did not, of course, represent an unbroken string of successes. Inevitably, some percentage of new products does not survive the test markets, and some are withdrawn from the marketplace even after entering national distribution. Neither Pillsbury nor its competitors was immune to this phenomenon. General Mills had failed with its Pyequick, and Pillsbury had tried, without success, to market a dry biscuit mix; in 1955 it also withdrew a waffle mix from a test market.[11]

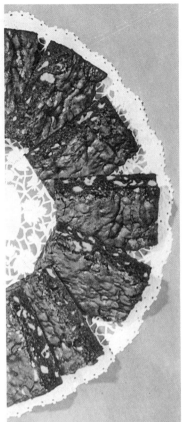

NEW!
Pillsbury
Fudge
Brownie
MIX

Makes the rich, chewy kind.
Country-fresh eggs are right in
the mix. **Water is all you add.**

Moist and fudgy and full of rich chocolate flavor. Now you can bake 'em with this new Pillsbury mix — the complete brownie mix with choice, country-fresh eggs right in the mix. All you add is water. Easier, quicker—costs less than homemade. Your package is at your grocer's now—just waiting for you to come along and pick it up. New Pillsbury Fudge Brownie Mix.

Pillsbury brownie (above, left) and frosting
(above, right) mixes came onto the market in
1955. A line of potato products (bottom)
followed.

Pillsbury made extensive use of the leading radio and television programs of the 1960s to advertise its consumer food products. When Ed Sullivan (above) introduced the Beatles to America on his Sunday night television show, Pillsbury was one of the sponsors. That night the Beatles brought to the American airwaves "She Loves You" and "I Want to Hold Your Hand."

A joint venture with the Kellogg Company of Battle Creek, Michigan, led to the introduction of Pillsbury dry grocery products in Canada. Kellogg was a leader in the ready-to-eat cereal business in Canada, where it owned manufacturing facilities and employed an excellent sales force. In 1954 the two companies formed Kellogg-Pillsbury of Canada, Ltd., to manufacture Pillsbury's line of consumer mixes for distribution through the Kellogg sales organization. The new corporation began manufacturing in Kellogg's plant at London, Ontario, distributing the products under Pillsbury labels with a Kellogg-Pillsbury signature. Concurrently, the two companies initiated a market study in England, with a view to forming a similar partnership there.

Both ventures terminated two years later when the Canadian market proved too thin to make the joint operation profitable. Pillsbury Canada, Ltd., the company's Canadian subsidiary, took over the business, building a new grocery products mix plant and refrigerated foods plant in 1958, next to its Midland flour mill in Ontario. Kraft also began to distribute the Pillsbury refrigerated line in Canada that year. For many years, however, distribution of Pillsbury consumer products in Canada was limited largely to the relatively populous province of Ontario.

The company fueled its sales of refrigerated and dry grocery products with an ever-increasing program of marketing and advertising. The Home Service Center, started in 1944, moved into new, larger quarters in 1958 as the company's staff of home economists grew. Advertising expenditures escalated sharply. The company became a principal sponsor of radio and television programs hosted by two of the decade's best-known media personalities, Arthur Godfrey and Art Linkletter. And when on February 9, 1964, Ed Sullivan introduced the Beatles to America on his popular Sunday night show, Pillsbury was one of its sponsors.[12]

Gerot insisted that the wave of new mix products not submerge efforts to gain a greater share of the profitable family flour market. The Pillsbury Bake-Off® contest, which had been an annual event since its successful introduction in 1949, continued to stimulate consumer interest in home baking and to supply new recipes for insertion in bags and packages of Pillsbury's Best® Family Flour. To add even more interest, in 1953 a team of experts directed by the Home Service Center sought out famous Old World recipes in Europe to augment the library that homemakers could build by regular purchases of Pillsbury's Best®.

After a decade of intense competition, Pillsbury could point to the highly successful performance of its refrigerated and grocery products divisions. The company's line of refrigerated products, benefiting greatly from the distribution arrangement with Kraft, was the undisputed leader of the growing refrigerated dough market. Pillsbury shared the lead in the cake mix market with General Mills and Procter & Gamble, which had acquired the Duncan Hines line in 1957. Pillsbury and General Mills were running neck-and-neck at the front of the new frosting mix field. Pillsbury's Best® was locked in second place in family flour sales, holding a respectable 15.1 percent of the national market in 1962 as compared to the leader's 29 percent.[13]

Gerot had more than met the critical challenge of establishing Pillsbury as a major processor of consumer food products. It was significant that consumer product sales in 1960 accounted for more than 80 percent of the company's pretax profits, and that in two of Gerot's first eight years as chief executive officer they produced more than 100 percent of pretax profits.

When Gerot became chief executive officer in 1952 he had assumed responsibility, of course, for the other businesses of the company as well. Each of these functioned as separate sales and marketing divisions. The number or designation of divisions changed occasionally as, for example, when the bakery division was reorganized into separate bakery flour and bakery mix divisions, or when a new institutional foods division was formed. Two staff departments, each managed by a vice-president reporting to Gerot, carried out the bulk of the production and procurement functions for all of the divisions.[14]

As the company's volume of business and numbers of products grew, it became apparent that management would have to be decentralized in order to further delegate authority and responsibility. In preparation for this the board on June 1, 1956 elected three executive vice-presidents—Robert J. Keith, Ben J. Greer, and Dean McNeal. Keith had joined the company as a grocery products salesman in 1935. After leaving the company to work for two years as an advertising agency account executive, he returned in 1938 and began moving upward in increasingly demanding consumer advertising and marketing assignments. Greer started as a grain buyer in 1926, transferred to California where he ultimately became president of the old Globe division, and then returned to Minneapolis to head the company's production department. McNeal, who managed the company's procurement department, had been a Ralston Purina executive; he came to Minneapolis after the war from his position as deputy price administrator in the Office of Price Administration.[15]

On June 1, 1958, the several businesses of the company were organized into three segments, identified as the consumer, industrial, and agricultural areas. Keith was assigned the consumer area, consisting of the refrigerated and grocery divisions. Greer became head of the industrial area, which included the bakery flour, bakery mix, institutional foods, and overseas, or export, divisions. McNeal assumed responsibility for the agricultural area, made up of the formula feed, soy, grain merchandising, and feed ingredient merchandising divisions. Major staff departments such as research and development, human relations, and the controller's office reported directly to Gerot, but each of the three business areas now carried out its own procurement and production functions.[16]

The company's new, broader purpose gained impetus and widespread publicity from an action taken by the shareholders at their annual meeting in 1958. After 14 years as Pillsbury Mills, Inc., the company changed its name on September 9, 1958, to The Pillsbury Company. The action reflected shareholder approval of the company's new directions, while wisely preserving for the total enterprise the identity of the familiar Pillsbury name. At the same meeting, the shareholders elected John S. Pillsbury, Jr., president of Northwestern National Life Insurance Company, to the board. He succeeded his father, John S. Pillsbury, Sr., who retired after 49 years as a board member of the company.

During the first eight years of Gerot's administration, profits from the company's industrial and agricultural areas were unimpressive. The industrial area's best performer was the overseas division, whose earnings fluctuated widely from year to year but which, unlike other area divisions, always produced a profit. Pillsbury led the world in wheat flour exports, and it exported formula feed, feed ingredients, family flour, and consumer mixes. One of its principal sources of revenue came from sales under the Agricultural and Trade Development Assistance Act of 1954, commonly called Public Law 480. Part of a program to reduce farm surpluses, the law authorized the award of contracts on a bid basis to fulfill government sales of flour, feed, and commodities to foreign nations. In 1957 the division assumed responsibility for exports from the Calgary and Midland mills.[17]

Still, the road ahead for the overseas division seemed anything but clear. As the 1950s progressed, many less-developed countries, influenced by emerging nationalism, began to build their own food processing facilities, particularly formula feed plants. This trend threatened many of the company's oldest and best export markets. The division decided that, rather than build overseas feed plants of its own, it would seek license agreements with indigenous companies, exchanging Pillsbury know-how and trademark licenses for agreements to buy Pillsbury feed and feed ingredient imports. By 1956 Pillsbury had four such licensees in Latin American countries and was negotiating for two more.

Next came the building of flour mills in many of the less developed countries. In June 1959, the construction of a number of flour mills in Guatemala closed that market to flour imports. The overseas division contracted to provide technical assistance and trademark li-

A Pillsbury institutional food products salesman and a dietitian at Minneapolis's Northwestern Hospital sampled cake baked from the institutional division's new Swiss-style chocolate-flavor cake base. The knife, fork, and spoon on the package label were the division's logo.

censes to one of the principal new mills in Guatemala in return for fees based on the mill's sales. The company reached similar agreement in the same year with Molinos de El Salvador, a new mill in San Salvador, in which Pillsbury purchased a 10-percent interest.

The bakery mix and institutional food products divisions followed the overseas division in profitability. Bakery mix was a low-margin business to begin with, and many bakers perceived of Pillsbury as a competitor because of its consumer cake mixes, piecrusts, and related products. The bakery mix operation was not a significant contributor to profits during the 1950s, although a slow upward trend accelerated at the end of the period, offering hope for the future. At the same time, the institutional food products division formed in 1955 handled sales to hotels, restaurants, and institutions, becoming profitable in 1959 and 1960. Profits were small in both years, but this business too offered some hope for significant earnings. Initially its product line consisted of flour-based mix products, but it gradually added products such as tomato juice, syrups, pie fillings, bread and batter mixes, and, in 1959, dehydrated potato flakes.

Bakery flour, the industrial area's largest division in terms of sales, was its least profitable, with five consecutive years of loss from 1954 through 1958. Although Pillsbury was one of the largest flour millers in the country, bakery flour was a commodity business, highly dependent on year-to-year wheat crop conditions and prices. The industry was plagued with overcapacity, and millers frequently engaged in ruinous rounds of price cutting in order to keep their mills in operation. Early in 1954 the company stopped milling durum flour, unprofitable for several years. The following year it withdrew from the macaroni business, closing down its single plant in Los Angeles.

A ray of hope was the company's development of a new "turbo grinding and turbo separation" process, announced early in 1957. Pillsbury had been experimenting with the process since 1953 in Springfield, and in 1957 turbo milling facilities were installed at Enid. The discovery, heralded as the century's first important breakthrough in milling technology, promised lower manufacturing costs and the capability of producing new kinds of flour, differing chemically and physically from that produced by conventional methods. The news led to favorable reports in 1957 and 1958 by business publications and brokerage houses, at least one of which envisioned an opportunity for developing lines of differentiated products. Other companies soon adopted the process or variations of it, however, and turbo milling did little to improve the profits of either Pillsbury or the industry generally.[18]

In 1955, Pillsbury leased a feed mill in Gainesville, Georgia (left, top), in order to supply broiler operations in the area, and four years later it announced plans to construct a new feed plant at Jasper, Alabama (above). In 1962 the company entered the broiler processing industry at Gainesville and Guntersville, Alabama. Chickens for the plants were raised at broiler-growing operations such as the one at left, bottom.

The agricultural area's four divisions also produced mixed results during the first eight years of Gerot's administration. The large formula feed division had substantial losses in the first five years, then registered minimal profits in 1958 and 1959. The much smaller soy division produced fewer earnings swings than formula feed, but over the eight-year period it just about broke even.

Numerous factors contributed to the formula feed division's poor showing. Demographic changes in California brought relocation of the cattle and poultry raising centers served by the Los Angeles and San Francisco plants, forcing the closing of both facilities. The cost of rejuvenating the old Minneapolis feed mill proved excessive, and it was dismantled in 1953. Ballard's large Louisville plant, designed to produce continuous high-volume runs of basic feeds for shipment by rail throughout the Southeast, closed in 1955. Customers now required a broad range of specialized feeds, and resultant increases in manufacturing costs and freight charges had rendered the Louisville plant uneconomical.

Aside from the formula feed division's own special problems, major change was taking place in the feed industry. Emphasis was shifting from the development of individual plants to serve wide geographic areas to the location of plants in close proximity to important customers. Thus in 1955, Pillsbury leased a feed mill in Gainesville, Georgia, in order to supply major broiler operations in the vicinity; and in 1959 it announced plans to construct a new plant at Jasper, Alabama, the heart of another leading broiler production area. The new strategy had occasional drawbacks. The broiler industry was highly cyclical. When the cycle was at its bottom, credit losses frequently occurred when a grower could not sell his birds at a profit and pay for his feed. At the end of the 1950s, the company owned almost a dozen formula feed plants across the country and faced another year of heavy losses.[19]

The agricultural area's other two divisions were both under ten years old when Gerot became president. Both were trading divisions, engaged in relatively esoteric operations for which the personnel either possessed or quickly acquired special skills. Traders' salaries were augmented by incentive payments, and the large dollar and volume amounts of their trades required careful structuring and management, with preagreed trading limits.

In addition to trading, the grain merchandising division derived substantial revenues from the handling and storage of grain. Government grain storage programs were an integral part of the agricultural economy, and the division's grain inventories, stored in leased and owned elevators and steel bins, often exceeded a billion bushels during the 1950s. The division was creative in searching out new operations to increase the volume of its transactions. For several years it

In the late 1950s, Pillsbury shipped grain in "Big John" hopper cars (at left, top, a hopper car is pulled up beside a ship for overseas loading) and bakery mix products in trucks (left, bottom). On March 2, 1958, the first barge of flour ever shipped from Minneapolis was loaded for Guntersville, Alabama, where it was stored for transfer to the New Albany refrigerated plant as needed.

countered high rail rates from the Midwest to the South, Southeast, and East by shipping grain in truck "back-haul" movements. Truckers bringing steel, produce, and lumber to the Midwest, rather than returning empty to their points of origin, carried back grain shipments by Pillsbury. The practice ended when the railroads offered lower rates through newly developed unit trains and giant "Big John" hopper cars.[20]

In 1959 the division initiated its first river operation, leasing an elevator in Florence, Illinois. From there it shipped grain by barge via the Illinois and Tennessee rivers to its feed customers, or via the Illinois and Mississippi rivers for export from the Gulf ports. To facilitate handling of its river business the company purchased six barges in 1963 and another six the following year.[21]

The feed ingredient division confined its operations to the purchase and sale of feed ingredients, in effect acting as a middleman. Its growth depended on increasing the volume of its trades and the number of ingredients in which it dealt. By 1960 the division had grown to 12 offices, and in the last three years of the decade it surpassed the grain merchandising division in earnings. The grain merchandising division's principal competitors were the major international grain companies, Cargill, Continental, Bunge, Dreyfus. The feed ingredients division's competitors all were local or regional companies, and at the end of the 1950s the division had become the only nationwide feed ingredient trading organization in the United States. During the first eight years of Gerot's administration, the combined earnings of these two divisions averaged about $500,000 per year, roughly offsetting losses of the formula feed division during that period.

Gerot had many reasons to be pleased with the company's accomplishments over his first eight years. Pillsbury had met the challenge of becoming a major consumer food processor. Its refrigerated and grocery product lines were established with grocer and consumer, and a majority of its products stood first or second in their markets. Its research and development laboratories and its commercial research operations were well managed and adequately staffed. Modern management techniques and tools, including long-range planning, industrial engineering, and advanced computer systems had been adopted. The company's physical properties were in good order, and although strikes of short duration had occurred at Buffalo, Springfield, and Enid, labor relations could be described as generally healthy. Corporate profits had doubled, and shareholders had benefited from a two-for-one split in April 1959; invested capital had grown from $78,521,000 in 1952 to $103,108,000 in 1960.

In 1960 the company acquired the assets of Tidy House Products Company, which produced a noncaloric artifical sweetener, Sweet*10®, made with calcium cyclamate. Use of calcium cyclamate in food was banned in 1969, and the company reformulated Sweet*10® with saccharin.

Soon after the start of the 1961 fiscal year, however, it became apparent that the year's earnings would not equal those of the previous year. It appeared that both the formula feed and bakery flour divisions would report substantial losses, after turning in small profits the year before. Even the grocery products division seemed in danger of falling sharply behind its all-time high of the previous year. The company had experienced two down years since 1952, and now there loomed a third. It was time to implement some of the major strategies Gerot had considered and planned for years. The second period of his leadership was about to begin, and it would carry the company to enviable new heights.

The changes brought about during the second period of Gerot's administration probably appear more dramatic now than they seemed then. While eye-catching, the developments of the early 1960s were direct responses to a clearly recognized need for new avenues of corporate growth. It would be three years before the company's earnings would reflect the change. Then in fiscal 1964 the company's profit line began a sharp ascent, carrying through to the end of the decade and allowing Gerot to retire in September 1967 with the company on an accelerating path of record earnings.

Gerot had pointed out to the board in March 1957 the company's need for new product lines, stressing his readiness to accept temporary reductions in earnings if that was what was necessary for expansion. The 1959 introduction of dehydrated potato products in the grocery products and institutional products divisions was a start. In July 1960 the company acquired the assets of Tidy House Products Company, the only acquisition during the first eight years of Gerot's administration. Located in Shenandoah, Iowa, Tidy House manufactured and distributed regionally a line of household cleaning products including dry bleach, liquid starch, and powdered detergent.

Tidy House's plant at nearby Omaha, Nebraska, produced a single food product, a noncaloric artificial sweetener containing calcium cyclamate and called Sweet*10.® Initially the product was sold through both grocery and drug stores. Pillsbury soon sold Tidy House's cleaning products business, but Sweet*10® started Pillsbury on a path leading to a formidable position in low-calorie foods.

In May 1961 the company made a second acquisition in the consumer area, buying Gibbs Goodies Company of Ludington, Michigan. Gibbs manufactured two excellent frozen products, Apple Dumpling and Apple Crisp, both in limited regional distribution. Gibbs presented an opportunity to test both the growing frozen foods market and some of Pillsbury's own new technology. This was not Pillsbury's first experience with frozen foods. In 1951 it had inherited from Ballard a small frozen pie business using a leased plant in Atlanta, Georgia. Conditions in the plant were unsatisfactory, and their correction would have been time consuming and costly. The com-

Ghana was one of the company's major customers for export flour (above) but loss of the market loomed when the Ghanian government decided to build its own flour mill at Tema.

pany discontinued the business in 1953 with the observation that for the time being Pillsbury could watch the frozen business more economically from the sidelines.

The acquisitions of Tidy House and Gibbs evidenced Gerot's determination to continue building Pillsbury's consumer franchise. The food processing industry was reaching out for new product markets, especially in the dessert field. The cake mix market had stabilized in about 1960, with Pillsbury, Procter & Gamble, and General Mills alternating in the lead. Pillsbury had experienced the tremendous advantage of being first in the market with a new product and at the same time had seen its product attract competitors determined to share in its success. Gerot told the Springfield Twenty-five Year Club in June 1963, "You can well ask . . . what caused this [cake mix] market to stabilize. The answer can be found in that one all-encompassing term: competition. In the cake mix field we are now competing with a large and growing number of dessert products. Each product and producing company is fighting desperately for a share of the consumer's food dollar. New and different products have entered the arena."[22]

With efforts underway to broaden the company's product line in the United States, Gerot had his sights set on another kind of expansion—in the consumer food products market abroad. Returning from Europe in 1959 he told the board that the mix market there, except for a small start made in England, was practically nonexistent. Nevertheless, he reported, major opportunities existed in the Common Market and elsewhere for acquiring food companies that would open new markets to Pillsbury and allow it to spread research costs over a larger sales base. The board agreed, authorizing management to explore foreign consumer product markets, particularly in Europe.

Before that was accomplished, however, the loss of the very lucrative Venezuelan flour export market and the threatened loss of the Ghanian market required attention. In June 1960 the company signed an agreement with the Ghanian government to build and operate a flour mill at Tema. Mill ownership would be split 60/40 between Pillsbury and a Ghanian government subsidiary. Unfortunately, complications in connection with the project necessitated termination of the contract with the Ghanian government before the mill was built.

In Venezuela local interests had constructed a number of flour mills, and the Venezuelan government had issued import license restrictions to protect the infant industry. In 1959 Pillsbury negotiated to build a mill in partnership with Venezuelan business interests. Negotiations the next year came to an end when the company had the

In 1961 the company acquired control of Etablissements Gringoire, S.A., a manufacturer of cookies, cakes, and rusks in France (above). The next year it purchased H. J. Green & Co. in Hove, England (top, left, and far left, bottom), Doria, S.A., in Switzerland, and Erasco in West Germany. In addition it bought 50 percent of White Wings Pty., Ltd., in Australia (left, bottom) and a 32-percent interest in a flour mill in the Philippines.

opportunity to purchase a majority interest in a two-year-old mill at Maracaibo, near Caracas. On August 14, 1960, Pillsbury became a 70-percent owner of Molinos Caracas Maracaibo, S.A., commonly known as Mocama.

Ownership of Mocama, the technical assistance agreements in Latin America, and the 10-percent interest in Molinos de El Salvador, S.A., all were taken in the name of Pillsbury Holdings (Canada) Limited. Pillsbury Holdings had been formed to hold certain of the company's foreign assets for tax purposes. The overseas division initially managed its operations.

After the Venezuelan acquisition, Gerot announced at the September 13, 1960, shareholders' meeting that the company was exploring opportunities in Europe's Common Market countries. This market exceeded the United States domestic market in population. In April 1961, the company acquired control of Etablissements Gringoire, S.A. Headquartered southwest of Paris at Pithiviers, the company employed more than 1,000 people in the manufacture of cookies, honey cakes, rusks, and macaroni. The Gringoire trade name had existed in France for more than a century, and some of its products were market leaders. That winter the *Magazine of Wall Street* reported that "The food companies are beginning to make dramatic gains abroad, penetrating the 270 million population Free European market as never before. This does not mean that the U.S. market of 180 million is fully saturated, but it is true that the going is getting progressively tougher here. Total sales of foreign subsidiaries of domestic food companies are expected to jump 15 percent in 1961 over 1960, and industry sources look for a minimum further gain in 1962 of 10 percent."[23]

In 1962 Pillsbury purchased three more European companies. The largest was Paul Erasmi, G.M.B.H., known as Erasco, a West German manufacturer of canned fruits and vegetables, marzipan, chocolate, and other confections. The company, located in Lubeck near Hamburg and the Baltic Sea, was slightly larger than Gringoire in both sales and number of employees. The other two companies, H. J. Green & Co. in Hove, England, and Doria, S.A., in Geneva, Switzerland, were substantially smaller than Gringoire and Erasco. Doria was a cookie manufacturer, and Green's principal lines were baking and other mix products.

In addition to its European acquisitions, in 1961 the company acquired a 50-percent interest in White Wings Pty., Ltd., an Australian manufacturer of consumer mix products, and in 1962 a 32-percent interest in Pillsbury Mindanao Flour Mills Company, operators of a new flour mill at Iligan in the Philippines. In all, the foreign acquisitions from 1960 through 1962 added about $40 million to Pillsbury's total sales.

In January 1963 the company consolidated management of its growing international interests into a fourth business area. Terrance Hanold, who had been treasurer of the company since 1956, was elected executive vice-president to head the new, international area. The man in charge of the Pillsbury Holdings (Canada) Limited portion of the foreign operations was William H. Spoor, who in 1973 would become the company's ninth chief executive.

And so in the early 1960s Gerot moved the company forward solidly on two fronts, increasing the diversity and size of the consumer products area while creating a new international presence. At the same time he realized that simply broadening the productive parts of the business would not be enough. Something would have to be done with the businesses that were failing to produce.

The most obvious offender was the formula feed division. Dating from 1942, when Pillsbury set out to establish a place for itself in the country's expanding animal feed business, the division had succeeded in reaching high sales levels, but its earnings were disappointing. Since at least 1950 its loss years had exceeded its profit years. When it was apparent that the division would record another loss in 1960, Dean McNeal proposed to the board that if the company wanted to stay in the feed business, it should become an integrated producer of protein, with feed manufacturing only one of several steps.

The company elected to follow McNeal's advice. In 1961 it purchased a poultry processing plant under construction at Guntersville, Alabama, near its new feed plant at Jasper. Georgia Broilers, Inc., a poultry processor at Gainesville, Georgia, where Pillsbury operated a major feed plant, was engaged to operate the Guntersville facility. The following March Pillsbury purchased a controlling interest in Georgia Broilers, Inc., and on June 1, 1962, the company formed a protein division. The remaining interest in Georgia Broilers was acquired two years later.

The new protein division included the Pillsbury feed mills at Gainesville and Jasper, the breeding hen, hatchery and broiler-growing operations of Georgia Broilers, and the Guntersville and Gainesville processing plants. A third processing plant, at Ellijay, Georgia, was added the following year. The new division's principal product was ice-packed broilers, marketed east of the Mississippi. In addition it began to develop a frozen chicken processing capability at Gainesville, and by 1964 it had four frozen products in regional test markets.

The company was not yet ready to terminate its formula feed operation. It had begun in 1960 to review the business plant by plant, in order to center operations in areas where actual and potential sales would be the greatest. In doing so, it moved division headquarters from Clinton to Minneapolis, reorganized management, and closed or remodeled various plants. But the division continued to lose money, and finally in 1964 the decision was made to close. All the plants except that at Ogden, which was transferred to the industrial area, were sold, and the 22-year-old division was dissolved.

The soy division had ceased business a year earlier, in 1963. Diminished soybean production near the Centerville and Clinton plants in the early 1950s was the beginning of its demise. The badly outmoded Centerville plant was shut down in 1953. Reduced to a single plant and confronted with a questionable future for two of its customers—the company's feed manufacturing plants at Clinton and Centerville—Pillsbury sold the Clinton soy plant and discontinued the division.

Increasing the profitability of the flour milling side of the business presented an entirely different set of problems. About 40 percent of the company's flour production was ingredient flour, used in producing Pillsbury's Best® Family Flour and the company's mixes and refrigerated products. Another portion filled export sales, although it often was advantageous to fill part of these orders with flour milled to Pillsbury's specifications by outside millers. The principal targets for improving profits were the bakery flour and bakery mix divisions. It had proven impossible to achieve any meaningful differentiation between Pillsbury's products and those of its competitors, advertising was of little value, and flour was always in great supply.[24]

Gerot's approach to increasing the profitability of industrial flour sales was twofold—to become a more efficient, lower-cost producer and to increase bakery mix sales. In the 1950s the company had begun extensive cost-cutting efforts, including installation of the turbo process in certain of its mills, addition of special equipment to enable the more economical bulk handling of flour, and introduction of a number of industrial engineering changes in the mills. It was time to take the next step, that of reorienting the mills to meet major changes in the country's agricultural and commercial economies. The company's objective was to relocate its mills in the best proximity to current wheat supplies and customers. In 1961 a mill was built in East Los Angeles to better serve the California market. The Ballard flour mill at Louisville, in need of extensive rehabilitation since acquisition, could not be renovated because of uncertainties in the still-undetermined FTC case. Rather than continue its uneconomical operation, the company closed it in May 1961. That December the Astoria mill, acquired to serve foreign markets in the Orient that no longer existed, was closed. In 1964 the small Sacramento mill and the Springfield C mill were shut down, too. The company renovated the Springfield B mill, and Pillsbury continued to be as large a flour miller as it had been before the changes. The changes simply made it more efficient. In 1965 the company regained its place as the country's largest wheat flour miller when General Mills closed nine of its mills.

It's bottoms up with these Funny Face mugs. Collect all eight, including our two new flavors, Rudy Tutti Frutti and "With It" Watermelon. Each one holds 8 ounces. They're made from break-proof plastic and can be placed in the dishwasher. Just send five presweetened package fronts for each mug.

While the agricultural and industrial areas dealt with the problems of their ailing members, both divisions of the consumer area were getting stronger. A new dietary product market had developed in the grocery store, occasioned by the public's newfound interest in diet and weight control. The grocery products division saw an opportunity to introduce a noncaloric drink mix made from calcium cyclamate, the principal ingredient of Sweet*10®. The result was a series of six flavors of Funny Face drink mix, targeted to the children's market, sold in low-priced packages complete with cartoon caricatures and supported by heavy television advertising. The products moved quickly into the national market in 1965.

Packages of Funny Face Injun Orange, featuring an Indian caricature, and Chinese Cherry, displaying a grinning, pigtailed Oriental figure, brought complaints from ethnic groups, and immediately the flavors were redesigned as Jolly Olly Orange and Choo Choo Cherry. The products survived but the company had learned its second lesson in labeling. Years earlier, under heavy pressure from the Food and Drug Administration, the company had withdrawn from the market a new blueberry pancake mix that contained fruit particles fabricated to taste and look like the real thing. The label had omitted to assert the artificial character of the "blueberries." The two labeling problems manifested growing consumer and governmental interest in food marketing practices.[25]

Soon after acquiring Tidy House, Pillsbury discontinued drugstore sales of Sweet*10® in order to concentrate on a more familiar market, that of the grocery store. The strategy paid off, and by 1965 liquid Sweet*10® led the grocery store noncaloric sweetener market. Pillsbury had equipped the Omaha plant to manufacture calcium cyclamate, establishing a new chemical division in 1962. When the Omaha plant could no longer meet the company's volume requirements, the chemical division purchased and rehabilitated a manufacturing plant at Painesville, Ohio, where it produced calcium cyclamate for both the company and the industry generally. Meanwhile Pillsbury had concluded that the cost of introducing the Tidy House cleaning products into the national market would be prohibitive, and it sold the line to a group of former Tidy House employees in 1964.[26]

The refrigerated fresh dough market continued to grow. By 1965, according to a Pillsbury press release, 70 percent of American families were purchasing refrigerated dough products. It had been only 12 years since Gerot had brought to the board the good news that 7 percent of the population was buying refrigerated biscuits, the only refrigerated dough product on the market at the time.

Midway through Gerot's fourteenth year as president and chief executive officer, on September 14, 1965, the board elected him chairman of the board. Philip Pillsbury, who had been board chairman since 1952, became co-chairman, and Robert J. Keith was elected president and chief operating officer. Gerot continued as chief executive officer.

Another major event of that year was the introduction of Poppin' Fresh®, the Pillsbury Dough Boy. The brainchild of the Chicago advertising agency, Leo Burnett Company, Inc., Poppin' Fresh® was intended to pull all the company's refrigerated dough products together under one symbol. The Dough Boy soon became one of the company's best-known ambassadors, both in the United States and abroad. The refrigerated division continued to bring new products, from doughnuts to pizza crusts, to market; a year after Poppin' Fresh® was born, General Mills withdrew from the refrigerated dough market, closing its four plants and leaving Pillsbury even more solidly positioned as the market leader.[27]

The grocery products division introduced a wider and wider spectrum of products, although in 1965 the company sold the Gibbs Goodies line and dropped out of the frozen food market. In 1965 it began production of cake and cookie decorators as well as a line of gravy mixes, and it entered the new light dessert market. In 1967 the division introduced two new drink mixes—Tart 'n Tangy, a packaged, presweetened dry mix for adults, and Moo Juice, a child-oriented milk-shake mix. In the same period it test-marketed an unprecedented simultaneous offering of 20 one-dish suppertime convenience foods. Six were "heat and serve" products, such as Beef Stew and Chili with Beans, eight were "cook and serve," items such as Noodles 'n Chicken, and the others were "bake and serve" casserole dishes. The experiment, code-named "Project 20," failed when the grocery trade would not provide shelf space for such a deluge of new products. Nevertheless, the undertaking symbolized the company's unflagging efforts to continue growth in the grocery market.[28]

The new age of computer technology, marching along almost in step with Pillsbury's own growth in size and complexity, provided attractive new tools for Pillsbury's management. In 1957 the company began using two separate computer systems, one for research problems and one for the routine order, invoice, and billing cycle. Pioneering in the new technology, Pillsbury kept reaching for higher levels of computer usage. In 1960 it established a study team to work with computer professionals in identifying company needs. The result was reported in a *Minneapolis Star and Tribune* story on June 11, 1964: "The 'gee whiz' age of computers has come to a sub-basement of the Pillsbury building. The Pillsbury Co. has tied together there a communications and computer network that exceeds the capacity of any electronic data processing combination except the 'way out yonder' multi-million dollar systems."

Two years later, on April 1, 1966, a subsidiary of the company began offering a computer time-sharing service to both internal and external customers. Users with telephone terminals could connect into and use one of Pillsbury's computers for a fee based on minutes of usage. The service was offered to all commercial users, but special emphasis was placed on sale of the service to Minnesota high schools and colleges. That year the company purchased its largest computer to date, at a price of $2.6 million—about half the sum paid by the English in 1889 for the entire Pillsbury company.

The following year Pillsbury and Occidental Life Insurance Company of North Carolina formed Pillsbury-Occidental Company to offer a national time-sharing service under the trade name Call-A-Computer. Both Pillsbury and Occidental transferred their existing time-sharing businesses to the new company, in which Pillsbury held a 65- and Occidental a 35-percent interest. Call-A-Computer started up on March 1, 1967, in Raleigh, North Carolina, and in Minneapolis, and it soon opened a third office in Atlanta.

Pillsbury's earnings began to rise again in 1963, as both the new foreign operations and the domestic consumer area became increasingly profitable. In 1965 the shareholders voted the second two-for-one stock split during Gerot's administration. A Pillsbury share on May 28, 1952, the last market date of that month, had a market value of $34.75. On May 31, 1966, after the two splits, the one share had grown to four shares, each valued at $31.50.[29]

Then, in the summer of 1966, Gerot started the company on a quest that would culminate in the purchase of Burger King Corporation on June 21, 1967. The acquisition was a major strategic step, ranking in its long-term consequences with two other Gerot-inspired strategies—building a powerful consumer food franchise and becoming an important international company.

For years the company had been striving to increase its return on investment, the ratio of profits to invested capital. Although its efforts were not wholly unsuccessful, they were not bringing the company close enough to its goals. The new protein division helped in some years but hurt in others, as the cyclical nature of the poultry industry produced sharp rises and falls in profitability. Accordingly, Gerot and his associates believed that in order for the company to enjoy steady growth in the food industry, it would have to establish itself in another new and growing market.[30]

The management firm of Booz, Allen & Hamilton was engaged in 1965 to survey the field of food marketing opportunities. The consultants' strong recommendation was for the eating-away-from-home market, and particularly the fast-food restaurant field. In 1966 the company began searching for a suitable entry. That winter, after several prospective acquisitions had been examined, the company began discussions with representatives of Burger King.

In 1967 Pillsbury bought Burger King Corporation, a Florida-based hamburger restaurant chain. Its first store (above) opened in 1954; by 1957 its signage proclaimed it the Home of the Whopper® (left, top); its first drive-through window units appeared in 1975 (far left, bottom), and today Burger King is a worldwide operation (near left, bottom, in Hong Kong).

Burger King was a Florida-based hamburger chain founded by James L. McLamore and David R. Edgerton, Jr., former classmates at Cornell University. The two partners commenced business with the opening of a small self-service restaurant in Miami in 1954. They added several new stores and in 1957 entered the relatively new field of franchising, granting several franchises for Burger King® stores in Miami. From there they expanded franchising to other parts of Florida and in 1961 to locations outside the state. By 1967 Burger King was operating or franchising some 275 stores in about 28 states as far west as Colorado. Their company was flourishing, but the partners realized that large amounts of capital would be required if the business was to reach its full potential.

After thorough exploration of the compatibility of the two managements and the mutual advantages that a merger could bring, Pillsbury agreed on June 21, 1967, to acquire Burger King for shares of Pillsbury common and preferred stock valued at approximately $19 million. Another $2,550,000 in cash was paid to purchase the Burger King® trademarks from their owner, a franchisee who was licensing the marks to Burger King for a royalty based on sales. Addressing the Pillsbury shareholders on September 12, 1967, McLamore predicted that by 1975 there would be over 1,250 Burger King® restaurants with $400 million in annual sales. His prediction was modest. On May 31, 1975 there were 1,395 stores, and total sales for the year were $706 million.

When the Burger King purchase was completed, Gerot announced his plans to step down from active management on reaching retirement age. At the September 12, 1967, board of directors meeting, both Gerot and Philip Pillsbury were elected honorary co-chairmen of the board. Robert J. Keith was elevated to the office of chairman and chief executive officer, and Terrance Hanold was elected president.

Except for his two years as president, Bob Keith had spent his entire Pillsbury career in the consumer products business. He joined Pillsbury in 1935, during the company presidency of Harrison H. Whiting. He was on hand when research and development was given its start in 1942 under Philip Pillsbury, and he worked closely with Paul Gerot when the latter spearheaded Pillsbury's strategic postwar entry into the piecrust, hot roll, and cake mix markets. After Gerot became president and began to implement the Ballard acquisition, Keith became the leading figure in the development of the refrigerated food business. He had been elected executive vice-president in charge of the total consumer business in 1955.

Terry Hanold's career bore no resemblance to Keith's. After graduating from the University of Minnesota law school in 1936, Hanold worked as clerk to a Minnesota Supreme Court justice and as an attorney, first for the Wisconsin Central Railroad and then for the

Robert J. Keith was elected chairman and chief executive officer of the company in 1967. He brought to the job a highly successful career in the company's consumer foods operations, together with a high respect for the rights of consumers.

Minneapolis Star. He moved to Pillsbury's law department in 1946 and rose rapidly through the legal and financial areas, becoming treasurer in 1956. In 1963 he was elected executive vice-president responsible for international operations. At the time he was elected president, he was executive vice-president for finance and planning, and treasurer.

On becoming chairman, Keith established the company's first executive office, comprised of himself and Hanold. Keith was chief executive officer and Hanold, chief financial officer. Neither one took on the mantle of chief operating officer. Instead they acted together on matters brought to them by the operating officers, and they jointly led the company's planning efforts.

The new executive office immediately instituted a number of managerial changes. Dean McNeal, executive vice-president for the agricultural area, became group vice-president, administration, charged primarily with public affairs, public relations, purchasing, and transportation. For several years McNeal had been an active and prominent community leader, and Keith, especially, felt an increasing need for the company to become more closely involved in public affairs. George S. Pillsbury, executive vice-president of the industrial area, added McNeal's former responsibilities to his own, and was elected group vice-president, agricultural and industrial. George Hosfield, a longtime associate of Keith's in the consumer business, became a third executive vice-president, in charge of the refrigerated and grocery divisions. International operations, formerly divided into separate export, European, and Pillsbury Holdings (Canada) Limited sectors, were consolidated under William H. Spoor, who became vice-president and general manager of the international area.

Keith was still not satisfied with the company's organization. He appointed an employee task force to study the management systems used in a number of selected United States corporations. As a result, on June 1, 1969, the company established a "family of free-standing businesses." As Keith and Hanold stated in the 1969 annual report to shareholders: "Our goals in this program are . . . to develop a group of harder hitting competitive companies to increase the corporation's profitability. We have a strong feeling that this separate business concept, within the guide lines of a few clearly understood corporate policies, will serve to foster a number of management teams that will have expanding goals and independent discretion within their separate fields, and that this . . . will bring out their very best entrepreneurial spirit."

Initially there were seven such businesses. The archetype was Burger King, whose managers had been promised complete autonomy by Keith at a Miami meeting a few months after he was elected chairman. The others were industrial, Pillsbury Farms (formerly the protein division), food service, and commodity merchandising, all reporting to George Pillsbury; consumer food reported to George W. Hosfield; and the international company reported to the executive office.

The year 1969 marked completion of The Pillsbury Company's first 100 years. When the company began, the state of Minnesota was 11 years old, and Minneapolis was only 14 years old. Before the company reached its fourteenth year, it had become the largest flour miller in the world. It went on to survive 34 years of foreign ownership, including a particularly bitter receivership, before returning to American ownership in 1923. From there a succession of six chief executive officers had guided its evolvement into a broadly diversified international company.

Sales and earnings in the anniversary year hit new highs for the company of $569 million and $14.4 million, respectively. The source of 1969 sales, according to the annual report, was 43 percent from the consumer area, 35 percent from the agri-products group, 14 percent from international operations, and 8 percent from the newly acquired Burger King.

Burger King had grown from 273 outlets on June 1, 1967, to 489 two years later, of which 424 were franchised and 65 company-owned. Earnings came from franchise royalties, profits from the company-owned stores, one-time franchise fees, and sales of equipment, supplies, and food to the franchisees. In addition many of the restaurant sites, including 68 of those opened in 1969, were owned by Burger King real estate subsidiaries and leased to franchisees or the company. Sales in the fast-food market had been growing at an annual average rate of 14 percent for five years, and in 1969 it was predicted that this pace would continue for another five years. Burger King was gearing for its share of this growing market. It had under construction a new $3 million headquarters in Miami, from which it planned to direct its first entry into California and other West Coast markets in 1970.

The company's other major new business, Pillsbury Farms, was having a more difficult time. From the time the operation started in 1962, Pillsbury management recognized the production of ice-packed broilers as a commodity business, subject to cyclical swings in earnings. In 1969 Pillsbury Farms recorded earnings of $5.6 before taxes. But as 1970 began the cycle started moving down again. Pillsbury Farms' management strove tirelessly to develop products that would not be subject to the broiler cycles. It worked with branded fresh chicken and fully cooked and frozen products for the retail trade, precooked chicken products for the institutional market, and take-home chicken for the fast-food industry. Progress was slow, however, and the character of the business remained essentially unchanged. In January 1970 the company acquired J-M Poultry Packing Company, Inc.

Specially packaged food developed in Pillsbury's research and development laboratories accompanied F. Scott Carpenter on his May 1962 mission in *Aurora Seven* (above, right). In 1965, the company's consumer food products were displayed by Helen Wolcott Horton (left), director of the Home Service Center. In 1969 Pillsbury Space Food Sticks were introduced nationally after a successful polar expedition (above).

J-M owned processing plants in Louisiana and Arkansas, marketing its fresh chicken through its own sales and distribution facilities in the Southwest and in southern California. The acquisition made Pillsbury the second largest broiler processor in the United States.[31]

The company's other operations proceeded on the courses set for them during Gerot's administration. In January 1968 Keith announced a plan to double the size of the research and development laboratories, and in July construction started on the first phase. The consumer area continued to broaden its line of dry grocery and refrigerated products, giving special attention to low-calorie and other contemporary products. One of the new products was Space Food Sticks, introduced in 1969. The product traced its origin to food cubes developed for the space program in Pillsbury's research and development facilities in the early 1960s. The cubes had been the first solid food consumed in space, accompanying F. Scott Carpenter on his May 1962 mission in Aurora Seven.[32]

The consumer area suffered a sharp blow on October 18, 1969, when the Food and Drug Administration banned all uses of calcium cyclamate in food. When consumed in extremely large quantities, the chemical was found to produce cancer in rats, requiring its removal from the food chain even though it had not been known to cause harm to humans. The government action brought immediate withdrawal from the market of Funny Face, Sweet*10®, and Sprinkle Sweet®, a $4.5 million loss. But the consumer management rallied quickly, reformulating all three products. Sweet*10® and Sprinkle Sweet® were presweetened with saccharin, and Funny Face drink mix was reintroduced in both unsweetened and presweetened form.

The company purchased a flour mill in St. Louis (left, top) in 1968 to help meet its increasing internal requirements for flour, and to become more competitive in the southeastern and midwestern markets. The same year it expanded its foreign consumer operations with acquisitions of Etablissements Brossard, S.A., a processor of packaged baked goods in France (bottom), and Cora, a leading pasta manufacturing company in Mexico.

The company's flour milling business was benefiting from two favorable shifts in the industry's economy. The first was a recent reduction in the number of the nation's flour mills; the other was the apparent stabilization of per capita flour consumption after many years of decline. The company proceeded to streamline its plants to take advantage of the changed climate. It purchased a large St. Louis flour mill, advantageously situated to serve Pillsbury's consumer product plants in Springfield and New Albany; it also constructed a new bakery mix plant in Los Angeles to replace an outdated facility there. Pillsbury International entered the Mexican consumer food market in 1968, purchasing one of Mexico's best-known pasta companies, and in France Gringoire acquired Etablissements Brossard, S.A., making Gringoire the largest French producer of cookies and pastries. The international group continued to build its strong line of consumer products in Venezuela, where in 1965 it had acquired Milani, the country's leading pasta processor.

The executive office conducted an active program to bring more diversity to the company's operations. Its strategy was to seek out emerging consumer trends that the company could meet either by acquisition or through one of its existing businesses. In November 1969 Pillsbury took the first of several steps that in less than 19 months involved it in four new and unrelated fields. On the West Coast an expanding restaurant chain featured freshly baked pies that could also be purchased for take-out. After exploring acquisition of the company, Pillsbury decided to make its own test of the concept in the Midwest market. It entered into a joint venture with a prominent Des Moines, Iowa, restaurateur and his associates to open a pilot restaurant in Des Moines under the name Poppin Fresh® Pie Shop. The restaurant was a success, and in January 1971 Pillsbury, as the majority owner, and its partners opened a second shop in Hopkins, Minnesota, a Minneapolis suburb.

In January 1970 Pillsbury acquired two nationally circulated magazines, *Bon Appetit* and *Bon Voyage*. The consumer area had started a centralized publications business in 1968 to manage the company's growing line of hard- and soft-cover cookbooks and related publications; *Bon Appetit* and *Bon Voyage* were purchased to form a nucleus for further expansion in the publishing field. By the end of fiscal 1971, however, the company found it more profitable to publish cookbooks for product promotion within the separate operating divisions. The centralized publications operation was closed down, and *Bon Voyage* ceased publication in 1973.

The third new business was Pemtom, a Minneapolis-based community developer and builder of moderate-priced housing, in which Pillsbury purchased a 20-percent share in January 1970, agreeing to provide a line of credit. Lastly, in June 1971 the company purchased

Bachman's European Flower Markets, a Minneapolis retailer of cut flowers, plants, and accessories. Its sales were conducted at attractive floral outlets leased in grocery stores and shopping malls, principally in Minneapolis and the Twin Cities area.

That July, Call-A-Computer Company was sold to a manufacturer of computer hardware in California, and Pillsbury exited from the computer time-sharing business. Pillsbury Management Systems, a Pillsbury subsidiary established in 1967 to offer computer programming and consulting service to small businesses, was discontinued in 1971. Time-sharing was in its infancy when Call-A-Computer was formed in 1967, and the company accurately foresaw the magnitude of the opportunity. What it did not anticipate was the heavy capital requirements and the even heavier need for top management involvement and expertise to survive in the computer industry.

In 1970 the company again reached new highs in sales and earnings. The following year, however, earnings suffered their largest decline in the company's history. The broiler industry reached the bottom of its cycle, and a combination of the overproduction of broilers, the low prices of competing meats, and the increased costs of feed resulted in a loss of $9 million for Pillsbury Farms. Total company earnings fell to $9.3 million from the previous year's $17 million.

The five years of Keith's chairmanship were a period of turmoil and ferment in the United States. The overriding preoccupation was the war in Indochina and the deep emotional divisions it was creating. But there were other threatening issues: escalating inflation, school integration problems, civil rights protests and the assassination of Martin Luther King, Jr., student protests culminating in the deaths at Kent State University and Jackson State College, growing concern over the extent of poverty in the country, and serious questions about the safety and quality of the environment. It was an unsettling time, a time when corporate business leaders in the United States were coming face-to-face with an unprecedented range of social and ethical issues.

Consumerism had become a broadly supported national movement, as individual consumers and their organizations sought greater protection against useless, inferior, or dangerous products, misleading advertising, and unfair pricing. Keith was an unwavering champion of the consumer, and he saw much in the movement that was right. He led the company in a determined campaign to assure the safety of its products, so successful that in 1973 the company was employed to teach the Pillsbury product safety system to a number of Food and Drug Administration supervisors and inspectors. A carefully designed nutritional policy governed formulation and labeling of all company food products. Close attention was given to the style and

In addition to the 854 Burger King® stores in 1972, the restaurant group included two Poppin Fresh® Pie Shops (right), a restaurant concept Pillsbury had begun to test in 1969.

content of the company's advertising, in keeping with Keith's warning at a national advertising workshop that, "The freedom to advertise can be shredded by backlash, the same as any other freedom."[33]

During Keith's tenure as chief executive officer, all levels of government gave increasing attention to the conduct of American business. Pillsbury and other companies developed and constantly monitored programs to meet clean air and water standards, comply with occupational health and safety regulations, and accomplish energy conservation. The executive office audited on a regular basis the company's compliance with its programs to provide equal employment opportunity for minorities and women. Keith, determined that these activities would not diminish, appointed a public responsibilities committee of the board of directors in September 1970. It was one of the first such committees in American industry.

In 1972 the company bounced back from its disappointing performance of the preceding year, posting earnings within $100,000 of the all-time high reported in 1970. The restaurant group (854 Burger King® stores and two Poppin Fresh® Pie Shops) passed the agriproducts group to become the company's second largest profit producer behind the consumer group, accounting for 27.5 percent of 1972 net income as compared to the consumer area's 43.8 percent. Burger King, not yet 20 years old, began to remodel its restaurants from slower cafeteria-style service line to more efficient multiple sales positions. It also authorized the first Burger King® dessert item—hot apple pie.

PILLSBURY* NET PROFITS 1953-1972

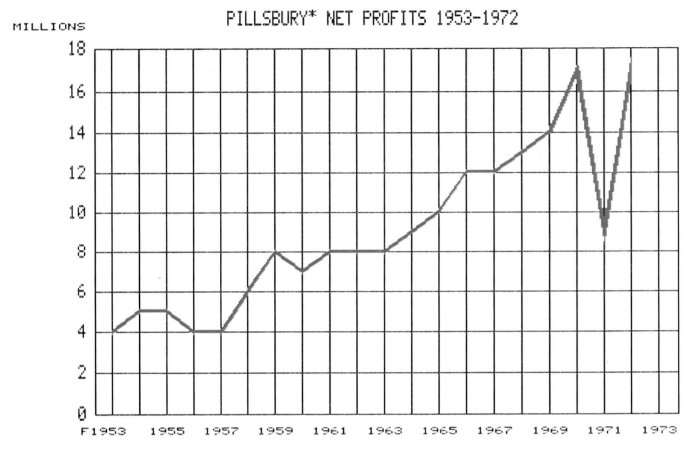

MILLIONS

*PILLSBURY MILLS, INC. 1953-1958
THE PILLSBURY COMPANY 1959-1972

For at least two years Pillsbury had been seeking a suitable entry in the wine market, and a few days before the September shareholders' meeting in 1972 the company announced its purchase of a California winery, Souverain Cellars, Inc. Souverain Cellars had been producing premium Napa Valley varietal wines in a tiny winery near Rutherford, California, since 1942. At the time of the purchase it had a new winery under construction at Rutherford and planned to construct a second, larger winery in the Sonoma Valley.[34]

That fall Bob Keith fought a lonely battle on another front. After surgery revealed a malignancy, he proceeded with treatment, returning to his regular duties. But early in November further surgery became necessary, keeping him from the November 9 board meeting, the last regularly scheduled one of the year. On December 6 Keith announced his retirement as chairman and chief executive officer, and he died the following May 23 at age 59.

The company had made giant strides under the leadership of Paul Gerot and Bob Keith. The magnitude of gains in their combined 20 years of stewardship is reflected in this table:

	Year Ending May 31, 1952	Year Ending May 31, 1972
Net Sales	$314,907,567	$717,837,000
Net Profits	3,209,893	16,914,000
Net Current Assets	31,977,721	90,062,000
Number of Shareholders	8,098	12,821
Number of Employees	8,130	18,818

Another table demonstrates that over the same period the company had also kept pace with its competitors:

	1972 Pretax Profit in Millions	1952–1972 Increase in Pretax Profit (%)
Procter & Gamble	$ 515	557
Campbell Soup	113	219
General Foods	221	433
Ralston-Purina	120	561
General Mills	104	493
Quaker Oats	68	425
Pillsbury	33	467
Average		451

Keeping pace, however, is not always enough. Fortune usually smiles her broadest on the winners. Pillsbury was again very much in the race; but it had not reached the top.

America's No. 1 selling frozen vegetable.

That's right! Green Giant® 4 Ear Corn-On-The-Cob is the No. 1 selling frozen vegetable item in retail dollar sales...according to the "SAMI Top 200" report for 52 weeks ending April 1, 1983. And Green Giant® 6 Ear Nibblers™ ranks No. 2. The reason: people like to enjoy the sweet taste of summer year 'round.

You can substantially increase your sales and profits with America's No. 1 and No. 2 frozen vegetable items – Green Giant® Corn-On-The-Cob.

So:

- Carry the leading brand – Green Giant.®
- Stock both 4 and 6-ear Corn-On-The-Cob.
- Give Corn-On-The-Cob the space it deserves.
- Promote Corn-On-The-Cob year 'round.

Green Giant®

Niblet Ears.

7 A Bold New Strategy
1973–1984

The scale of the company increased dramatically as the number of its at-home and away-from-home food businesses increased. Green Giant Company, with a rich Minnesota heritage dating from 1903, became part of The Pillsbury Company in 1979. Norman Rockwell painted the picture used in this retrospective advertisement in 1983.

In early 1971 Bob Keith had begun work on a plan for eventual executive office transition. His concepts were put into a memorandum for the board of directors' nominating committee, and this committee reviewed them preceding the regular November 9, 1972, board meeting. Toward the end of the month Keith's declining health prompted William T. French, the committee's chairman, to call a special meeting on Wednesday, December 6. French also sent his own memorandum to the committee, outlining a number of specific alternatives for consideration.

All but one of the 11 nominating committee members convened in Minneapolis that Wednesday. Keith, who had decided the previous day to retire as chairman and chief executive officer, joined them. The committee debated its alternatives for structuring the company's top management and then came to a decision, asking Keith to inform those who would be affected.[1]

On the following Saturday morning, Keith asked William H. Spoor, Terrance Hanold, and James R. Peterson, the 45-year-old vice-president of the consumer group, to meet at his home. There Keith told them that the committee intended to recommend the election of Spoor as chairman and chief executive officer and Peterson as president. The committee also proposed that Terry Hanold become chairman of the board's executive committee, and that all three act as a team in changing from old management to new. Keith asked Spoor and Peterson to present their strategy for the company to the nominating committee on January 3.

Spoor already had in hand the essential elements of such a presentation. Toward the beginning of 1972, at one of his regular meetings with Keith to discuss the international group's operations, Spoor had raised the issue of employee stock options. His own two-year-old options, he complained, were of little value, since Pillsbury shares could be purchased on the open market for only a dollar or two more than his option price. Keith, who held some of the same stock options, shared Spoor's concern. He had already decided to ask Spoor and a few other general managers to make a critical study of the company and develop recommendations for improving its performance. The small group began a series of monthly meetings, analyzed the operations and course of several competing companies and of Pillsbury itself, and arrived at strategies they believed would strengthen Pillsbury. They had completed their assignment in November.

Spoor and Peterson adopted many of the study group's conclusions as the basis for their presentation to the nominating committee. They both attended the nominating committee meeting, where Spoor presented the program he had organized, embellished, and had approved by Peterson. Later, a member of the committee recalled that "the presentation was so complete and well considered that it appeared to confirm the judgments we had made the month before."

The board met the next day, January 4, and shortly before noon announced the elections of Spoor, Peterson, and Hanold. William J. Powell, the company's chief legal officer, was elected senior vice-president to form a four-man executive office with them.

The swiftness of events coupled with the busy holiday season and the absence of newspaper publicity had minimized speculation as to Keith's successor. Nonetheless, the board's selection of Spoor came as a surprise to many knowledgeable observers, both inside and outside Pillsbury. Spoor was not as well known within the company as either Peterson or Hanold, and the board itself had seen more of the other two than of Spoor. The directors best acquainted with the new chairman, however, perceived him as a man who would stir up and energize the organization and provide it with a strong leadership.[2]

Spoor had been in Minneapolis about ten years when he was elected chairman. Born in Colorado on January 16, 1923, Spoor graduated from high school in Denver and then entered Dartmouth College on a track and football scholarship in 1942. He left college for 42 months' service in the army during World War II, returned to Dartmouth in 1946, and graduated in 1949 with a history major. His interest in joining a company with international operations led him to accept a job as assistant sales supervisor in Pillsbury's New York City export office. Four years later he became manager of the export division, where he was instrumental in arranging Pillsbury's participation in several new flour and feed milling businesses starting up in former Pillsbury export markets. In 1962 the export division and Spoor moved to Minneapolis. Only Paul Gerot's argument that becoming part of headquarters would increase Spoor's chances of promotion could persuade him to leave New York City, where he had worked 14 years. He was made vice-president of the company's non-European foreign operations in 1966, and two years later was promoted to vice-president and general manager of the international group.

The strategies Spoor presented to the board were simple and straightforward. Pillsbury must concentrate on building its considerable strengths and refuse to be diverted by undertaking ventures in unfamiliar fields. It must attract the most highly qualified people to

William H. Spoor was in charge of the company's international operations when he was elected chief executive officer in 1973. His dream was to build Pillsbury into a great company, a true industry leader, and he achieved it with a strategy that produced repetitive, predictable, and steadily growing earnings.

its key positions and board. It must produce substantial and, above all, steady growth in sales and earnings, anticipating and avoiding obstacles that might interfere with this course.

The ultimate objective was to transform Pillsbury into an industry leader, gaining for its shareholders the corresponding rewards. Spoor was confident that the program could be carried out. But first, he realized, Pillsbury's new management must establish credibility with the employee body, the directors, and the investing public. It had to persuade and demonstrate that it could change the company from an in-and-out performer to one with a solid, continuing capacity for growth.

As luck would have it, there were no major projects or problems demanding Spoor's attention in the first months of 1973. The company was riding the wings of a bullish national economy, and it appeared that Pillsbury's sales and earnings would almost certainly surpass those of the year previous. Consequently Spoor spent the first few weeks in his new job preparing for the future. He solicited from each board member and from a few selected security analysts a list of Pillsbury's strengths and weaknesses. He devoted time to increasing his knowledge of the company and its personnel. And, finally, he began to plan for the implementation of the strategies he had outlined to the board.

By the end of April, with strong results for the fiscal year virtually assured, Spoor decided it was time to take the first step toward raising the investment community's level of interest in Pillsbury. In early May the board agreed to his proposal that management ''go public'' with its major strategies and goals. A meeting was arranged in New York City on July 19 with the New York Society of Security Analysts. Spoor, Peterson, and Arthur A. Rosewall, president of Burger King, made a detailed presentation of Pillsbury's current business and its plans for the future. Spoor spoke to the new management's need to establish a consistent record of growth in sales and earnings and of its objective to grow at an annual rate of 10 percent in sales and earnings per share. He said that this course was the one that management had set for itself; by following it he expected Pillsbury to exceed $1 billion in sales and reach per-share earnings of $5 in fiscal 1976. The fiscal 1973 results, announced the following month, showed sales of $816 million and earnings per share of $3.74.[3]

Back in Minneapolis Spoor and Peterson began to talk more and more at management meetings and with the press about Pillsbury's goal of becoming a great company. They adopted the word ''quality'' to describe the levels the company must attain in every aspect of corporate activity. There must be quality people, quality products, quality earnings, and quality performance of its public responsibilities.

There was, however, one cloud hanging over the company's ability to produce quality earnings, the consistent, year-by-year increases that Spoor had talked about to the security analysts. As recently as fiscal 1971 the company's sizable poultry operations, Pillsbury Farms, had incurred a loss of $7.8 million, causing Pillsbury's total earnings that year to drop about 45 percent. Early in 1973 Pillsbury Farms discontinued its unsuccessful precooked frozen chicken business. The fresh ice-packed broiler operation that remained was a commodity business, subject to the industry's historical pattern of cyclical earnings. It was the same kind of difficulty that had plagued earlier managements in the days of the unpredictable formula feed business.

There was sharp disagreement within the company as to what should be done about Pillsbury Farms. The business provided an important part of the company's sales, nearly 14 percent in fiscal 1973. On the other hand, losses like those in fiscal 1971 could play havoc with the company's need for consistent growth in earnings. Spoor asked two of management's principal advocates for continuing with Pillsbury Farms to give him their views in writing; he made the same request of two of the leading proponents for selling the business. After reading their arguments, he concluded to recommend sale. There was no way, he believed, for the broiler business to provide a steady stream of increased earnings, and the lost sales would simply have to be made up in some other way. The board adopted his recommendation with only one dissenting vote, and the property was sold to an English company in March 1974 for $23.1 million.

Profits from the sale of Pillsbury Farms combined with an up-cycle in the broiler industry to help the company record net earnings of $5.04 per share on sales of $1 billion in fiscal 1974. Suddenly the company was two years ahead of the growth path projected to the New York security analysts in July 1973.

These excellent results came despite a sharp drop in earnings of the consumer products group. A government price freeze imposed during parts of June and July 1973 included consumer food products, but even apart from the freeze the company was unable to pass through to its customers the rapidly escalating cost of such key ingredients as vegetable oil, cocoa, and sugar. Then in October the Arab oil embargo began, sending fuel prices skyward and compounding the group's earnings problems. The agri-products group, however, doubled its profits from any previous year in history, while the restaurants group posted a 29-percent gain in profit over 1973. Agri-products' principal contributor was its grain merchandising division. An expanding world demand for grain, coupled with volatile markets

During the recession of the mid-1970s shoppers were especially attentive to the price-value of their food purchases. Sales of basic products like Pillsbury's Best® Family Flour flourished.

and high commodity prices, pushed the division's trading profits to record levels. Burger King sparked the restaurant group's growth by adding 223 new stores during the year and substantially increasing its average sales per unit.

The fiscal year also brought a major change in the company's research and development leadership. Spoor and Peterson both felt a need to build the status and productivity of the function, and in January 1974 they recruited Philip D. Aines, food research vice-president at Procter & Gamble, to head the research and development department at Pillsbury. It was the beginning of a number of significant additions to the company's top management ranks. A few weeks later Bert S. Cross, retired chairman of the board of Minnesota Mining and Manufacturing Company and a strong research and development advocate, joined Pillsbury's board of directors.

Fiscal 1975 was another record year despite continuing double-digit inflation, higher production costs, and the sixth recession since World War II. The consumer products group rebounded, demonstrating the recession-resistant nature of its product line. The weakened economy caused grocery shoppers to be especially attentive to the price-value of their food purchases, and sales of such basic, less expensive products as Pillsbury's Best® Family Flour, pancake mix, refrigerated biscuits, instant mashed potatoes, and dry beverage mixes flourished. The group also benefited from a full year of operations by Wilton Enterprises, Inc., acquired by the company in the last half of fiscal 1974. Wilton, headquartered in Chicago, was the country's leading marketer of cake decorating products. Originally it had sold

Halt the "Hungries" in a hurry!

With the great-tasting microwave foods from Pillsbury.

When sudden hunger hits, try great-tasting Pillsbury Microwave Foods: New Pillsbury Microwave Pizza...with a revolutionary crust that's really crisp! Pillsbury Microwave Popcorn...frozen for incredible flavor and great taste that pops up in less than five minutes. And Pillsbury Microwave Pancakes...fluffy, light pancakes anytime, with no mess. They're all in your grocer's freezer to keep them fresh and full of flavor.

Now you can, now you should...

Pillsbury Microwave is **Pillsbury** *Good!*

©TPC 1984

By 1975 the agri-products group's transportation fleet included 80 barges (above) and 800 rail hopper cars (top). The group was also engaged in exploring new technologies, and its pioneering led to introduction of a number of consumer microwave products in the 1980s (left).

to bakers through distributors and to consumers by mail order, but by 1975 it had substantially expanded its distribution system through direct sales "to such mass merchandisers as J.C. Penney, Sears, and Wards."

The agri-products group's earnings fell below those of the previous year but were still the second largest in its history. Again the grain merchandising division's earnings stood out. For several years the division had been acquiring a fleet of rail cars and barges, both leased and owned. The original purpose was to reduce its reliance on common carriers and to establish its own capability for shipping grain. Then it moved into the business of transporting bulk commodities such as coal, coke, salt, and fertilizer, for which it bought or leased more barges and hopper cars. By 1975 it was operating a system of 35 grain elevators, 80 barges, and 800 rail hopper cars.

The agri-products group was exploring a broad range of new businesses and technologies. It had two microwave products, popcorn and pancakes, being tested in the vended foods market. Bitsyn, a nutmeat replacement developed in the company's research laboratories, went into production in Minneapolis in 1972, and in fiscal 1975 another plant was constructed at Atchison, Kansas. The product, consisting mostly of wheat germ and hydrogenated oil, was sold in the consumer and industrial markets for use in candy, ice cream, and snacks. The group was engaged in the development of hydroprocessing, its patented wet milling process for producing gluten directly from the wheat berry for the bakery, breakfast cereal, and pet food industries. The process also resulted in a starch by-product for the paper and other industries. Ultimately the vended foods test market was terminated and the microwave popcorn product transferred to the consumer products group. Bitsyn also was transferred to the same group, marketed for a time under the name Wheatnuts, and then sold in 1982. The work with hydroprocessing was discontinued in 1978 when neither the process nor its products measured up.

Both Burger King and Poppin Fresh® Pie Shops met their targeted expansion figures in fiscal 1975. By the end of the year Burger King had grown to 1,395 franchised and company-owned stores, more than five times the number existing at purchase in 1967. It had begun in 1972 to convert existing stores from cafeteria-style service lines to the more efficient multiple sales positions. Now all its stores were being built in the new mode, and the process of converting the old stores continued. In fiscal 1975 at Lake Park, Florida, and Poway, California, Burger King opened its first two drive-through window units, inaugurating a popular service and boosting the all-important level of per store sales. The first overseas Burger King® was opened at Madrid, Spain, in June 1975. With only four stores in Canada and two in the Bahamas, the number of Burger King's foreign stores lagged far behind the approximately 354 McDonald's units outside the United States. Poppin Fresh® Pie Shops recorded a second consecutive profitable year, entering the Chicago market and extending to 11 the total number of its restaurants in the Twin Cities area, Chicago, and Des Moines. The next year Pillsbury would purchase the outstanding minority interest in the business.

Although the company's international business had a fairly wide geographical base, it still constituted a relatively small part of Pillsbury. In fiscal 1975 the international group, including the export division, accounted for only about 9 percent of the company's sales and 5 percent of its profits. Growth opportunities in the United States loomed larger than those abroad, and foreign expansion, for the time being at least, had little appeal. The only exception was the company's continuing effort to create a refrigerated fresh dough market in Europe, where the products were unknown. The undertaking began in 1972 with product shipment from Canada to England, followed by construction of a plant at Thurcroft, near London. Introduction of the product line in England was only moderately successful. A promising German test market, however, led in 1975 to national distribution of a line of such Knack und Back products as Sonntag's Brötchen, Apfeltaschen, and Kirschtaschen. France was next, but refrigerated fresh dough failed entirely to win Gallic acclaim. By 1978 the company concluded that Europe was not a suitable market for the product, and the Thurcroft plant was converted to other production by Pillsbury's English subsidiary.

No need, short- or long-term, was more strongly felt within the company than that of adding to the size and importance of the consumer products operations. Fiscal 1974 results made this even more evident. For the first time in many years, earnings of the agri-products group were greater than those of the consumer foods group, and the latter's lead over the restaurant group continued to narrow.

The surest course to new business, given the uncertainties and long lead times of internal development, lay in a stepped-up acquisition program. The frozen foods business continued to provide the strongest attraction. Although Pillsbury was well represented in the dry grocery and refrigerated sections of the store, it had closed down its small Gibbs Goodies operation in 1965, and it was notably absent from the frozen foods section. In 1974 and 1975 the company explored a number of acquisitions in the frozen food field, from Mrs. Smith's Pies to John's Pizza to Mrs. Paul's Fish. But none materialized, and the only proposed acquisition to reach the newspapers was a nonfrozen food company, Weight Watchers International, Inc. An agreement in principle with Weight Watchers was announced in April 1975, but the transaction was never completed.

With the recession coming to an end, prices on the New York Stock Exchange began to climb in 1975. The price of Pillsbury stock also rose, buoyed by recognition of the company's recent performance. By the close of fiscal 1975 Pillsbury had exceeded its sales and earnings goals for three successive years. Moreover, since the start of new management, each quarter had been better than the same quarter a year before. Spoor had introduced the term ''repetitive, predictable and steadily growing'' to define quality earnings, and it was becoming a company watchword. When the company's board of directors met on September 8, 1975, Pillsbury stock had reached 67⅜, almost double the price a year before. Management recommended and the board authorized a two-for-one split of the company's stock.

This third split (the others had occurred in 1959 and 1965) was reported at the stockholders' meeting on September 9, 1975. Shortly thereafter the company mailed its stockholders a letter including two media releases. The first, on October 7, announced an agreement in principle for the acquisition of Steak and Ale Restaurants of America, Inc. The second, dated October 15, announced an agreement in principle to acquire Totino's Finer Foods, Inc.

Steak and Ale® and Totino's® were the American dream come true, glittering examples of the opportunities and rewards of the free enterprise system. Both companies started from scratch in the 1960s. In each case, major businesses grew out of the entrepreneurial drive of a pair of individuals dedicated to making an idea work. Pillsbury was to benefit immensely from the two acquisitions, as well as from the decisions of the principal founders to become Pillsbury employees and to watch over their enterprises after the mergers.

The Totino's acquisition capped Pillsbury's quest for a viable line of frozen products. After a long search for a suitable partner, the company found a match right in Minneapolis. James and Rose Totino, both children of Italian immigrants, had opened a small shop in northeast Minneapolis in 1951 to sell homemade pizzas to takeout customers. Their business grew, and they converted the little shop to a restaurant called Totino's Italian Kitchen. In 1962 Jim and Rose considered retiring, but they decided instead to invest their savings in a small factory to produce frozen pasta-based entrees for the retail market. Frozen pizza, their first choice, was ruled out because of the unmanageable cost of building a bakery to produce the crusts.

Totino's frozen entree business was struggling in 1961, when Jim fortuitously found a firm to supply prebaked pizza crusts. He and Rose took a Small Business Administration loan to install equipment to top and package pizza. Reunited with the product they knew best, they soon found that product demand exceeded the capacity of their original factory. In 1971 they built a $2.5 million plant, complete with its own bakery, in the Minneapolis suburb of Fridley. By 1975, when Pillsbury initiated talks, Rose and Jim had succeeded in building a little take-out shop for fresh, homemade pizza into the nation's

ANNCR. (VO): It took a great cook . . .
Rose Totino . . .

to finally do a deluxe pizza right!

Introducing "My Classic Pizza" by
Rose Totino.

ROSE (VO): The secret of my new
pizza is perfect balance.

A marvelous crust . . . rich tomato
sauce with real Italian herbs . . .

and lots of fantastic toppings.

I cook from the heart, for pizza
lovers!

ANNCR.: Finally. A deluxe pizza that
did it right. "My Classic Pizza"
by Rose Totino.

ROSE: Enjoy!

second-largest producer of frozen pizza. The acquisition was completed in November 1975, with Jim and Rose and their two daughters receiving Pillsbury stock valued at about $20 million.[4]

Totino's was still far from reaching its potential in 1975. Frozen pizza was one of the largest and fastest-growing categories in the retail food store, its sales greater than those in either the total cake mix market or the refrigerated fresh dough market. Totino's number-two position had been attained with product distribution confined to areas doing only 55 percent of the nation's grocery business, and it had yet to enter the populous eastern United States market. On completion of the acquisition Rose became a Pillsbury vice-president, the first woman in the company to hold that position. Jim died in 1981, but in 1984 Rose continued as an officer of Pillsbury and as a valued adviser and ambassador for its products.[5]

Steak and Ale, still a year short of its tenth birthday in 1975, was the premier company in one of the fastest growing sectors of the restaurant business, the limited-menu, dinnerhouse segment. John Whitehead, one of Pillsbury's outside directors, told Spoor that the principal owners of the chain of about a hundred company-owned restaurants might be considering a merger with a larger company. Although Pillsbury was not contemplating another restaurant acquisition at the time, the chance to purchase the leading company in its field was worth pursuing. After assuring himself of the young organization's soundness, Spoor opened a dialogue with its cofounder and chief executive officer, Norman Brinker. Shortly thereafter negotiations began.

Brinker had been in the restaurant business since graduation from college in 1957, first with the Jack-in-the-Box chain and then as co-owner of Brink's Coffee Shop in Dallas. In February 1966 he and his partner, Peter G. Wray, a Phoenix investor, opened the first Steak and Ale® restaurant in Dallas. Sales rose from $400,000 to $101 million in nine years, the partners having raised additional capital with a public stock offering in 1970. Although the company's future seemed assured, Brinker foresaw greater opportunities for its employees by joining with Pillsbury. He also perceived that a merger for Pillsbury stock would afford Steak and Ale shareholders, of which he was the largest, "a continued growth opportunity with a diversified, quality company." For Pillsbury it meant adding a new dimension to its restaurant offerings and establishing itself even more firmly as a leader in the industry. When the acquisition was completed on May 28, 1976, Steak and Ale shareholders received Pillsbury shares valued at approximately $100 million, and Pillsbury owned a vigorous, expanding company with 113 restaurants in 26 states and Canada. Brinker and his team continued to manage the company from its headquarters in Dallas.[6]

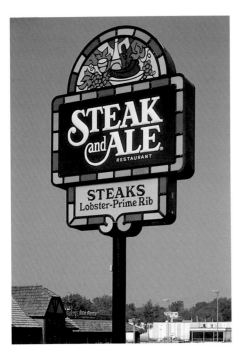

The company acquired Steak and Ale Restaurants of America, Inc., in 1976. Norman Brinker had expanded the full-service restaurant firm from one store in Dallas (left, top) in 1966 to 113 restaurants in 26 states and Canada. Today its sign (above) and appetizing entrees (left, bottom) are known from coast to coast.

As 1975 drew to a close Terry Hanold, after a 29-year career with the company, reached age 64 and elected to take early retirement at the end of December. Then on January 5, 1976, Jim Peterson resigned as president and director of the company, ending an uneasy relationship with Spoor that had existed through most of their three-year association. Spoor was then elected president. For the next 30 months he acted both as chairman and chief executive officer and as president.

The acquisition of Steak and Ale necessitated sale of the wine business. Substantially all of the Steak and Ale® restaurants served liquor, and "tied house" laws in most states prohibited a company from selling alcoholic beverages at both the wholesale and retail levels. Souverain had expanded after Pillsbury bought the company in late 1972 by purchasing the assets of Frank Schoonmaker Selections, Inc., a well-known importer of French and German wines, and Schoonmaker joined the Souverain board in 1973. In the fall Souverain opened a new winery at Geyserville in California's Sonoma Valley. The wines produced at the Napa and Sonoma Valley wineries were of excellent quality, but Souverain's share of the national market was infinitesimal, and efforts to build an effective marketing program in the face of extensive, well-established competition never succeeded. Consequently, even before negotiations with Steak and Ale began, plans were being made to get out of the business. The commencement of discussions with Steak and Ale accelerated the effort to sell. Disposition of Souverain was completed within a few days after the Steak and Ale merger became effective, May 28, 1976. A palliative for the losses realized on the sale was that they could be charged off in fiscal 1976 without interrupting the company's lengthening string of improved annual earnings.

Divestment of the wine business completed the disposal of the diverse group of toehold acquisitions the company had made in 1970 through 1972, and the consumer products group became the consumer foods group. In describing the new management's strategic posture to the New York security analysts in July 1973, Spoor had asserted the company's intention "to be diversified beyond our food base." But after a year, management decided that the company's future lay in being exclusively a food company. As Spoor was to say later, "As we looked back, that was the only thing that we'd really made money on. Once we'd agreed on that . . . we got rid of all the sideshows." *Bon Appetit* was sold in March 1975 when the company decided against trying to carve out a place in the publishing field. The company's interest in Pemtom, Inc., the Minneapolis housing developer, was liquidated in May 1975. Sale of European Flower Markets was completed in June 1976. That venture had never achieved profitability, despite expansion from the Twin Cities to Houston, Dallas, Chicago, Milwaukee, and Detroit.[7]

At the annual stockholders meeting on September 14, 1976, after less than four years as the company's chief executive officer, Spoor was able to tell the stockholders: "Pillsbury is quite a different company than it was just 12 months ago . . . [and] the task of refocusing and refining the strategic thrust of our company is now largely finished. Our basic portfolio of businesses is in place; our management team is in position; and our finances stronger than at any time in our history . . . The underlying reason for our business health is the clear definition of ourselves as being a food company dedicated to the food business—not incidentally the largest and most basic industry in the United States. Pillsbury is uniquely positioned in three major food sectors and has a solid base for expansion." The 1976 annual report described Pillsbury as "an international company participating in three major aspects of the food business—Agri-Products, Consumer Products, and Restaurants," a description repeated with minor editorial changes in succeeding annual reports.

During the first four years of Spoor's leadership there were major changes in the board of directors. Of the 16 board members elected at the 1976 shareholders meeting, only seven had been on the board when the new management was elected in January 1973. The board had changed from a majority of inside or employee directors (8 of 15) in 1972 to a majority of outside directors (11 of 16) in 1976. In accordance with the board's mandatory retirement policy, Philip Pillsbury and Paul Gerot, who had a combined total of 70 years service on the board, did not stand for reelection in 1974.

The search for highly qualified managers, begun with the selection of Philip D. Aines, continued. In May 1975, Walter D. Scott, an associate director of the U.S. Office of Management and Budget, joined the company as senior vice-president and chief financial officer. Raymond F. Good, president of Heinz U.S.A., the domestic subsidiary of H. J. Heinz & Co., moved to Pillsbury as executive vice-president of the consumer foods group in August 1976. The following January Donald N. Smith, executive vice-president of McDonald's, became a vice-president of Pillsbury and president and chief executive officer of Burger King.

In 1977 Spoor decided that the time had come to relinquish some of his responsibilities, and on June 7, 1977, the board elected Winston R. Wallin president and chief operating officer. Wallin was 51 years old and had joined the company as a grain buyer after graduation from the University of Minnesota in 1951. He had risen rapidly through the company's agri-products operations, heading the commodity merchandising division from 1970 to 1974, when he was elected vice-president and general manager of the agri-products group. Wallin was assigned responsibility for the restaurant and agri-products groups. Ray Good, as executive vice-president of the consumer foods group, continued to report to Spoor.

For several years the 13-story Pillsbury Building, the company's headquarters for more than 30 years, had been too small to house all the headquarters personnel. The company rented additional space in a half-dozen downtown and suburban office buildings. In 1973 Investors Diversified Services, Inc., invited Spoor to consider locating Pillsbury's headquarters in the IDS Tower, Minneapolis's newest and largest downtown office building. Negotiations, premised in Pillsbury's case on renaming the tower, began but were broken off in 1975.

By that time Pillsbury's employee count had reached 27,000, and it was clear that a solution for the headquarters problem would have to be found. The company commenced a study of its options, including expansion and renovation of its existing space as well as construction of new offices in downtown or suburban Minneapolis or in another state. Motivated in large part by the desire to help maintain the vitality of the Minneapolis downtown area, the management decided to stay there. In early 1978 the company signed an agreement to become the primary tenant of a two-towered Pillsbury Center, to be constructed in the block directly northeast of its existing headquarters. Ground was broken for the new center in the summer of 1978, with the Pillsbury World Headquarters scheduled to occupy most of the larger 40-story tower.

The research and development laboratories, located in southeast Minneapolis on the street behind the old A mill, were also overcrowded. When Phil Aines joined the company in 1973 he counseled Spoor that the facilities would have to be materially enlarged and upgraded before the company could expect to obtain a satisfactory

Ground for Pillsbury Center in Minneapolis was broken in 1978. When the company's new world headquarters building was completed in 1981, employees took advantage of an open house to inspect the board room (right).

Pillsbury continued expansion with acquisition of Fox Deluxe Foods, as well as of American Beauty Macaroni Company whose products are shown above. The addition of new employees along with new businesses made the new headquarters building (left) imperative.

return on its research and development investment. Rather than remodel the existing structures, a research and development task force supported by outside consultants recommended building an entirely new complex; an option was taken on a proposed site in Eden Prairie in the fall of 1976.

About 12 miles from downtown Minneapolis, the site was large enough to accommodate a headquarters building as well. But when the decision to locate the new world headquarters in the heart of the city was reached, support for the Eden Prairie research and development facility waned, and the option was allowed to expire. In its place the company acquired lands adjacent to the existing facilities in southeast Minneapolis and began construction of a four-story addition to the laboratories. Work was completed in 1981, and in September the new building was dedicated. The research and development staff had grown to 395, a significant increase from the 229 employed when Spoor became chairman eight years earlier.

Pillsbury continued to make acquisitions to strengthen the consumer products group. In November 1976 it acquired Fox Deluxe Foods, Inc., a Joplin, Missouri, pizza manufacturer. American Beauty Macaroni Company, a manufacturer of pasta products and sauce mixes marketed primarily in the Midwest and on the West Coast was added in September 1977, and Speas Company, producers of a line of vinegar and apple juice products, was acquired in May 1978.

A still-larger acquisition, however, was on the drawing boards in the summer of 1978. The subject was the Green Giant Company, 40 miles away from Minneapolis at Le Sueur, Minnesota, in the mythical valley of the Jolly Green Giant. Green Giant's sales for the fiscal year ended May 27, 1978, its seventy-fifth year, were almost half a billion dollars, and its net earnings were $10.4 million. The Green Giant product lines complemented those of Pillsbury, both in the dry grocery and the frozen sections of the grocery store, where the Green Giant® logo was as well known as Poppin' Fresh®. A leading processor of canned and frozen vegetables, Green Giant was also developing a line of frozen entrees.

Pillsbury management initiated studies of Green Giant's business early in 1978, concluding with a decision to recommend acquisition. The board concurred at its September 1978 meeting and authorized commencement of negotiations. After protracted, price-centered discussions, Pillsbury agreed to purchase Green Giant's stock for approximately $156 million in cash and Pillsbury stock. At a meeting of the Pillsbury stockholders on January 30, 1979, the acquisition was approved with a vote of 13,453,555 shares for and 264,612 against. The acquisition became effective a month later.

Americans who had watched the Green Giant grow up (left, top) now saw him advertising Pillsbury's Hungry Jack® products along with his own. Little Green Sprout™ (near left, bottom) made his first appearance in 1973.

Robert C. Cosgrove, chairman of Green Giant, and Thomas H. Wyman, president, both joined the Pillsbury board. Cosgrove's father, Edward B. Cosgrove, had served on the Pillsbury board from 1944 to 1961, and had been a major contributor to the development of Pillsbury's consumer marketing capabilities in the 1940s. Wyman had been an executive of Polaroid Corporation and Nestlé before coming to Green Giant in 1975. He was elected vice-chairman of the Pillsbury board and charged with responsibility for the consumer foods group, joining Spoor, Wallin, and Scott in the company's executive office. John M. Stafford, who had been Wyman's principal assistant at Green Giant, was named an executive vice-president of Pillsbury and chief operating officer of Green Giant.

The Green Giant acquisition did not meet with universal acclaim. A number of financial writers and analysts thought that the price of about 15 times Green Giant's earnings was excessive; others saw the canned vegetable business as another cyclical business in which Pillsbury could become enmeshed. The acquisition, however, resulted immediately in Pillsbury becoming a $1-billion supplier to the grocery business. Pillsbury's management maintained that the in creased scale and additional product lines would make Pillsbury a stronger competitor in the grocery market and materially strengthen the company's basic business for the decades ahead.[8]

The overabundance of talent at the top of the company soon became evident. As Spoor told a *Wall Street Journal* reporter, "When we got Green Giant, we got two of everything and three of some things." Good, believing that his importance to the company had lessened, resigned in July 1979, and within a few weeks he was named chairman and chief executive officer of Munsingwear Company. A few months later Scott accepted a position as president of Investors Diversified Services, Inc. And in May 1980 Wyman resigned to become president and chief executive officer of CBS, Inc. His responsibilities for the consumer products group were assumed by Jack Stafford. The same month Don Smith left Burger King to join PepsiCo as president of a newly formed foods service division.[9]

These and other management changes at Pillsbury drew querulous comment from a few local and national business writers, including a reference on the cover of *Fortune* magazine to "The Management Caldron at Pillsbury." Whether there were more such comings and goings at Pillsbury than at other firms in the 1970s is a moot question. The period was one in which skilled corporate managers were in great demand. The changes that did occur at Pillsbury highlighted the outstanding qualifications of the people Spoor attracted to the company, as well as the greater mobility of top corporate officers that had developed in recent years.[10]

Historically, the company has viewed its corporate responsibility as extending beyond the accomplishments reflected in financial statements. In 1973, Ray M. Eiland (above) joined Pillsbury as the company's first director of affirmative action, and he became a vice-president in 1975. (Left, top) a warehouse employee loads part of a 100,000-pound food shipment donated by the company to needy families on Minnesota's Iron Range. Pillsbury also is a cosponsor of the Twin Cities Marathon (left, bottom).

Another measure of a quality company, voiced by the 1972 study group and accepted by the Spoor management, was its attitude toward social issues. Corporate responsibility has two aspects—the company's response to legal mandates and its entirely voluntary commitments. Post-World War II legislation, especially in the 1960s and early 1970s, imposed new legal requirements on corporate management in such fundamental areas as employment practices and employee and product safety programs. Bob Keith had instilled in the company a determination to comply with the spirit as well as the letter of such new legislation as the Equal Employment Opportunity Act of 1972, the Occupational Safety and Health Act of 1970, and the Consumer Product Safety Act. Under Spoor the company continued to support and develop programs transcending the bare demands of the law.

As Pillsbury's earnings accelerated during the 1970s and as its presence expanded throughout the country, the company developed an increasingly sophisticated program for supporting higher education, food distribution, nutritional education, community services, and cultural organizations. In fiscal 1980 the company made charitable gifts of $1,569,000—up from $201,000 in fiscal 1973. Many grants were made on a matching or challenge basis to encourage broad participation in the funding; others were ''seed money'' for new nonprofit organizations or programs. Concurrently the company encouraged employees to provide voluntary services to charitable organizations, particularly to programs supported by the company.

Pillsbury became one of the first companies to form a Political Action Committee to foster employee involvement in the political process and complement management's advocacy of specific legislation at federal and state levels. In fiscal 1974 the company began to include in its annual report to stockholders a section detailing the company's response to its public responsibilities. Spoor termed it a ''scorecard'' of Pillsbury's performance in one of its foremost areas of commitment.

The company finished the decade of the 1970s on a high note. Net sales in fiscal 1979, aided by three months of Green Giant ownership, were $2.16 billion, easily reaching the $2 billion target set five years earlier. The following year, the last one of the decade, sales passed the $3 billion mark and earnings per share on a pre-split basis reached $10.44. The first eight years of Spoor management had seen compound annual growth rates of 20.5 percent in sales and almost 17 percent in earnings per share. As Spoor and Wallin wrote the shareholders on July 10, 1980, the decade ''brought Pillsbury a period of success unmatched in its history and solidified its stature as one of America's premier food companies.''

"Who says you have to be a Grandma to bake like one."

"I get old-fashioned scratch taste without the old-fashioned fuss.

With Pillsbury Plus."

"I thought nobody could bake a cake like my Grandmother. But I can with Pillsbury Plus cake mix. Pudding in the mix makes my cakes turn out moist and delicious—like I made them from scratch."

Pillsbury Plus
Yellow Cake Mix
Pudding in the mix

The freshest ideas are baking at Pillsbury.

Hot Buttered Soul!!

Hungry Jack® Flaky Biscuits. They're the big biscuits made with dozens of butter-meltin' flaky layers. Great-tasting flaky layers that come together to give you a big, flaky biscuit that satisfies even the heartiest appetites.

Hungry Jack
BUTTERMILK
FLAKY BISCUITS

Hungry Jack® Biscuits.

©1981 The Pillsbury Company

It's time!

[The fleeting moment of perfect flavor.]

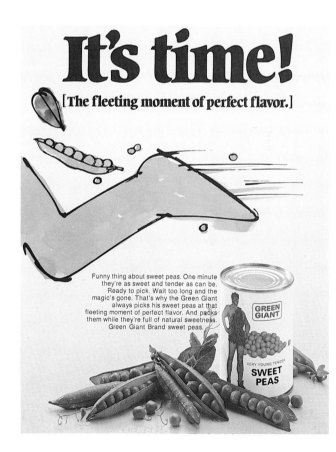

Funny thing about sweet peas. One minute they're as sweet and tender as can be. Ready to pick. Wait too long and the magic's gone. That's why the Green Giant always picks his sweet peas at that fleeting moment of perfect flavor. And packs them while they're full of natural sweetness. Green Giant Brand sweet peas.

GREEN GIANT
VERY YOUNG TENDER
SWEET PEAS

The Le Sueur Label.
Young peas wear it at a very tender age.

That distinctive silver foil Le Sueur Brand label says a lot about the peas that wear it. It says they're small, tender peas with a delicate flavor all their own. Le Sueur peas are every bit as special as they look.

LE SUEUR is a trademark of the Green Giant Company. © 1982 GGCo.

Pillsbury advertising built sales by appealing to diverse segments of the consumer market (far left and left, top). Other ads noted that peas (above, and far left, bottom) and other vegetables packed by Green Giant are picked at "the fleeting moment of perfect flavor," a claim backed by night harvesting operations (near left, bottom).

The success of Spoor's first eight years at the company's helm was manifest, and its causes were as evident as the success itself. The first, perhaps the most important, reason for favorable results was the sharp definition of company objectives and strategies to attain them. The second was the driving, insistent, uncompromising force Spoor brought to his job. He did not suffer failure easily, and he seldom encountered it. The third cause was timing, attributed largely to luck by some, but actually due to the prescience to recognize and seize upon transient opportunity.

In the mid-1980s indications were that the company's growth was not about to slow. There were clear signs, however, that its pattern would be different from that of the 1970s. Through the 1970s and into the 1980s the company spoke of its balanced portfolio of businesses —restaurants, consumer foods, agri-products. This balance is a logical and tidy concept, practical assurance that a below average performance by one group will not prevent an overall corporate gain. Its corollary precept was that no one group's profits should account for more than 50 percent of the company's total earnings. In fiscal 1984, however, earnings of one group exceeded 50 percent of company earnings for the first time, while those of another group continued far below their fiscal 1980 peak.

During the 12 years of Spoor's chairmanship (see the chart on page 228), the consumer foods and the restaurant groups waged a seesaw battle for leadership in profitability. A narrow consumer foods edge in the first four years gave way to four years of restaurant leadership once the 1976 acquisition of Steak and Ale took hold. The addition of Green Giant and other consumer companies enabled the consumer group to retake the lead for the next three years. But in fiscal 1984, earnings of the restaurant group took flight, producing 51 percent of the company's profits. This was accomplished without Poppin Fresh® Pie Shops, sold in April 1983. After acquiring the outstanding minority interest in the company in 1976, Pillsbury built the business to 69 shops in seven midwestern states. But although they produced a profit, the pie shops were not believed promising enough to justify major expansion.

The star of the restaurant group in 1983 and 1984 was Burger King. Don Smith's program of restaurant remodeling, menu additions, and improved store operations produced outstanding results in the last years of the 1970s, making Burger King the industry's top performer in 1979. Following his departure in April 1980, however, Burger King's progress in per store sales growth slowed perceptibly, virtually coming to a halt in the 1980–1982 recession.[11]

Spoor and Wallin, chafing over Burger King's lackluster results, began asking "Why isn't there more competition between the leaders in the fast food field?" As the recession ended Spoor prevailed upon Norman Brinker to become chief executive officer of Burger King while continuing in the same capacity at Steak and Ale. Brinker,

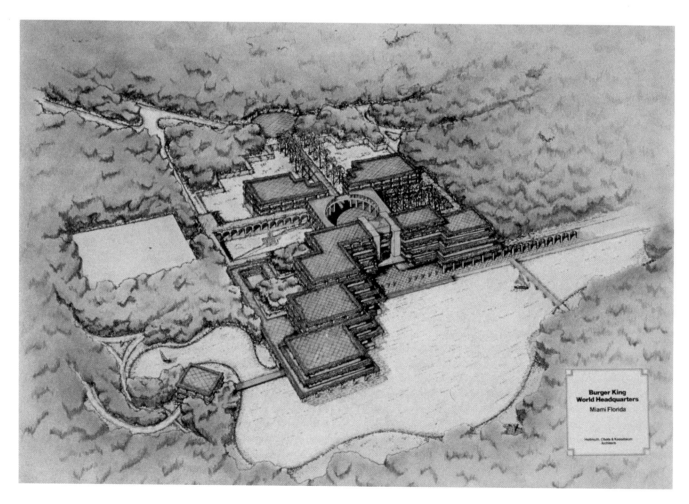

Burger King
World Headquarters

Miami Florida

Hellmuth, Obata & Kassabaum
Architects

commuting to Miami from his home in Dallas, guided a new Burger King management team until July 1983, when he turned over the reins to 39-year-old J. Jeffrey Campbell, a 13-year veteran of Burger King.[12]

The new Burger King management team's answer to Spoor and Wallin was a plan carefully designed to give Burger King primacy in the hamburger segment of the fast food market. Their first step was to put Burger King's own house in the best possible order. Concentrating on the basics, they tightened the efficiency of the restaurants, once more invested in physical changes to make the stores more attractive, and worked relentlessly to raise the level of quality and service. At the same time they intensified a search for unconventional restaurant sites, locating Burger King® restaurants at military bases including Pearl Harbor and Governors Island, and at facilities owned by such institutional franchisees as F.W. Woolworth, Howard Johnson's, and Greyhound Corporation. When the management was satisfied that its product had become fully competitive, it launched a heavily supported national television campaign proclaiming the superiority of Burger King's broiler-cooked hamburgers over the fried hamburgers sold by McDonald's and Wendy's, their principal competitors. Dubbed the "Battle of the Burgers," the hard-hitting advertising and promotional assault received extensive media coverage across the country, attracting countless converts to Burger King®. By the end of fiscal 1984 average sales at Burger King's 3,827 domestic franchised and company-owned stores had reached $944,000, a whopping 25 percent above the $751,000 per store average two years earlier.

Only in the foreign field was Burger King still lagging. After a late start it had about 300 stores in 25 foreign countries, but international operations had yet to become profitable. Campbell and his team were working on that, too. Promising that what he called "a long seven-year disappointment for Pillsbury" would break even by 1986, Campbell predicted that thereafter international operations would be a vehicle for significant capital infusion.[13]

Meanwhile Pillsbury's full-service restaurant business, renamed S&A Restaurant Corp., was pursuing a uniquely successful course. When Pillsbury acquired the chain of 113 Steak and Ale restaurants in 1976, Norman Brinker and his associates were already looking for new dining concepts to complement their dinnerhouse restaurants. There was, they believed, room for innovative ideas to provide opportunities in other segments of the expanding full-service restaurant market. Late in 1975 they began to design a restaurant that would be more casual than a Steak and Ale®, finally adopting a format that offered a wide variety of medium-price entrees in a restaurant featuring a Gay Nineties exterior and, inside, growing plants, antiques, and natural lighting. The new concept, called Bennigan's®, was tested in

LESS THAN 300 CALORIES

LOOK WHO'S COUNTING CALORIES.

Green Giant Entrees have always had "thinner dinners." We've just made them easier to find.

Green Giant Entrees line includes 9 items below 300 calories, and 5 items less than or equal to 350 calories.

Green Giant Entrees, with the new yellow "less than" flags, are flowing in at retail, NOW!

Green Giant Entrees. Fewer calories for your consumers. More profit for you.

Green Giant ENTREES

Steak and Ale management was already looking for new dining concepts when it was acquired in 1976. This led to the opening of Bennigan's® (left, top) in 1978 and JJ. Muggs® (left, bottom) in 1984. Meanwhile, the consumer foods group appealed to calorie-conscious customers with its Green Giant frozen entrees (above).

1978 by opening seven restaurants at Dallas and other southwestern locations. Bennigan's® was an immediate success. By the end of fiscal 1984 there were 148 Bennigan's® establishments in 33 states, boasting average annual sales per unit of $2.3 million.

Bennigan's® success encouraged the testing of a third theme in 1983, a ''gourmet hamburger'' restaurant stressing fast service and a limited, high-quality menu including ribs, salads, sandwiches, soft tacos, and appetizers. By May 31, 1984, five new JJ.Muggs® restaurants were being tested in Florida and Texas. Steak and Ale® dinnerhouse restaurants numbered 178 and were located in 33 states. Reflecting four consecutive years of real sales growth, their average annual sales per unit stood at $1.5 million. All S&A Restaurant Corp. units served alcoholic beverages and, except for two franchised Steak and Ale® restaurants, all were company-owned.

Neither Spoor nor Wallin had any question about the competitiveness of the packaged food industry. Management's strategy for the consumer foods group was to hold it on a steady, single-minded course of higher visibility for Pillsbury in the grocery store, accomplished with an ever-broadening line of number-one or number-two performers. The extent to which this strategy succeeded was reported in the September 1983 issue of *Processed Prepared Foods*, a leading trade publication: ''Every industry has a standard bearer—a company that sets the pace for sales and earnings growth, return on investment, innovation and management. In the prepared foods industry, an industry with a gang of robust competitors, one company has consistently shown itself to be such a leader—The Pillsbury Company.''

The group's sales doubled to almost $1.5 billion in fiscal 1980, the first full year of Green Giant's operations as a part of Pillsbury. The profitability of Green Giant that year, however, was curtailed sharply by a drop in the total market for frozen entrees and a severe oversupply of peas, corn, and beans in the canning industry. These factors combined with the losses of the recently acquired Speas Company to produce disappointing fiscal 1980 earnings for the consumer foods group. Fortunately a totally unprecedented performance by the agri-products group enabled the total company to post a remarkable 25-percent gain in net earnings.

The following year Pillsbury sold the Speas operations and set about restructuring Green Giant's canning business to make it more stable and predictable. The cost of making these changes adversely affected the dry grocery segment's profitability during the year. This was more than offset, however, by the group's frozen and refrigerated areas. In 1980 the hedges provided by the company's three-group portfolio preserved the company's unbroken string of growth years. Now intragroup diversity had enabled consumer foods to overcome a down performance by one of its segments and to post the group's largest earnings in its history.

In 1983 the company acquired Häagen-Dazs, the country's leading producer of super-premium-category ice cream (above).

In 1983 the company made another major addition to its diversified line of products when it paid $76 million for the assets of the family-owned Häagen-Dazs® ice cream companies, the nation's leading producer of superpremium-category ice cream. Based in New Jersey, Häagen-Dazs® products were sold in stores and restaurants nationwide and in franchised ice cream parlors called Häagen-Dazs® Dipping Stores. Häagen-Dazs® sales were growing at a rate of 30 percent a year, and its owners needed more capital to maximize its growth potential. From a long list of suitors the family elected to sell to Pillsbury because of its long experience in both consumer foods and franchising. By the end of fiscal 1984 the number of franchised dipping stores had risen from 244 at acquisition to 316 units in 32 states, and plans were underway to construct a production facility in California to supplement the Woodbridge, New Jersey, plant.

The Häagen-Dazs® purchase was one of a number of steps taken from 1982 through 1984 to add muscle to the consumer foods group. Wilton Enterprises, Inc., was sold in 1982, when its line of cake baking and decorating products no longer fit the group's profile. In 1984 three more companies were purchased: Apollo® Foods, a producer of high quality ethnic foods; Azteca® Corn Products Corporation, a manufacturer of refrigerated corn and flour tortillas; and Sedutto® Ice Cream Corporation, a manufacturer and supplier of a premium line of ice cream, principally serving the institutional market. One acquisition got away. In an effort to add to the Green Giant line of canned goods, Pillsbury acquired a minority position in Stokely-Van Camp Inc., a large canning company in Indiana, and offered to buy a majority of its shares. Pillsbury was outbid by Quaker Oats, who paid a price that, according to a company spokesman, "wouldn't be in the best interests of Pillsbury stockholders."[14]

The list of Pillsbury consumer food products with a first- or second-place market share grew longer. In the dry grocery area these products included at the end of fiscal 1984 Pillsbury's Best® Family Flour (#2), large specialty cake mixes (#1), ready-to-spread frostings (#2), pancake mixes (#2), dehydrated mashed potatoes (#1), measured solid diet meals (#1), canned corn (#2), canned peas (#1), canned beans (#2), and canned mushrooms (#1). Pillsbury had never relinquished its lead in the refrigerated fresh dough market, and it added such new products as loaves of bread and Azteca® refrigerated tortillas that year. In the frozen area the Totino's® and Fox Deluxe® brands held a firm lead in the pizza market, and Green Giant's® corn-on-the-cob and vegetables in sauce were first in their respective markets. Attuned to changing lifestyles, the research and development laboratories continually introduced new products, from a ready-to-eat nutritional snack for the dry grocery shelves to All Ready Pie Crust in the refrigerated case to a new line of Pillsbury's frozen pizzas and popcorn designed exclusively for microwave ovens.[15]

The agri-products group was active in the grain exchange (right).

Until fiscal 1981 the agri-products group contributed handsomely to the company's balanced portfolio. In fiscal 1981, earnings of the agri-products group commenced a sharp decline, materially lessening the group's importance in the portfolio. The underlying cause for the decline was a deteriorating agricultural economy that began in 1981 and 1982 to have serious consequences for the group's grain merchandising division and especially for the division's transportation system.

The first sign of trouble came in fiscal 1981 when the volume of the division's grain transactions fell off because of reduced United States crop production and continuation of the Russian grain embargo. As the domestic farm economy continued to worsen, foreign demand for United States grain continued to shrink, and these factors cut seriously into the division's grain handling and trading profits. The turndown in the farm economy had an even more disastrous effect, however, on the division's transportation business. The division managed a fleet of 513 owned, leased, or controlled barges and 1,907 railroad hopper cars, increased by an additional 200 barges and eight towboats when it purchased American Barge Company in 1981. Beginning in late 1981 and 1982 precipitous declines in movements of raw materials and finished products caused large surpluses of transportation equipment, leading to a much lower rate structure in the depressed industry and a severe underutilization of Pillsbury's extensive fleet. The rail transportation segment began to show improvement in fiscal 1984, but the barge transportation business was still weak at the end of the year, and the company's efforts to reduce its equipment commitments continued.

Plans to convert the historic A mill (left, top) to a national museum of flour milling were in the works in 1984.

In 1983, Pillsbury's West German subsidiary, Erasco, acquired Jokisch (the plant, bottom), and together the two firms supply more than half of the dish-ready meal market.

The company's flour mills, located in Minneapolis and seven other strategic points across the country, operated near capacity at the end of 1984, with about 25 percent of production going to the consumer foods group as ingredient flour. The rest was sold as family flour, exported, or sold to commercial bakers in the form of bakery flour and bakery mix. The country's per capita consumption of flour showed minor variations offering little prospect of significant market growth. Mill maintenance and modernization in the tradition of Charles A. Pillsbury enabled the company's 115-year-old-flour milling business to continue providing a good return on investment. Although the main Minneapolis milling operations were carried on in the "new" South A mill built in 1916 and 1917, the historic A mill still produced graham flour and served as a bulk flour storage and packaging facility. The only flour mill still operating at the Falls of St. Anthony, it was placed on the National Register of Historic Buildings in 1966, and planning began for converting it to a national museum of flour milling.[16]

A third division of the agri-products group grew out of the company's strategy to maintain the relative size of its three groups. In 1979 Pioneer Food Industries, Inc., an Arkansas-based rice miller and grain processor was purchased, and in 1982 the company acquired Wickes Corporation's agricultural division, processors of dry edible beans, peas, and lentils. Toward the end of 1982 Pillsbury entered into a joint venture to operate a sunflower-seed oil-processing plant in North Dakota. These three operations were combined with the company's long-established feed ingredient merchandising business to form the special commodities division.

In the years from 1981 through 1984 the agri-products group accounted for only 11 percent of the company's profits, as compared to an average of 31 percent during the first four years of Spoor's administration. Speaking to students at Dartmouth's Amos Tuck School of Business in November 1983, Spoor reported the company's "reluctant conclusion" that because of the agri-products group's deep and unpredictable cycles it would have to be restructured in a major way. He predicted that "probably never again would the group be as important a part of our portfolio as in the 1970s."[17]

Pillsbury's international operations did not change appreciably after Bill Spoor shed direct responsibility for that function to become the company's chief executive officer. Sales and earnings represented in 1984 a somewhat smaller percentage of company sales and earnings than they did in fiscal 1973, a condition due in some part to the current strength of the United States dollar. With one or two minor exceptions there was no geographical expansion of the company's holdings. The two Canadian flour mills were sold, and in Australia the company's 50-percent interest in White Wings Pty., Ltd., was divested. In 1982 the Cora-Rex pasta operations in Mexico merged with two flour mills to form a joint venture called Grupo Ola-

zabal Pillsbury S.A. de C.V. In 1984 it was the number-one company in the premium segment of Mexico's pasta market.

In Europe a number of acquisitions by Pillsbury's subsidiaries in England, France, and Germany strengthened those operations. In West Germany, Erasco was joined by a second subsidiary, Jokisch; together they held over 50 percent of the country's canned dish-ready meal market in 1984. They also produced gourmet soups and entered the frozen food market that year. In France and Belgium the Gringoire/Brossard group of companies maintained a strong position in the wafers, ready-made cakes, and egg cookies markets. H. J. Green & Co. in England continued to lead the cake mix market, and in 1982 Pillsbury acquired a second English company, Hammonds Sauce Company, Ltd., producers of sauces, vinegar, herbs, and spices. One other foreign market, that for canned sweet corn, continued to grow, and Green Giant lines held a dominant market position in several of the world's key markets for the product.

An Asian-Pacific team sought out opportunities in the Far East, focusing attention on Japan, Taiwan, Hong Kong, and Korea. In June 1981 Pillsbury joined with Tokyo's Snowbrand Company to market Totino's® Crisp Crust pizza in Japan, and in 1984 it purchased a 50-percent interest in a Hong Kong-based producer of Chinese sauces and frozen specialties.

In fiscal 1984 Pillsbury passed the $4-billion mark in sales, a long leap from the $718-million figure of only 12 years before. Agri-product group's miseries in 1982 and 1983 caused a temporary slowdown in the company's growth, but in fiscal 1984 sales and earnings per share growth of 13 and 22 percent put the company back on the track of its earlier successes. The strategies Spoor proposed to the board in January 1973 had produced for the company the quality earnings he had forecast to the New York Society of Security Analysts a few months later. As *Fortune* magazine said, "More than anything, Spoor wants Pillsbury to 'make its numbers' on growth and profitability. Anything else is losing."[18]

At the September 1983 stockholders meeting, Pillsbury management announced another two-for-one stock split, the second in eight years. When Spoor had complained to Keith in the spring of 1972 about the value of his stock options, the market price of a share of Pillsbury stock hovered around $52. Adjusting for two stock splits, each 1972 share was worth a total of $151.50 on May 31, 1984. The appreciation in the shares, together with the dividend yield for the 12-year period, provided a 13.1 percent compounded annual rate of return. Even allowing for a compounded inflation rate of 7.9 percent during the period, such performance was good news to the company's 20,800 shareholders. Fiscal 1984 was the company's twenty-sixth consecutive year of increased dividends and its fifty-sixth year of uninterrupted dividends.

At the end of fiscal 1984 the company had 79,400 employees, an increase of almost 50,000 in 12 years, due largely to the company's burgeoning restaurant operations. The new Pillsbury world headquarters, opened in August 1981, housed 1,900 exployees. On February 23, 1984, Spoor and Wallin were joined on the executive committee by John M. Stafford, who was elected president when Wallin became vice-chairman of the board of directors.

During the 1980s corporate responsibility, and particularly the depth and extent of a company's community involvement, attracted more public interest and scrutiny than it had in the past. Recent cuts in public funding, the pillar for many nonprofit institutions and organizations, increased the pressures for greater corporate support of these groups. The dollar amount directed by the company to civic, educational, cultural, and social programs more than kept pace with its growth and earnings, and in fiscal 1984 the company's contributions rose to $4,250,000.

The years from 1972 through 1984 were part of a vibrant period for corporate America. A constant flow of mergers and acquisitions, major and minor, changed the nature of hundreds of established com-

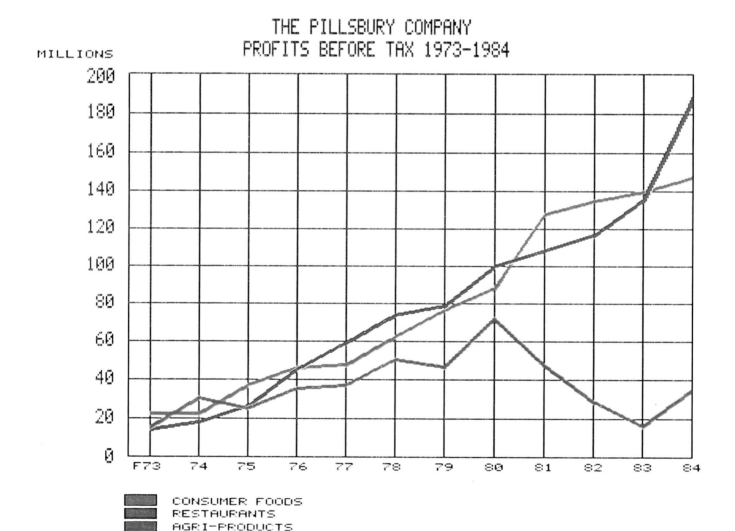

THE PILLSBURY COMPANY
PROFITS BEFORE TAX 1973-1984

CONSUMER FOODS
RESTAURANTS
AGRI-PRODUCTS

panies and ended the independent existence of many others. Pillsbury was an active participant, concentrating single-mindedly on building its strengths in the food industry, to the exclusion of other areas of business.

Since 1952 the company had been tracing its performance against the records of six competitors. The results below show dramatically the gains made by Pillsbury in the 12 years from 1972 to 1984:

	1972 Pretax Profit in Millions	1984 Pretax Profit in Millions	1972–1984 Increase in Pretax Profit (%)
Procter & Gamble	$515	$1,427	277
Campbell	113	332	294
General Foods	221	573	259
Ralston-Purina	120	438	365
General Mills	104	399	384
Quaker	68	260	382
Pillsbury	33	304	921
Average			412

This performance should satisfy even the most demanding of Pillsbury's shareholders—a distinction indisputably held by Bill Spoor. As the company moved into its one-hundred-and-sixteenth year, the time-honored trademark Pillsbury's Best® was never more appropriate.

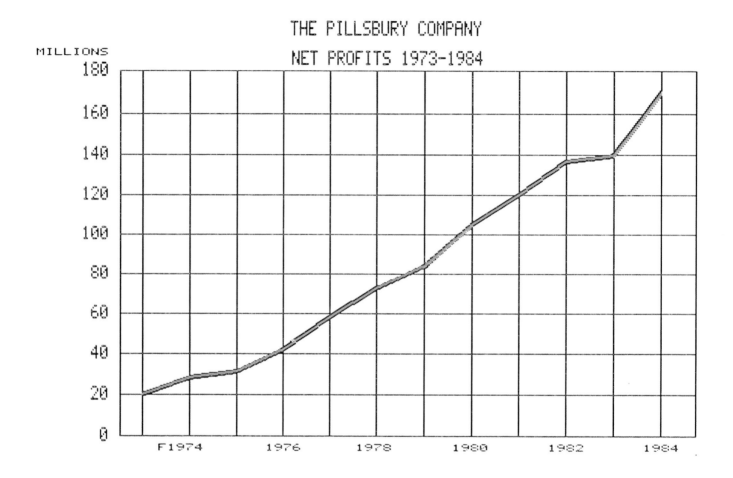

Epilogue

One can expect that this will not be the last history of The Pillsbury Company. Today the company is on a rising tide, its future brighter than at any other time in this century. Not since the sale to the English in 1889 has the company ranked higher in the world of American business. Indeed, the April 1985 *Fortune* magazine, listing the country's 500 largest industrial companies, reports Pillsbury's move into the top 100 of that select group.

This book has concentrated on the strategies, decisions, and fortunes of the successive chief executive officers, to the virtual exclusion of the hundreds of other employees who have made major contributions during The Pillsbury Company's 116 years. But it is, after all, the chief executive officer who provides the leadership, sets the pace and tone, and, alone, answers to the stockholders. It is on him or her alone that high praise, modest applause, or unfeeling criticism ultimately rests.

The company's original greatness resulted from Charles A. Pillsbury's determination to produce a product of unsurpassed quality, advertise it so that it would be universally recognized, and sell it in all available markets. To accomplish this he seized on every invention and innovation he or any of his competitors could develop, and he always marshalled the capital resources at his command to gain any advantage of timing. These principles enabled him to make his company the largest flour miller in the world and then to sell the mills to the English at their peak value.

The 50 years that followed saw the company's business fall and rise without approaching the level of importance enjoyed during the first 20 years. Shortly after the death of the last of the company's founders, an attempt to bolster sagging flour milling profits by speculating in the wheat market brought the company to the brink of bankruptcy. Rescued by a receivership, it was reacquired from the English several years later by the newly constituted Pillsbury Flour Mills Company, which achieved moderate profitability. By 1940, however, Pillsbury seemed destined to a future as a regional flour miller, undistinguished except for its old and respected brand name.

John M. Stafford became the company's tenth chief executive officer on May 7, 1985. Combining superb leadership qualities with a strong background in both packaged food and restaurant operations, he is ideally suited to guide Pillsbury's progress in an increasingly competitive industry.

It was then that Philip W. Pillsbury, a grandson of Charles, became the company's sixth chief executive. Determined to break the firm's inertia, he immediately extended operations to the West Coast through a major acquisition in California. In Minneapolis he built and staffed the company's first foods research laboratory. Six years later a revitalized organization brought onto the consumer market a line of Pillsbury cake and pie crust mixes, creating a brand new company image with America's homemakers. Still expanding, the firm in 1950 acquired a long-established southeastern flour milling company, owner of a patented process for producing a new product—refrigerated fresh dough biscuits. Philip, his objective accomplished, stepped aside as chief executive officer.

His handpicked, market-driven successor, Paul S. Gerot, soon built the infant refrigerated fresh dough biscuit business into a multi-product line, establishing a market leadership it has not relinquished. The company continued to add to its flour-based dry grocery product line, and it entered the dietetic field as well. Gerot extended the geographical reach of the company's consumer foods business by purchasing companies in Europe, Mexico, Venezuela, and other foreign countries. Then, in 1967, Pillsbury became the first consumer foods company to enter the burgeoning field of away-from-home eating by acquiring Burger King, a rising new star in the firmament of franchised food restaurants.

Bob Keith's brief period as Gerot's successor saw further extension of existing product lines, mixed with several small-scale ventures into various nonfood areas. When Bill Spoor became chief executive officer in 1973, he reasoned that the stockholders would enjoy their greatest advantage if the company's principal goal became that of achieving uninterrupted gains in sales and earnings, at a rate of at least 10 percent per annum. He began to fashion the company's portfolio to this end, divesting the nonfood businesses and the last of its highly cyclical enterprises—the ice-packed broiler business. He invested instead in existing and new restaurant enterprises, in major, strategic additions to consumer foods, and in the process brought acquisition and divestiture planning and execution into the mainstream of Pillsbury's operations. Sales and profits increased every year, although it seemed once or twice that it was only Spoor's strong will that brought them about.

With the company's sales and earnings at an all-time high, its financial base secure, and a portfolio of businesses divided almost equally between the vast away-from-home and at-home eating markets, Bill Spoor has announced that he will retire as chief executive officer on May 7. On that day John M. Stafford, the company's president, will become Pillsbury's tenth chief executive officer, while Spoor will continue as chairman of the board of directors. Still in his forties, Jack Stafford is an able and dedicated leader, possessed of marketing skills sharply honed by advertising agency and fast-food restaurant company experience before coming to Pillsbury in the Green Giant acquisition. Now his job will be to continue Pillsbury's climb back to the top of the world's food companies.

APRIL 1985   WILLIAM J. POWELL

Pillsburys Active in the Company

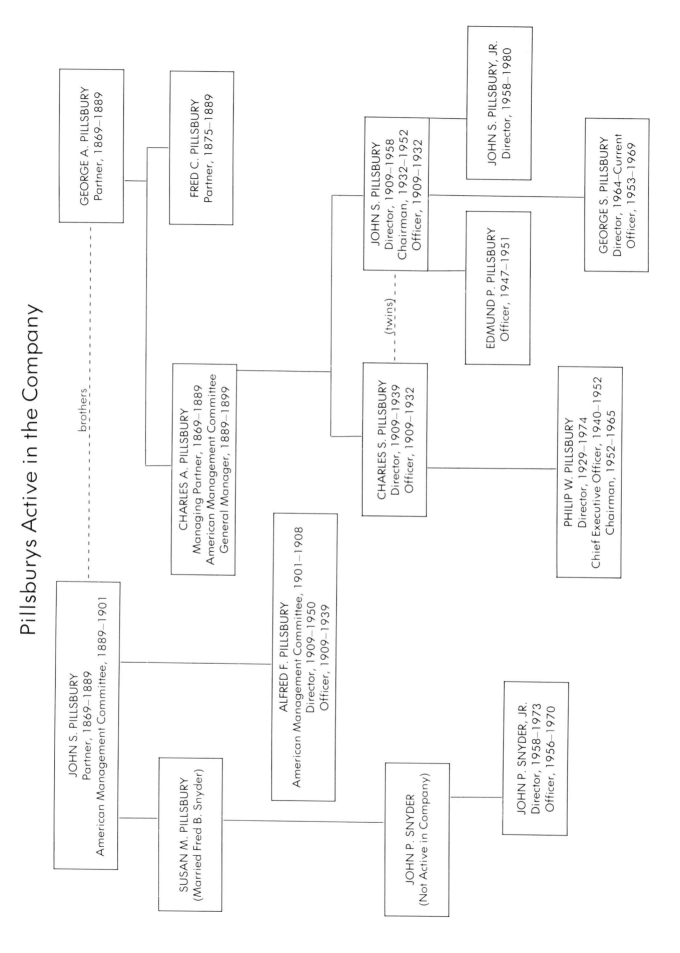

GEORGE A. PILLSBURY
Partner, 1869–1889

FRED C. PILLSBURY
Partner, 1875–1889

brothers

CHARLES A. PILLSBURY
Managing Partner, 1869–1889
American Management Committee
General Manager, 1889–1899

JOHN S. PILLSBURY
Director, 1909–1958
Chairman, 1932–1952
Officer, 1909–1932

JOHN S. PILLSBURY, JR.
Director, 1958–1980

GEORGE S. PILLSBURY
Director, 1964–Current
Officer, 1953–1969

EDMUND P. PILLSBURY
Officer, 1947–1951

CHARLES S. PILLSBURY
Director, 1909–1939
Officer, 1909–1932

(twins)

PHILIP W. PILLSBURY
Director, 1929–1974
Chief Executive Officer, 1940–1952
Chairman, 1952–1965

JOHN S. PILLSBURY
Partner, 1869–1889
American Management Committee, 1889–1901

ALFRED F. PILLSBURY
American Management Committee, 1901–1908
Director, 1909–1950
Officer, 1909–1939

SUSAN M. PILLSBURY
(Married Fred B. Snyder)

JOHN P. SNYDER
(Not Active in Company)

JOHN P. SNYDER, JR.
Director, 1958–1973
Officer, 1956–1970

Governance of The Pillsbury Company and its Predecessors
1869–1985

C. A. PILLSBURY & CO. (1869–1889)
Partners

Charles A. Pillsbury	1869–1889
John S. Pillsbury	1869–1889
George A. Pillsbury	1869–1889
Fred C. Pillsbury	1875–1889

PILLSBURY-WASHBURN FLOUR MILLS COMPANY, LTD. (1889–1909)
Board of Directors

Richard H. Glyn, Chairman	1889–1909
J. Flower Jackson	1889–1906
Sydney T. Klein	1889–1909
E. T. Rose	1889–1891
Frank Spencer	1903–1909
George Cloutte	1906–1909
Sir William B. Forwood	1892–1902
Charles T. Fox	1900–1903

American Management Committee

Charles A. Pillsbury, General Manager	1889–1899
John S. Pillsbury (Chairman, 1899–1901)	1889–1901
William D. Washburn (Chairman, 1901–1908)	1889–1908
Henry L. Little (General Manager, 1899–1908)	1898–1908
Charles M. Amsden	1898–1908
William de la Barre	1899–1908
Alfred F. Pillsbury	1901–1908

PILLSBURY FLOUR MILLS COMPANY AND SUCCESSORS (1909–1984)
Board of Directors

Albert C. Loring	1909–1932
Charles S. Pillsbury	1909–1939
Alfred F. Pillsbury	1909–1950
John S. Pillsbury (Chairman, 1932–1952)	1909–1958
Clark Hempstead (Co-Chairman, 1940–1952)	1923–1951
Max A. Lehman	1923–1951

Harrison H. Whiting	1923–1936
Dwight K. Yerxa	1923–1941
George A. Zabriskie	1923–1936
J. W. Avery	1923–1928
Cornelius O'Donnell	1923–1924
	1935–1941
Margaret E. McSwiggen	1923–1924
Charles H. Dennison	1923–1924
Harry C. Piper	1924–1961
Robert Lehman	1924–1925
Henry S. Bowers	1924–1946
James Jennison	1925–1933
	1935–1936
Howard W. Files	1928–1957
Philip W. Pillsbury	1929–1974
(Chairman, 1952–1965)	
(Co-Chairman, 1965–1967)	
Stanley Partridge	1929–1953
A. E. Mallon	1933–1947
E. H. Mirick	1933–1951
J. Irl Beatty	1935–1944
	1948–1959
James R. McNamara	1935–1941
Mortimer H. Matschke	1935–1940
Emory J. Price	1935–1941
Harry F. Young	1936–1941
William E. Derrick	1937–1941
Patrick J. McKenney	1936–1941
Paige Lehman	1939–1941
	1951–1963
Clive T. Jaffray	1941–1956
Edward B. Cosgrove	1944–1961
James F. Brownlee	1946–1953
Paul S. Gerot	1950–1974
(Chairman, 1965–1967)	
Rogers C. B. Morton	1951–1970
	1977–1979
Samuel N. Stevens	1950–1966
B. J. Greer	1951–1964
Clyde H. Hendrix	1951–1955
Robert J. Keith	1953–1973
(Chairman, 1967–1973)	
R. J. Pinchin	1953–1956
Dean McNeal	1955–1974
Robert V. Horton	1956–1970
J. L. Rankin	1958–1960
John P. Snyder, Jr.	1958–1973
J. Cameron Thomson	1958–1963
John S. Pillsbury, Jr.	1958–1980
Terrance Hanold	1961–1975
J. Cy Rapp	1961–1963
Robert B. Fiske	1961–1970
Ernest C. Arbuckle	1961–1966
Paul Christopherson	1963–1970
George S. Pillsbury	1964–

Willys H. Monroe	1966–
William T. French	1967–1979
James W. McLamore	1967–
George W. Hosfield	1968–1973
John H. Perkins	1969–
John C. Whitehead	1970–
Thruston B. Morton	1971–1974
James R. Peterson	1973–1976
William H. Spoor	1973–
(Chairman, 1973–)	
Bert S. Cross	1973–1975
Caro E. Luhrs	1973–
William J. Powell	1973–1978
Leo H. Schoenhofen	1975–1982
Norman Brinker	1976–1983
Walter D. Scott	1976–1980
Peter G. Wray	1976–
Winston R. Wallin	1977–
Donald R. Dwight	1977–1983
Raymond F.Good	1978–1979
Thomas H. Wyman	1979–1980
Robert C. Cosgrove	1979–1981
W. Michael Blumenthal	1979–
Robert A. Schoellhorn	1981–
George J. Sella, Jr.	1982–
John M. Stafford	1983–
Donald F. Craib, Jr.	1983–
Allen Jacobson	1985–
Kenneth A. Macke	1985–

Notes

Unless otherwise noted, contracts, board meeting minutes, market data, interview transcripts and notes, and other such materials are in the possession of The Pillsbury Company. Names of companies and corporations are listed as they were commonly noted in contemporary news articles. Publication data is included in notes in lieu of a bibliography.

Chapter 1

1. E. B. Barnes, ''The Milling History of Minnesota,'' *Northwestern Miller*, Holiday Edition, 1890; Isaac Atwater, ed., *History of Minneapolis and Hennepin County, Minnesota* (New York: Munsell Pub. Co., 1895), 1:607; Charles B. Kuhlmann, *The Development of the Flour Milling Industry in the United States with Special Reference to the Industry in Minneapolis* (Boston: Houghton Mifflin Company, 1929), 131.
2. Gristmills were small mills that ground grains into flour or feed, for use primarily by the owner of the grain. Merchant mills purchased wheat and milled it into flour for sale to the general public. Accounts vary as to whether the sawmill, built to produce lumber for the fort, was constructed in 1821 or 1822. It is fairly well established that the gristmill followed it by a year. Accounts also differ as to whether the gristmill originally was installed in the sawmill building or whether it always had its own building. For general history of the state, see Theodore C. Blegen, *Minnesota: A History of the State* (Minneapolis: University of Minnesota Press, 1963).
3. William Watts Folwell, *A History of Minnesota* (St. Paul: Minnesota Historical Society, 1956), 1:351–52; *Northwestern Miller*, Aug. 22, 1879; Harry S. Alford, ''Milling of Flour Produces Much Rail Traffic,'' *Illinois Central Magazine*, March 1942, 13.
4. For biographies of John S., George A., Charles A., and Fred C. Pillsbury, see Marion D. Shutter and J.S. McLain, eds., *Progressive Men of Minnesota* (Minneapolis: *Minneapolis Journal*, 1897), 56–57, 155–56, 195–97; Lucile M. Kane, *The Waterfall that Built a City: The Falls of St. Anthony in Minneapolis* (St. Paul: Minnesota Historical Society, 1966) 29.
5. For population see Bureau of the Census, *Compendium of the Tenth Census, 1880* (Washington, 1880), 4–5, and for improved farmland and wheat production, 654–55, 664–65; for percentage of land in wheat, see Folwell, *History of Minnesota*, 3:60.
6. Kuhlmann, *Development of Flour Milling*, 108. Flour was packed in 196-pound wooden barrels, the common unit of production until much later, when the hundredweight replaced it. Approximately four and one-third bushels of wheat produced one barrel of flour.
7. *Minnesota Executive Documents*, 1870, 2:1051.
8. Kane, *Waterfall that Built a City*, 49, 57.
9. Copy of Charles A. Pillsbury's courses and grades, Dartmouth College; John Scales, ed., *Biographical Sketches of the Class of 1863* (Hanover, N.H.: Dartmouth College, 1903), 418.
10. Charles A. Pillsbury to Alfred F. Pillsbury, Dec. 11, 1897; *New York Tribune*, Sept. 4, 1892; Scales, *Biographical Sketches*, 424.
11. The Minneapolis Flouring Mill is shown in the alphabetical section of the 1869 *Minneapolis City Directory* as owned by the firm of Frazee, Gardner and Brown. George A. Pillsbury acquired Frazee's one-third interest in June 1869, according to records of the Hennepin County recorder. These records also show that in August 1869 William B. Brown sold his one-third interest to George M. Crocker, who in October 1869 sold half his interest to John S. Pillsbury. Begin-

ning about that time the mill was described as that of Gardner, Pillsbury & Crocker. In about 1872 Gardner sold his interest to Woodbury Fisk, a brother of Mrs. John S. Pillsbury, and the mill became known as Pillsbury, Crocker & Fisk. Fisk was associated in the hardware business with John S. Pillsbury. Crocker had been engaged in flour milling in Minneapolis for a number of years.

The Minneapolis Board of Trade in its report of manufacturing interests, Jan. 1, 1870, noted a combined daily flour capacity of 3,380 barrels for both cities. The Gardner, Pillsbury & Crocker mill was shown as having a capacity of 300 barrels a day, seven employees, and an area of 45 by 60 feet. See *Minneapolis Daily Tribune*, Apr.17, 1870. For a 200-barrel per-day capacity when Charles and George purchased their one-third interest, see *Northwestern Miller*, Aug. 24, 1883; Holiday Edition, 1893; Philip W. Pillsbury, *The Pioneering Pillsburys* (New York: The Newcomen Society in North America, 1950), 13.

12. Pillsbury, *Pioneering Pillsburys*, 13.
13. Minneapolis Board of Trade, Annual Report, 1870, showed the Taylor and Pillsbury mill as having a capacity of 300 barrels a day and an area of 45 by 60 feet. See *Minneapolis Daily Tribune*, Mar. 16, 1871. The Taylor Brothers had a year in which to redeem their property from the foreclosure sale, but the period ended on Apr. 12, 1871, without redemption. During the year the Pillsburys leased the mill, and it was operated as Taylor & Pillsbury.
14. The area referred to here as the "Northwest" might more properly be called the Upper Midwest. But Northwest was the name given to the hard spring wheat area of North and South Dakota, Minnesota, and Montana, before statehood was achieved by what we now call the "Northwest" states.
15. E. V. Smalley, "The Flour Mills of Minneapolis," *Century Magazine*, May 1886, 46; *Northwestern Miller*, Holiday Edition, 1893; Feb. 24, 1915.
16. Paul R. Fossum, "Early Milling in the Cannon River Valley," *Minnesota History* 11(1930):27.
17. For description of the middlings purifier see B. W. Dedrick, *Practical Milling* (Chicago: National Miller, 1924), 187–204.
18. George D. Rogers, "History of Flour Manufacture in Minnesota," *Minnesota Historical Society Collections*, 10 (1950): 48; *Northwestern Miller*, Holiday Edition, 1884; Dec. 15, 1915.
19. Atwater, *History of Minneapolis*, 584; *Northwestern Miller*, Export Edition, Oct. 15, 1882; Nov. 8, 1889.
20. *Northwestern Miller*, Oct. 1, 1875; Oct.22, 1875.
21. Robert M. Frame III, "The Progressive Millers: A Cultural and Intellectual Portrait of the Flour Milling Industry, 1870–1930, Focusing on Minneapolis, Minnesota," (Ph.D. diss., University of Minnesota, 1980), 99.
22. *Northwestern Miller*, July 12, 1878; Oct.4, 1878; Nov.4, 1881; Export Edition, Oct. 15, 1882.
23. Ibid., Feb. 11, 1881; *Flour and Grain Statistics*, (Minneapolis: Miller Publishing Company, 1907).
24. *Northwestern Miller*, Nov. 4, 1881.
25. *St. Paul Pioneer Press*, Mar. 12, 1880; *Northwestern Miller*, Mar. 25, 1881.
26. William de la Barre, "Recollections of a Milling Engineer," *Northwestern Miller*, July 15, 1936.
27. W. D. Gray, "The Golden Era of Milling," *Northwestern Miller*, Sept. 12, 1950.
28. See Charles E. Flandrau, *The History of Minnesota and Tales of the Frontier* (St. Paul: E. W. Porter, 1900), 195–96; and John Storck and Walter Dorwin Teague, *Flour for Man's Bread* (Minneapolis: University of Minnesota Press, 1952).
29. Charles A. Pillsbury, "American Flour," in Chauncey M. Depew, ed., *One Hundred Years of American Commerce* (New York: D. O. Haynes, 1895), 1:269.
30. Richard L. Ferrell, "Pillsbury's 'A' Mill, Part One," *Hennepin County History*, Spring 1981, 6; Horace B. Hudson, "A Public Servant of the Northwest," *The American Monthly Review of Reviews*, 24 (Dec. 1901):696.
31. *Northwestern Miller*, Export Edition, Oct. 15, 1882; Ferrell, "Pillsbury's 'A' Mill," 11; Frame, "Progressive Millers," 124.
32. *Northwestern Miller*, July 24, 1885; Mar.15, 1899; Holiday Edition, 1888; Mar. 8, 1889. C. A. Pillsbury & Co. leased the Empire mill property from 1873 to 1885.
33. Ibid., Oct. 31, 1884.

34. Ibid., Dec. 7, 1883.
35. Ibid., Oct. 28, 1881; May 8, 1940.
36. Ibid., July 9, 1886; Dec. 31, 1886; Nov. 8, 1889; May 8, 1940.
37. See accounts of decision in *Northwestern Miller*, Apr. 17, 1885; May 8, 1885. The decision by the U.S. Circuit Court for the Southern Dist. of New York was rendered orally.
38. Document of unknown origin in files of The Pillsbury Company.
39. *Northwestern Miller*, Jan. 22, 1936; Dec. 7, 1932.
40. Herman Steen, *Flour Milling in America* (Minneapolis: T. S. Denison & Co., 1963), 48; *Northwestern Miller*, Oct. 20, 1926; Kuhlmann, *Development of Flour Milling*, 142.
41. Amended Bill of Complaint, *The Second National Bank of St. Paul, et al. v. Pillsbury-Washburn Flour Mills Company*, U.S. Circuit Court, Dist. of Minn., Fourth Div., Oct. 6, 1908, 3,4.
42. Kuhlmann, *Development of Flour Milling*, 229–30.
43. See note 20.
44. For wages in other manufacturing establishments, see Bureau of the Census, *Historical Statistics of the United States: Colonial Times to 1957*, (Washington, 1960), series D728–734, 165; for Pillsbury wages, see *Manufacturing Census of 1880*, roll II, frame 522.
45. For a description of the profit-sharing plan see *Review of Reviews*, September 1891, and *Northwestern Miller*, Sept. 11, 1891; for other stories concerning the plan see *Northwestern Miller*, Oct. 2, 1885; Oct.15, 1886; Sept. 21, 1888.
46. Smalley, ''The Flour Mills,'' 47; Kuhlmann, *Development of Flour Milling*, 134; Steen, *Flour Milling in America*, 63–64.
47. Clipping from unidentified English language European newspaper, 1886, in the files of The Pillsbury Company; Mrs. Augusta Harvey Worthen, comp., *The History of Sutton, New Hampshire: Consisting of the Historical Collections of Erastus Wadleigh, Esq., and A. H. Worthen* (Concord, N.H.: Republican Press Association, 1890), 130–31.
48. *Anoka Herald*, Mar. 22, 1890; *Northwestern Miller*, Apr. 24, 1891.

Chapter 2

1. *Northwestern Miller*, May 24, 1889; Pillsbury, ''American Flour,'' 272.
2. *Northwestern Miller*, July 12, 1889.
3. *Minneapolis Daily Tribune*, July 24, 1889.
4. Ibid., Sept. 29, 1889.
5. Pillsbury-Washburn sold its majority interest in the Atlantic Elevator Company, according to a letter from Charles A. Pillsbury to Mrs. Fred C. Pillsbury, Aug.8, 1899.
6. *Northwestern Miller*, July 18, 1890; Kuhlmann, *Development of Flour Milling*, 135.
7. *Northwestern Miller*, Oct. 3, 1900; July 19, 1895; Charles A. Pillsbury to John S. Pillsbury, Dec. 16, 1897; Charles A. Pillsbury to Mrs. Fred C. Pillsbury, Aug. 5, 1899; Charles A. Pillsbury to Richard Glyn, May 4, 1898.
8. *Northwestern Miller*, May 24, 1889; July 12, 1889; Nov. 29, 1889; Dec. 19, 1890; Jan. 9, 1891.
9. Ibid., Nov. 14, 1890; Oct. 30, 1885; Nov.24, 1885.
10. Allen Johnson and Dumas Malone, eds., *Dictionary of American Biography* (New York: Charles Scribner's Sons, 1959–60), 19:504.
11. *Northwestern Miller*, Nov. 29, 1889.
12. Ibid., Dec. 7, 1894; *Northwestern Miller Advertisers' Hand-Book No. 2* (1892), 6.
13. Statement of Expenditures, Receipts and Profits of the Pillsbury-Washburn Flour Mills Company, Ltd., for 14 Fiscal Years, from 1890–01 to 1903–04, Both Inclusive, in the files of The Pillsbury Company.
14. *Northwestern Miller*, Nov. 14, 1890.
15. *Anoka Herald*, Mar. 22, 1890.
16. *Northwestern Miller*, Feb. 6, 1891; Aug. 24, 1904; Holiday Edition, 1889.
17. Ibid., Dec. 7, 1894; see also Dec. 16, 1898.
18. Ibid., Dec. 7, 1894.
19. Ibid., Oct. 18, 1895; Nov. 1, 1895; Mar. 8, 1895.
20. *Minneapolis Daily Tribune*, Oct. 31, 1889; Kane, *Waterfall that Built a City*, 151; *Northwestern Miller*, Jan.4, 1895; May 15, 1896; Jan. 22, 1897.
21. *Northwestern Miller*, Jan. 4, 1895; Mar. 6, 1896; Mar. 26, 1897; Kane, *Waterfall that Built a City*, 154.

22. William H. Dunwoody to Thomas C. Jenkins, Nov. 15, 1899; William H. Dunwoody Papers, Letterbook 3: 4–5, Div. of Archives and Manuscripts, Minnesota Historical Society.
23. *Northwestern Miller,* May 24, 1899; Oct. 18, 1899; Mar. 7, 1900; Sept. 26, 1900; June 19, 1901; Oct. 15, 1882.
24. Ibid., Jan. 21, 1898; Jan. 19, 1894; for sales offices see, for example, Mar.7, 1906.
25. Ibid., Dec. 14, 1894; May 24, 1895.
26. Ibid., Jan. 20, 1904; Feb. 3, 1904.
27. Ibid., Dec. 6, 1895.
28. Ibid., Nov. 19, 1897; Dec. 24, 1897.
29. Ibid., Dec. 31, 1897; Feb. 4, 1898.
30. Charles A. Pillsbury to Charles D. Rose, Dec. 1, 1897; ''Leiter Claims Minneapolis Men Broke Corner,'' unidentified Dec. 13, 1914, newspaper clipping datelined Chicago, Associated Press, in the files of The Pillsbury Company.
31. ''Leiter Claims Minneapolis Men Broke Corner.''
32. *Northwestern Miller,* Dec. 16, 1898.
33. John S. Pillsbury to Alfred F. Pillsbury, Dec. 28, 1898; Henry L. Little to Alfred F. Pillsbury, Dec.31, 1898.
34. John S. Pillsbury to Alfred F. Pillsbury, Jan. 18, 1899; Henry L. Little to Arthur T. Safford, Jan. 14, 1899; Henry L. Little to Alfred F. Pillsbury, Jan. 12, 1899; *Northwestern Miller,* Feb. 22, 1899.
35. *Northwestern Miller,* July 5, 1899; Feb. 18, 1939.
36. *Ibid.,* May 10, 1899; May 31, 1899.
37. *American Miller,* Oct. 1, 1899.
38. Charles A. Pillsbury to Frank Spencer, Dec. 24, 1897.
39. Henry L. Little to Arthur T. Safford, Jan. 11, 1899.
40. *Northwestern Miller,* Dec. 26, 1900; July 10, 1901; Aug. 6, 1902; Oct. 8, 1902; June 3, 1903.
41. Ibid., June 3, 1903; Sept. 30, 1903; Oct. 7, 1903; Oct. 14, 1903; Oct.21, 1903; May 27, 1903.
42. For earlier efforts to change the company's domicile from England to the United States, see John S. Pillsbury to Alfred A. Pillsbury, Mar. 4, 1899; Cary & Whitridge to W. D. Washburn, Jan. 13, 1900; John S. Pillsbury to Sir William Forward [*sic*], Apr. 18, 1900; Cary & Whitridge to Henry L. Little, June 26, 1901; Frank Spencer letters to Henry Little, June12, 1901, and Aug. 9, 1901; for attempt in 1905, see Ralph W. Whelan to George A. Zabriskie, May 20, 1905.
43. *Northwestern Miller,* Oct. 26, 1904; Dec. 7, 1904; Dec. 14, 1904; May 24, 1905.
44. Ibid., Sept. 21, 1904; Nov. 2, 1904; Apr. 19, 1905; May 24, 1905.
45. Kane, *Waterfall that Built a City,* 156; *Northwestern Miller,* Oct. 9, 1907.
46. Unidentified 1902 newspaper clipping in the files of The Pillsbury Company; Johnson and Malone, *Dictionary of American Biography,* 4:188–89.

Chapter 3

1. George A. Touche, Proceedings at a Meeting of the Holders of Debentures, Oct. 27, 1908, 4.
2. Frank Spencer to William de la Barre, July 1, 1908; July 22, 1908; William H. de la Barre Papers, Div. of Archives and Manuscripts, Minnesota Historical Society.
3. Clive T. Jaffray Reminiscences, 1956, 65–66, Div. of Archives and Manuscripts, Minnesota Historical Society.
4. Albert C. Loring to Richard H. Glyn, ca. Apr. 8, 1910; Report of the Directors for the Year ending 31st August, 1908; Touche, Proceedings at a Meeting of the Holders of Debentures, 21.
5. The Pillsbury-Washburn Flour Mills Co., Ltd., Report of the Directors for the Year ending 31st August, 1908; Frank Spencer to William de la Barre, July 27, 1908; William H. de la Barre Papers, Div. of Archives and Manuscripts, Minnesota Historical Society.
6. Albert C. Loring to Richard H. Glyn, ca. Apr. 8, 1908.
7. *Minneapolis Tribune,* Aug. 10, 1908; *Minneapolis Journal,* Aug. 10, 1908; *Northwestern Miller,* Aug. 19, 1908.
8. William H. Dunwoody to James McDaniel, Aug. 19, 1908; William H. Dunwoody Papers, Box 3, Div. of Archives and Manuscripts, Minnesota Historical Society.

9. The Trustees, Executors & Securities Insurance Corp., Ltd., to First Mortgage Debenture-holders of The Pillsbury-Washburn Flour Mills Co., Ltd., Sept. 3, 1908; Touche, Proceedings of Holders of Debentures, 6.
10. *Northwestern Miller,* Aug. 26, 1918; Sept. 2, 1908; Sept. 9, 1908.
11. Marwick, Mitchell & Co. to Receivers of The Pillsbury-Washburn Flour Mills Co., Ltd., Sept.30, 1908.
12. Petition for Final Decree, U.S. Circuit Court, Dist. of Minn., Fourth Div., in *The Second National Bank of St. Paul, et al. vs. Pillsbury-Washburn Flour Mills Company, Limited,* July 8, 1909, 7; *Northwestern Miller,* Sept. 15, 1909.
13. *Northwestern Miller,* Sept. 9, 1908.
14. Albert C. Loring to Ralph Whelan, October 1908 (no further date); Creditors Committee to Sir Frank Crisp, Nov.7, 1908; Gilbert G. Thorne to Ralph Whelan, Dec. 18, 1908.
15. *Northwestern Miller,* Dec. 16, 1908.
16. Ibid.
17. George Cloutte to Shareholders, Aug.9, 1910, 2; Fidelity (Frank Spencer?) to William de la Barre, Apr. 1, 1901 (obviously dated in error, should be 1910); William H. de la Barre Papers, Div. of Archives and Manuscripts, Minnesota Historical Society; Office of Receivers to C. C. Wyman, Dec. 9, 1908.
18. Albert C. Loring to Richard H. Glyn, Apr.8, 1910, 3.
19. *Northwestern Miller,* Sept. 15, 1909.
20. Lucile M. Kane notes taken in 1950s from William de la Barre to Charles Lock, Jan.29, 1913, Special Letterpress Book, 1911–14, formerly in files of Minneapolis Mill Company, now unavailable; *Northwestern Miller,* Oct. 13, 1909; Nov.3, 1909; May 25, 1910.
21. Ralph Whelan to M. D. Koon, June 7, 1910.; Frank Spencer to William de la Barre, May 27, 1910, William H. de la Barre Papers, Div. of Archives and Manuscripts, Minnesota Historical Society; Ralph Whelan to John B. Niven, July 22, 1910.
22. *Northwestern Miller,* Aug. 10, 1910.
23. The market quotation spread on Aug. 15, 1910, was £¼–£¾ (in predecimal English coinage) for ordinary shares and £2–£3 for preference shares, according to a Pillsbury memo from Bruce Noble to Edward C. Stringer, Feb. 11, 1985.
24. Lucile M. Kane notes taken in 1950s from William de la Barre to Frank Spencer, Mar. 17, 1910, Special Letterpress Book, 1907–11, formerly in files of Minneapolis Mill Company, now unavailable.
25. Ralph Whelan to Charles W. Folds, July 8, 1910, 4.

Chapter 4

1. In order to keep the flour milling operations in focus, chapter 4 begins with the lease of the five flour mills in September 1909 to the newly formed Pillsbury Flour Mills Company. Since final disposition of the disputes created by the receivership did not occur until Aug. 3, 1910, this chapter overlaps the period discussed in chapter 3. See Bureau of the Census, "Abstract of the Census Statistics of Population, Agriculture, Manufacture and Mining for the United States, the States and Principal Cities With Supplement for Minnesota" in *Thirteenth Census of the United States Taken in the Year 1910* (Washington, 1913), 436, 443.
2. Mennonite immigrants are credited with bringing the Turkey Red seed wheat to America; see Steen, *Flour Milling in America,* 210; Victor G. Pickett and R. S. Vaile, *Decline of Northwestern Flour Milling* (Minneapolis: University of Minnesota Press, 1933), 30.
3. Pickett and Vaile, *Decline of Northwestern Flour Milling,* 58.
4. Kuhlmann, *Development of Flour Milling,* 136.
5. Steen, *Flour Milling in America,* 285.
6. Clark Hempstead, unpublished corporate history, ca. 1944, in the files of The Pillsbury Company.
7. Albert C. Loring to Ralph Whelan, October 1908 (no further date).
8. *Minneapolis Journal,* Dec. 8, 1913.
9. *Northwestern Miller,* Mar. 13, 1911; Dec. 3, 1913.
10. Ibid., June 28, 1916.
11. Ibid., Aug. 24, 1910; Oct. 26, 1910.
12. Ibid., 75th Anniversary Edition, June 1, 1948.
13. Ibid., Jan. 8, 1919.

14. Ibid.
15. Ibid., Feb. 20, 1918.
16. Ibid., May 13, 1942; Dec. 26, 1917.
17. Ibid., May 27, 1942.
18. Ibid., June 26, 1918.
19. *Northwestern Miller*, Feb. 28, 1923; Steen, *Flour Milling in America*, 74.
20. *Northwestern Miller*, May 21, 1924; Sept. 3, 1924.
21. *Minneapolis Journal*, Oct. 17, 1932.
22. *Pillsbury People*, January 1964.
23. Steen, *Flour Milling in America*, 124.
24. *Northwestern Miller*, Mar. 14, 1928.
25. *Pillsbury People*, 75th Anniversary Issue, June 1944, 15.
26. *Northwestern Miller*, Mar. 14, 1928.
27. Pickett and Vaile, *Decline of Northwestern Flour Milling*, 37, 53.
28. *Northwestern Miller*, June 18, 1924: *Interstate Commerce Commission Docket No. 17000*, Part 7, 1927.
29. *Northwestern Miller*, May 1, 1929.
30. *Minneapolis Journal*, Dec. 12, 1932.
31. "Roosevelt Saves Relief Bill with Message to Congress," *New York Times*, Mar. 17, 1933.
32. *Northwestern Miller*, Oct. 14, 1936.
33. Ibid., Sept. 23, 1936.
34. Ibid., Nov. 18, 1936.
35. Ibid., Aug. 4, 1937.
36. Ibid., July 5, 1933; May 31, 1939.

Chapter 5

1. Philip W. Pillsbury in taped interview by Kenneth D. Ruble, 1975.
2. Philip W. Pillsbury, "Relation of Technology to Company Management," to Seventh Annual Food Conference, Boston, June 2, 1947, reprinted in *Food Technology*, 2(January 1948):75–78.
3. Undated Paine, Webber, Jackson & Curtis market letter, published shortly prior to Aug. 18, 1952.
4. *P. G. and E. Progress*, August 1940, 1–2.
5. Philip W. Pillsbury, in private journal maintained during his tenure as president of the company.
6. *Minneapolis Tribune*, Aug. 14, 1940; Pillsbury's *Research and Development Laboratories*, 1956.
7. Bureau of the Census, *Statistics of Industry*, vol. 2 of *1947 Census of Manufacturers* (Washington, 1947), 101.
8. *Modern Miller*, July 25, 1942.
9. *Northwestern Miller*, Apr. 29, 1942.
10. Pillsbury Press Release, Mar. 24, 1941; *Northwestern Miller*, June 1, 1948.
11. Philip Pillsbury, "Milling Around," *Pillsbury Reporter*, September 1969.
12. Pillsbury News Bureau Release, Mar. 22, 1945.
13. Annual Report to Shareholders, 1943, 9; *A Message to Pillsbury Stockholders*, Dec. 1, 1942.; *Investor's Reader*, Feb. 13, 1952, 19.
14. Minutes of meeting of Board of Directors, Apr. 25, 1944; Annual Report 1949, 6; "The New Era at Pillsbury," *Tide*, Dec. 15, 1950.
15. *Business Week*, Dec. 15, 1945.
16. *Pillsbury Reporter*, November 1970.
17. Minutes of meeting of Board of Directors, June 29, 1943.
18. *Northwestern Miller*, Feb. 15, 1946; Feb. 19, 1946; Mar. 5, 1949.
19. "Three New Pillsbury Divisions," *Bakers Review*, June 1947, 83; Annual Report 1947, 5.
20. *Pillsbury Today*, Oct., 1951, 6, 7.
21. Minutes of meeting of Board of Directors, Dec.18, 1945.
22. Paul S. Gerot in taped interview by Kenneth D. Ruble, 1975, 3.
23. Minutes of meeting of Board of Directors, Apr.6, 1945, 139.
24. Undated Verne Burnett Associates memo suggesting Springfield opening announcement.
25. *Pillsbury People*, October 1945; *American Miller*, August 1946; *Feedstuffs*, July 27, 1946.
26. *Investor's Reader*, Feb. 13, 1952, 16.
27. Annual Report 1946, 11; 1947, 4.

28. Pillsbury Press Release, May 9, 1947.
29. Auditors Report, Internal Finance Statements D51, Pillsbury Vaults.
30. Bureau of the Census, *1975 Historical Statistics of the U.S.* (Washington, 1975); Cedric Adams, ''In This Corner,'' *Minneapolis Star,* Dec. 13, 1949.
31. ''The New Era at Pillsbury,'' *Tide,* Dec. 15, 1950, 45.
32. Steen, *Flour Milling in America,* 246.
33. Paul S. Gerot in taped interview by Kenneth D. Ruble, 1975, 7, 8.
34. Carl Schenker to John O'Connell, Dec.9, 1952.

Chapter 6

1. Undocumented information about personnel, products, earnings, and operations in this chapter is from Pillsbury Annual Reports, Stockholders' Meeting Reports, and Financial History and Financial History Library Index for the years stated.
2. Paul Gerot in taped interview by Kenneth D. Ruble, 1975.
3. Kenneth D. Ruble notes from interview with Lowell Armstrong, Jan. 15 and 16, 1976.
4. Ibid.
5. *Wall Street Journal,* Mar. 12, 1959.
6. *The Pillsbury Co. v. Federal Trade Commission, Trade Regulation Reports* (Commerce Clearing House, Inc., 1966), p.81,891, 71,646. Pillsbury acquired the assets of Ballard & Ballard and Duff, rather than its capital stock. Section 7 of the Clayton Act, which prohibits a company from acquiring the stock of another corporation when the effect might be to substantially lessen competition, was amended in 1950 to include acquisition of another corporation's assets. The proceeding against Pillsbury was the first to be brought under the newly amended section. In May and June of 1955 congressional subcommittees of both houses conducted hearings on the amended section, questioning commissioners and staff members about their enforcement of the section and specifically about their management of the Pillsbury case. This questioning, during the time when the commission was still deliberating the Pillsbury case, was the basis for the court's finding that Pillsbury's right to due process of law had been violated.
7. Pillsbury Management News Letter, No. 92, Aug.13, 1957.
8. Fiscal 1953 Pillsbury Internal Financial Statements: Summary of Revenue by Divisions, Compared with F 1952; Fiscal 1960 Pillsbury Internal Financial Statements: Operating Statement for Each Revenue Division.
9. Paine, Webber, Jackson & Curtis Market Letter, titled Pillsbury Mills, Inc., issued between May 31, 1952, and Aug. 18, 1952; James L. Rankin, Jr., memo, Nov. 26, 1952.
10. *Pillsbury People,* January 1954.
11. *Advertising Age,* Aug. 10, 1959.
12. Leo Burnett Company, Inc., to William Edgley, Feb. 14, 1964; *Atlanta Pillsbury Journal,* May 17, 1955.
13. Market data in the files of The Pillsbury Company.
14. *Forbes,* Feb. 1, 1960, 19–22.
15. Ibid.
16. Ibid.
17. Dana L. Thomas, ''Grain of Hope,'' *Barron's* June 3, 1957, 16.
18. Courts & Co., Investment Bankers, Report on Pillsbury, Sept. 6, 1957; Thomas, ''Grain of Hope,'' 3; *Forbes,* Feb. 1, 1960, 21.
19. Management News Letter No. 62, Mar. 25, 1955.
20. Edward P. Palmen, ''A Short History of Pillsbury's Grain Merchandising Operations,'' (unpublished), 6,7.
21. Ibid.
22. Paul S. Gerot remarks to Springfield President's 25-Year Club, June 9, 1963.
23. *The Magazine of Wall Street,* Dec. 16, 1961, 352.
24. Paul S. Gerot to St. Louis Society of Financial Analysts, May 5, 1966.
25. *Minneapolis Star,* Feb. 5, 1966.
26. ''Pillsbury Co.,'' *Advertising Age* reprint, Aug. 30, 1965.
27. *Minneapolis Star,* Feb. 16, 1967.
28. See note 26; also Susan M. Johnson to J.Levine, Apr. 19, 1979.
29. Stock prices in chapters 6 and 7 are the closing prices on the New York Stock Exchange for the date stated.
30. *Finance Report for Stillwater, Minnesota Management Meetings,* Nov. 9–11, 1960.

31. *Pillsbury People*, March 1970; *Minneapolis Tribune*, Sept. 10, 1969.
32. *Minneapolis Tribune*, Sept. 12, 1962; Pillsbury Management News Letter No. 157, May 24, 1962.
33. H. E. Baumann to Doniver Lund, Oct. 12, 1982; *Advertising Age*, Aug. 3, 1975.
34. Alan Magary and Kerstin Fraser Magary, *Across the Golden Gate: A Comprehensive Guide to California's North Coast, Wine Country, and Redwoods* (New York: Harper & Row, 1980), 140.

Chapter 7

1. Information about the selection process has been gathered from interviews with the principals by the author. Paul Gerot formed the nominating committee in 1966. Consisting of all the nonemployee members of the board of directors, it was formed to aid in the selection of new board members and to nominate officers required to be elected by the board. Bill Spoor increased the committee's functions substantially. Today it meets with the chairman before each of the board's six regularly scheduled meetings during the year, and every two years it conducts a full-scale review of its own operations.
2. *Fortune*, Nov. 5, 1979, 128.
3. Undocumented information in this chapter may be found in Pillsbury Annual Reports to Stockholders and Stockholders Meeting Reports for the years indicated.
4. *Pillsbury Reporter*, January 1984, 6; *Minneapolis Star and Tribune*, June 18, 1984.
5. *Wall Street Journal*, Dec. 6, 1976.
6. Pillsbury News Release, Oct. 7, 1975.
7. James Brian Quinn and Mariann Jelinek, ''The Pillsbury Company,'' (Hanover, N.H.: Amos Tuck School, Dartmouth College, 1980), exhibit 1, pp. 1, 7.
8. *Forbes*, Nov. 13, 1978, 138; *Wall Street Journal*, Oct. 21, 1980, Oct. 24, 1980, Jan. 31, 1979; *Minneapolis Tribune*, Nov. 8, 1981.
9. *Wall Street Journal*, Oct. 24, 1980.
10. Ibid.; *Fortune*, Nov. 5, 1979.
11. *Minneapolis Tribune*, May 13, 1980.
12. *Pillsbury Reporter*, March 1984.
13. Ibid.
14. *Wall Street Journal*, July 20, 1983.
15. Market research data in the files of The Pillsbury Company.
16. For description of Pillsbury flour mills in 1984, see *Pillsbury Reporter*, June 1984.
17. William H. Spoor remarks at Amos Tuck School, Dartmouth College, November 1983.
18. *Fortune*, Nov. 5, 1979, 126.

Index

References to illustrations are printed in italics.

Adams, Charles Francis, 9
Adomeit, Bernard L., 11
Advertising (*See also* Specific companies—Advertising): and development of export trade, 32–33
Agricultural Adjustment Act, 121–22
Agricultural and Trade Development Assistance Act (1954), and Pillsbury exports, 166
Aines, Philip D., and Pillsbury research and development, 199, 208–209, 211
Alaska mill (Minneapolis, MN). *See* Charles A. Pillsbury and Company—Mills
American Association of Cereal Chemists, 129
American Banker, on Pillsbury-Washburn receivership, 80
American Barge Company, Pillsbury acquisition of (1981), 223
American Beauty Macaroni Company, Pillsbury acquisition of (1977), *211*
American Federation of Labor, 124–25
American Home Products Corporation, Duff Baking Mix Division, Pillsbury acquisition of (ca. 1951), *152*–153, 159, 162; home mixes, sale of, Pillsbury rights retained, 162
American Miller, 64–65
American Red Cross, 139
Ames Mill (Northfield, MN), 22
Amsden, Charles M., 92–93, 235; American manager Pillsbury-Washburn Mills Co., *64*–65; and Minneapolis and Northern Elevator Co., receivership, 82; and Pillsbury-Washburn receivership, 76
Anchor mill (Minneapolis). *See* Charles A. Pillsbury and Company—Mills
Animal feed (*See also* Formula feed): F. Pillsbury, experiments with, 32; Pillsbury ads for, *67*; use of bran for, 31–32
Apollo® Foods, Pillsbury acquisition of (1984), 222
Arbuckle, Ernest C., 236
Armour, Philip, 64
Armstrong, Lowell, 158, 161
Association of Operative Millers, 129
Astoria (OR): Pillsbury mills, *118*–119; closed (1961), 177
Astoria Evening Budget (OR), 119
Atchison (KS): Pillsbury Bitsyn plant in, 201; Pillsbury mills, *108*–109
Atlanta (GA): Pillsbury-Occidental Company, Call-A-Computer service, 181
Atlantic Elevator Company: profits, 49; sale of, *43*, 45
Aunt Jemima pancake flour, 115
Aurora Seven space mission, use of Pillsbury foods, *187*
Avery, J. W., 236
Azteca® Corn Products Corp., Pillsbury acquisition of (1984), 222

Babson, Roger W., 119–20
Bachman's European Flower Markets: Pillsbury acquisition of (1971), 190; sale of (1976), 207
Bakeries, commercial: demand for flour, and profits, 113; rise of, and flour supply, 101–102, 113
Baking industry, commercial: development of flours for, 113
Ballard & Ballard Co., Inc. (Louisville, KY), 151, *152*–153; earnings, 161; frozen pie plant, Pillsbury lease of, 172–73; Gerot on acquisition of, 151, 153; H. Steen on, 151; Louisville plant, closed (1955), 169, 177; packaging, 159; Pillsbury acquisition of (1951), 158; plants closed (1961), 177; products: 151, 153, *160*–161
Ballard, Charles T., 151
Ballard, S. Thruston, 151
Beatles, 164
Beatty, J. Irl, 236
Belter, Judith A., 11
Bennigan's®, *220*–221; The Pillsbury Co., and success of, 219, 221
Berry, Rachel, 11
Blacksmiths, wages, 36
Black Tuesday (1929), 119
Blasing, Everett A., 11
Blumenthal, W. Michael, 237
Bon Appetit: Pillsbury acquisition of (1970), 189; sale of (1975), 207
Bon Voyage: Pillsbury acquisition of (1970), 189; sale of (1975), 207
Booz, Allen & Hamilton, 181
Borden, Inc., 161
Bowers, Henry S., 236
Bran (*See also* Milling industry, by-products): F. Pillsbury and, 32; use as cattle feed, 31–32
Breakfast foods, 54–56; competition, 55; Pillsbury brands, 54, *55*–56; Washburn Crosby Co., 55
Brinker, Norman, 237; and Bennigan's®, 219; and Steak and Ale®, 205; Pillsbury career of, 217, 219
Brink's Coffee Shop (Dallas, TX), 205
British: purchase of Minneapolis flour mills, 41–47
Brownlee, James F., 144, 236
Buck, Robertson & Co. (Montreal), 17, 19
Buffalo (NY): Crosby flour mills, 101; dominance of, in flour milling, 116, 125; Pillsbury Flour Mills Co. mill, construction, *108*–109, *110*–111; Pool elevator, Pillsbury acquisition of, *148*–149
Bunge, 171
Burger King Corp., *182*–183, 184, 191; advertising, television, success of, 219; and Campbell, 219; and D. N. Smith, 208; and fast food competition, 217, 219; and N. Brinker, 217, 219; drive-through windows, *182*–183, 201; earnings, 185, 191; foreign locations, *182*–183,

201; growth of, 185, 201; headquarters, *218*–219; Home of the Whopper®, *182*–183; Pillsbury acquisition of (1967), and success of, 181, *182*–185, 217; site locations, 219; stores updated, *218*–219
Business Week, on Pillsbury Flour Mills Co. diversification, 139

Calgary, Alberta (Canada): Renown Mills, Ltd., elevator, Pillsbury acquisition of, 153–*154*
Call-A-Computer. *See* Pillsbury-Occidental Company, Call-A-Computer Service
Cambridge Tile Company (Ohio), 139
Campbell, J. Jeffrey, and Burger King, 219
Campbell Soup, compared with Pillsbury, 157, 193, 229
Cargill, 171
Carnegie, Arthur, 64
Carpenter, F. Scott, use of Pillsbury foods, *187*
Carpenters, wages, 36
C. C. Washburn Flouring Mills Co., 41–42; McIntyre takeover attempt, 63–65; mills of, 42; proposed sale of, 41–42, 45
Chamberlain, Mr., 76
Charles A. Pillsbury and Company (1869–1889) (*See also* corporate entries under Pillsbury; and Minneapolis & Northern Elevator Co.), 9, 50, 65, 235; advertisements and advertising, *12*, *32*–34, *40*–41, *43*, 48; and competition, 50; brands and trademarks, *32*; *Carry-On* (house organ), 37; elevators, *24*, 41–42, *43*, 45–47; expansion of, 26; export trade, 32–33; F. C. Pillsbury and, 25; founding of, 20; grain supply, 35; mills of, *20*–*21*, *24*, 25–26, 28, *29*–*30*, 31, *37*–*38*, 42, 45; mills, capacity, 26, 31; partners, 235; products, 31, *32*–33; profit-sharing plan, 36; profits, 36, 39, 47–48, 52; roller mill, use of, *27*, 28–29; sale of, to Pillsbury-Washburn, *43*, 95; sales, 32; steam engines, use of, 31; storehouse, 23; wheat inventory and purchase, 52
Chicago Board of Trade, and suspension wheat futures (1917), 102
Chippewa (Ojibway) Indians, treaties, 13
Christian, George H., 22, 26
Christopherson, Paul, 236
Clinton (IA), Pillsbury Feed Mills, *136*–137
Cloutte, George, 92, 235; and Pillsbury-Washburn receivership, 83, 88; and Pillsbury-Washburn reorganization, 89–90; resignation, 91
Cobb, Albert C., and Pillsbury-Washburn receivership, *78*–79
Columbia Broadcasting Network (CBS, Inc.), 115, 213; "Cooking Closeups from Pillsbury's Model Kitchen in Minneapolis" (program), 115
Common laborers, wages, 36
Concord Railroad Corp., 17
Consolidated Milling Co., 79, 97; McIntyre takeover, 64

Consumer Product Safety Act, 215
Consumerism, rise of, and Pillsbury safety measures, 190–91
Continental, 171
"Cooking Close-ups" (radio program), Pillsbury ads for, 114–115
Copeland Flour Mills, Ltd. (Canada), Pillsbury acquisition of, 153
Cora (Mexico), Pillsbury acquisition of (1968), 189
Cora-Rex, merger with Grupo Olazabal Pillsbury S. A. de C. V. (1982), 225, 227
Cosgrove, Edward B., 144; Pillsbury career of, 213, 236
Cosgrove, Robert C., Pillsbury board member, 213, 237
Cosmopolitan, Pillsbury ads in, 56
Council Bluffs (IA), Pillsbury elevator, 149
Craib, Donald F., Jr., 237
Crisp, Frank, 83, 85
Crosby, Washburn, 101
Crocker, George M., 19
Crocker & Fisk, 30
Cross, Bert S., 199, 237
Crump, William, 83; and Pillsbury-Washburn reorganization, 90

Dallas (TX): Bennigan's®, 219, 220–221; Steak and Ale®, 206–207
Dart & Kraft, Inc., Kraft division, distributors, 158
Davenport (IA), Pillsbury elevator, 147, 149
Decker, Mr., 76
de la Barre, William, 55–56, 76, 81, 88, 93, 235; American Manager Pillsbury-Washburn, 65; and introduction of roller mill, 27; and Pillsbury C mill, design of, 65; and renovation Pillsbury A mill, 99; and reorganization Pillsbury-Washburn, 86–87; and waterpower development, 69, 71; Spencer to, on Pillsbury-Washburn receivership, 75, 93
Delaware: Pillsbury Flour Mills Co. incorporated in, 122
Deloitte & Co., 88–89
Dennison, Charles H., 236
Depression (1930s), 119; and New Deal agricultural programs, 121–22
Derrick, William E., 236
Des Moines (IA), Pillsbury restaurants, 189
Development of the Flour Milling Industry, The, on wheat mixing, 35
Doria, S. A. (Switzerland), Pillsbury acquisition of (1962), 175
Douglas, Henry F., and Minneapolis & Northern Elevator Co., receivership, 82
Dreyfus, 171
Duff Baking Mix Division. *See* American Home Products Corp.
Duluth Imperial Mill (MN), 49
Dunwoody, William H., and flour exports, 26; on Pillsbury-Washburn receivership, reasons for, 80
Dwight, Donald R., 237

East Los Angeles (CA), Pillsbury flour mill, 177
Edgerton, David R., Jr., 183
Ehlert, Nancy, 11
Eiland, Ray, 214–215
Electricity: transmission of, and power plants, 55; use of, 55
Ellijay (GA), Pillsbury poultry processing plants, 176
Ellwein, Michael D., 11
Empire mill (Minneapolis), 26; capacity of, 25;

Pillsbury acquisition of, 25; site of, 24
Engineers, wages, 36
England: income tax, and dividend payments, 69
Enid (OK): Pillsbury mill, 117; turbo grinding and separation, 167
Equal Employment Opportunity Act (1972), 215
Erasco (West Germany), 227; acquisition of Jokisch (1983), 224–225; Pillsbury acquisition of (1962), 175
Etablissements Brossard, S. A. (France), Pillsbury acquisition of (1968), 188–189
Etablissements Gringoire, S. A. (France), Pillsbury acquisition of (1961), 174–175
Excelsior Mill (Minneapolis). *See* Charles A. Pillsbury and Company
Export trade: development of, and advertising, 32–33; effect of Third World food plants on, 166–67

Falls of St. Anthony (MN), 13; waterpower, and milling industry, 16; waterpower rights, 45
Famine relief. *See* Food relief
Faribault (MN), flour mills, 22
Farm machinery, and wheat crop, increase of, 16
Fast food chains (*See also* Burger King; Jack-in-the-Box; McDonald's; Wendy's): competition, and Burger King, 217, 219
Federal Trade Commission, complaint of Pillsbury acquisitions, 159, 161
Feed industry (*See also* Formula feed): and formula feed, 135; plant location, changes in, 169; product value increased, 135
Ferrell, Richard, 11
Files, Howard W., 237
Financial Times (London), on Pillsbury-Washburn Flour Milling Co., Ltd., 49
First National Bank of Minneapolis, officers, 75–76
Fiske, Robert B., 237
Florence (IL), Pillsbury elevator, 171
Flour (*See also* Flour milling; Flour milling industry; Flour mills): exports of, 113; mixed-wheat in, 35; non-wheat, and government regulation, WWI, 105; quality control of, 35; packaging, 238; prices, 36, 53; railroad rate structure, and decline of exports, 95
Flour and Feed, Pillsbury-Washburn ads in, 67
Flour, Cereal and Elevator Workers Union, 66
Flour mill workers, 66
Flour milling: early process of, 20; expansion of, and exports, 26; "high grinding" process, 22; process of, 21; purification of middlings, improved, 22; roller mill process, 26–27, 28; spring wheat, difficulties, of, 20; turbo grinding process, 167
Flour Milling in America, 113
Flour milling industry: and publicly owned companies, 49; and trade-union movement, 53; and wheat processing taxes, 122; Buffalo (NY), dominance of, 116; C. A. Pillsbury on, 39; capacity, excessive, and competition, 39, 109; competition, 39, 49–50, 109, 116, 131, 133, 135; effect of Turkey Red on market, 95; expansion of, 16, 109; exports, 95, 144; food relief and, post WWII, 144; government regulation of, WWI, 102, 105, 107; government regulation of, WWII, 137, 144; hours of work, 66; importance of C. A. Pillsbury to, 64; McIntyre's takeover attempt, 63–65; marketing, 56; middlings purifier and, 22, 36; Minneapolis, development of, 39; Northern, J. S. Pillsbury on competitive position of, 116; *Northwestern Miller* on, 35; Pillsbury family and, N. G. Ord-

way on, 39; power sources, 16, 31; railroad rate structure, effect on exports, 95; railroads, growth of, and, 16; speculation and effect of WWI, 102; spring wheat, effect of on Minneapolis industry, 20, 22; Steen on, 36, 39; use of by-products, 31–32; wages, 36, 66; wheat supply, 35; winter wheat, and dominance of St. Louis, 20
Flour mills: British purchase of, 41–47; capacity of, 15–16, 25; early, in Minneapolis, 15; explosions, 21, 25–26, 30; increase in number of, 16; in Minneapolis, 21; naming of, 25; Pillsbury posters of, ca. 1888, 12
Fonfara, Allan E., 11
Food Control Act (1917), 102
Food relief: Pillsbury and, 214–215; post WWII, 144
Formula feed industry, Pillsbury prominent in, 147
Fort Snelling (MN), 15; established, 13
Fortune, 231; on Pillsbury management changes, 213; on Spoor and Pillsbury growth, 227
Forwood, William B., 59–61, 63, 235
Fox, Charles T., 235
Fox Deluxe Foods, Inc. (Joplin, MO), 211; Pillsbury acquisition of (1976), 211; products, 211
France: use of roller mill, 26
Frank Schoonmaker Selections, Inc., Souverain acquisition of, 207
Frazee & Murphy, 19
French, William T., 195, 237
Frey, Kathy, 11
Fridley, Russell W., 11
F. W. Woolworth, 219

Gainesville (GA), Pillsbury feed mill, 168–169, 176
Galaxy mill, 97
Gardner mill (Hastings, MN), 22
Gates, John Warner, 71
General Foods: compared with Pillsbury, 157, 193, 229; home-mixes, competition, 162; products, 115
General Mills, Inc.: compared to Pillsbury, 157, 193, 229; formation of (1928), 133; flour mill closings, 177; packaging, of flour, 143; products, 145, 161–62, 165, 173; refrigerated dough market, withdrawal from, 180; Sperry flour, acquisition of, 133
Georgia Broilers, Inc., Pillsbury acquisition of (1961), 176
Gerot, Paul S., 11, 159, 166, 181, 187, 193, 196, 208, 232, 236; and acquisition of Burger King Corp., 159, 181, 183, 232; and expansion of consumer food products, 157–58, 161–62, 165; and expansion of consumer franchises, 173; and family flour market, 164; and foreign expansion, 157, 159, 173, 175–76; and FTC case, 159, 161; and internal development of products, 162; and product expansion, 145–46, 172–73; and refrigerated dough, success of, 158–59, 160–161, 179; early career of, 158; on acquisition of Ballard & Ballard Co., Inc., 151, 153; on Pillsbury's prepared mix expansion, 145–46; on stabilization of cake mix market, 173; Pillsbury career of, 155, 157–58, 179–80; retirement (1967), 83, 157, 172; success of, 169, 171
Geyserville (CA), Souverain winery, Pillsbury acquisition of, 207
Ghana, Pillsbury flour export market, 173
Gibbs Goodies Co. (Ludington, MI): Pillsbury acquisition of (1961), 172–73; plant closed (1965), 202; products, 172; sale of Pillsbury line, 180

Globe Grain and Milling Co. (Los Angeles, CA), 144–45, 165; advertisements, *133*; capacity, 133; feed mills, 137; Pillsbury acquisition of, *130*–131, 133, 137; products, 131, 133

Glyn, Richard H., 47, 50, 52–53, 59–60, 65, 91, 235; and McIntyre takeover attempt, 63; and Pillsbury-Washburn receivership, 75, 85, 87–88; and reorganization, 90; as chairman, 61, 63; on earnings, 61

Godfrey, Arthur, 164

Good, Raymond F., 208, 237; and Munsingwear Co., 213; resignation, 213

Gopher Yearbook, Pillsbury ads in, *48*

''Gradual reduction process.'' *See* Roller mill

Grand Forks (ND), Pillsbury potato processing plant, 162

Gray, W. D., 27; and introduction of roller mill, 27–28

Great Northern Railway Company, 35, 45, 92

Green, Ellen B., 11

Green Giant Company (MN), 144; advertisements, *194*–195, *212*–213, *216*–217; Pillsbury acquisition of (1978), 211; products, *212*–213, *216*–217, 221; reorganization, 221

Green, William, 124–25

Greenville (PA), Pillsbury refrigerated dough plant, *160*–161

Greer, Ben J., 165, 237

Greyhound Corp., 219

Grinnell College (IA), 144

Gristmills, 238; early, 15; established on Mississippi River, 13

Grupo Olazabal Pillsbury S. A. de C. V. (Mexico), Cora-Rex merger (1982), 225

Guaranty Loan Bldg. (Minneapolis), 50–*51*

Guatemala: flour mills in and Pillsbury licensing agreements, 166–67

Guntersville (AL), Pillsbury poultry processing plant, *168*–169, 176

Häagen-Dazs®, *222*; Häagen-Dazs® Dipping Stores, 222; Pillsbury acquisition of (1983), 222

Hamilton (OH): Duff Baking Mix Division, Pillsbury acquisition of, *152*–153, 162

Hammond, Toni, 11

Hammonds Sauce Company, Ltd., Pillsbury acquisition of (1982), 227

Hanold, Terrance, 176, 184, 195, 236; career of, 183–*184*, 195–96; retirement, 207

Harvey Paper Co., Pillsbury acquisition of (1928), 119

Hatcher, Graham, 11

Heinz, U.S.A., 208

Hempstead, Clark C., 124–*125*, 235; career of, 125; on losses ca. 1938, 126; resignation of, 131

Henderson, Mr., 89

Hendrix, Clyde H., 236

Hill, James J., 45–46, 64

H. J. Green & Co. (England), Pillsbury acquisition of (1962), *174*–175

H. J. Heinz & Co., 208

H. M. Byllesby & Company, purchase of waterpower corporation from Pillsbury, 113

Homestead Act (1860), and settlement of Minnesota Territory, 16

Hoover, Herbert, 102; and food administration, WWI, 102, 105, 107

Horton, Helen Wolcott, *186*–187

Horton, Robert V., 236

Hosfield, George W., 184–85, 237

Howard Johnsons, 219

Hubbard, L. P., 63, 80

Hungary: use of roller mill, 26, 28

Industrial Research Institute, 135

Interstate Commerce Commission, J. S. Pillsbury testimony to, 116

Investors Diversified Services, Inc., 209, 213

Jack-in-the-Box, 205

Jackson, J. Flower, 47, 89–90, 235

Jacobson, Allen F., 237

Jaffray, Clive T., 75–76, 131, 144, 236

Jasper (AL), Pillsbury feed plant, *169*, 176

J. C. Penney, 201

Jennison, James, 236

JJ. Muggs®, Pillsbury and, *220*–221

J-M Poultry Packing Co., Inc., Pillsbury acquisition of, 185, 187

John's Pizza, 202

Jokisch (West Germany), Pillsbury acquisition of, 227

Jones, Ballard & Ballard. *See* Ballard & Ballard Co., Inc. (Louisville, KY)

Jones, Mr., 90

Kane, Lucile M., 11

Kansas City, dominance of, in milling, 125

Keith, Robert J., 141, 157, 165, 227, 232, 236; and expansion of Pillsbury research and development, 187; and government regulation of business, compliance with, 191, 215; and organization of management, 184; and refrigerated food business, 183; and separate business concept, 184; career of, 165, 180, 183, 190–91, 215; retirement and death, 193, 195

Kellogg Co., and Kellogg-Pillsbury of Canada, Ltd., 164

Kelsey, Paul J., 11

King, Martin Luther, Jr., 190

Klein, Sydney T., 47, *63*, 90, 235; and Pillsbury-Washburn receivership, 88

Koon, Whelan & Bennett. *See* Koon, Whelan & Hempstead

Koon, Whelan & Hempstead, 124–25

Kraft, distributor Pillsbury products in Canada, 164

Kuhlmann, Charles, on wheat mixing, 35

LaCroix, Edmund N., improvement of milling technique, 22

LaCroix, Nicholas, and milling technique, 22

Ladies Home Journal, Pillsbury ads in, *94*–95

Latin America, Pillsbury licensing agreements in, 166–67

Lehman, Max A., 235

Lehman, Paige, 236

Lehman, Robert, 236

Leiter, Joseph, 60, 65; and wheat market, 60, 63, 80

Leo Burnett Co., Inc., 180

Lewis, Robert J., 11

Lima (OH), Pillsbury feed mill, *147*

Linkletter, Art, *150*–151, 164

Little, Henry L., 59, 63, 65, 76, *80*, 97, 235; and Pillsbury-Washburn failure, 88–89, 92–93; and Pillsbury-Washburn receivership, 76, 80, 83, 87–88; as manager of Pillsbury-Washburn, 59–61, 64–66; resignation of, 80; success in wheat purchase, 71

Lock, Charles, 90

London Times, on Pillsbury A mill, 31

Loring, Albert C., *79*, 110, 129, 235; and expansion Pillsbury flour products, 101–102; and Pillsbury Flour Mills, Inc., 111; and Pillsbury-Washburn receivership, 79; and reclassification Pillsbury-Washburn shares, 109; and sales organization, 115; and U.S. Food Administra-

tion Millers' Committee, WWI, 102, 105; career of, 87, *96*–97, 120–21; on cost of change to small packages, 115; on dividends during depression, 120; on sale of waterpower companies, 113

Los Angeles (CA): Globe Grain and Milling Co., Pillsbury acquisition of, *130*–131, *132*–133; Pillsbury bakery mix plant, 189; Pillsbury feed plant, 147; Pillsbury refrigerated dough plant, 161

Louisville (KY): Ballard & Ballard Co., Pillsbury acquisition of, 151, *152*–153; Pillsbury plant in, 162; plant closed, 177

Lowry, Thomas, 55

Ludington (MI), Gibbs Goodies Co., Pillsbury acquisition of, 172–73

Luhrs, Caro E., 237

Lund, Doniver Co., 11

Lund, Ronald E., 11

McCormick, Cyrus, 64

McDonald Grain & Milling Co. (Los Angeles, CA). *See* Globe Grain & Milling Co. (Los Angeles, CA)

McDonald's, 208, 219; foreign units, 201

Machinists, wages, 36

McIntyre, Thomas A., 63, 97; and flour industry takeover attempt, 63–65

McKenney, Patrick J., 236

McLamore, James L., 183, 236

McNamara, James R., 236

McNeal, Dean, 176, 236; career of, 165–66, 184

McSwiggen, Margaret E., 236

Macke, Kenneth A., 237

Magazine of Wall Street, on food companies' European expansion, 175

Mallon, A. F., 236

Marwick Mitchell & Co., 82–83

Matschke, Mortimer H., 236

Mayer, Levy, 42

Metropolitan Life Bldg. (Minneapolis). *See* Pillsbury Bldg. (Minneapolis)

Miami (FL): Burger King, 183–85; Burger King headquarters, *218*–219

Middlings, 21

Middlings purifier, 22–*23*, 25; and expansion of Minneapolis milling, 26; and impact of, 27; and profits, 36; use in Pillsbury A mill, 29

Midland, Ontario (Canada), Copeland Flour Mills, Ltd., Pillsbury acquisition of, 153

Milani (Venezuela), Pillsbury acquisition of (1965), 189

Millers National Federation, 36

Minneapolis (MN): early history of, 13, *14*–15; electricity, transmission and use of, 55; flour milling industry (*See also* Charles A. Pillsbury Company *and* corporate entries under Pillsbury), 20, 26–28, 36, 39, 49, 95; flour mills, *21*, 25–26, 30, 41–47, 49, 239; G. A. Pillsbury, mayor of, 17, 64; milling district, *37*–38, *104*–105; power plant and dam construction, 55; strikes and lockouts, 124–25

Minneapolis & Northern Elevator Co., 35, 80; dissolved, 101; earnings, 61; in receivership, 82; Pillsbury acquisition of, 92; profits, 47, 49; sale of, *43*, 45

Minneapolis Chamber of Commerce. *See* Minneapolis Grain Exchange

Minneapolis Flouring Company, *21*

Minneapolis Flouring Mill, 9, *20*–22, 25; Pillsburys buy into, *18*–19

Minneapolis General Electric Co.: leases Pillsbury-Washburn Co. dam, 69; subleases to Twin Cities Rapid Transit Co., 69

Minneapolis Grain Exchange, and wheat purchase and distribution, 35

Minneapolis Journal, on Pillsbury A mill ca. 1913, 98

Minneapolis Mill Co., 16–17, *43*, 45, 47, 55

Minneapolis Millers Association, and wheat purchase and distribution, 35

Minneapolis Star and Tribune: on H. L. Little and wheat purchase, 71; on Pillsbury Co. computer systems, 180; on sale of flour mills, 41–42

Minnesota (*See also* Minnesota Territory): flour mills, use of spring wheat, 20, 22; food relief, Pillsbury and, *214*–215; senate, John Pillsbury member, 17

Minnesota Mining and Manufacturing Co., 199

Minnesota Territory: exploration, 13; farming in, and milling industry, 16; railroads in, and milling industry, 16; settlement, 15–16; wheat crop in, 16

Minnetonka Mill Co. (MN), 97

Mirick, E. H., 236

Mississippi River (in Minnesota): dams, 13; exploration and settlement, 13, 15, 28; first mills on, 13

Molinos Caracas Maracaibo, S. A. "Mocama," Pillsbury majority purchase (1960), 173, 175

Monroe, Willys H., 237

Montgomery Wards, 201

Moore, Allan Q., 147

Morrison, Dorilus C., 26; and rebuilding Excelsior mill, 31

Morton, David C., 151

Morton family, 158

Morton, Rogers C. B., 151, 236

Morton, Thruston B., 151, 237

Mrs. Paul's Fish, 202

Mrs. Smith's Pies, 202

Munsingwear Co., 213

National Broadcasting Co., Pillsbury ads, 15

National Council of Grain Processors, 124

National Register of Historic Places, Pillsbury A mill on, 225

National Research Council, 135

Nestlé, 213

New Albany (IN), Pillsbury refrigerated dough plant, *160*–161, 189

"New Deal," and aid to agriculture, 121–22

New York Curb Exchange, 119–120

New York Society of Security Analysts, 197

New York Stock Exchange, 120, 202

Niven, John B., *83*; and Pillsbury-Washburn receivership, 82

North American Newspaper Alliance, 115

North Dakota, Pillsbury plants in, 225

Northern States Power Co., 113

Northwestern Consolidated Milling Co. (*See also* Consolidated Milling Co.), 97; capacity, 49; F. Pillsbury manager, 50; staff, ca. 1890, *51*

Northwestern Miller, 25–26; ads, *32*–*33*, 49, *74*– 75, *84*–85, *112*–113, *142*–143; antitrust ads, *62*; on Ann Pillsbury, 143; on 1881 explosions, 30; on formation Pillsbury Flour Mills, Inc., 111; on milling industry competition, 50; on milling profits, 36; on Pillsbury A mill, 29, 31–32; on Pillsbury expansion, 117; on Pillsbury laboratories, *98*–99; on Pillsbury quality control, 35; on Pillsbury profit-sharing, 36; on Pillsbury-Washburn exports, 69; on Pillsbury-Washburn reorganization, 89; on rumors of Pillsbury move, 101; on sale of flour mills, 41–42, 45; on wheat regulation, WWI, 107; survey of milling industry, 56

Northwestern National Bank, 76; G. A. Pillsbury president, 64

Northwestern National Life Insurance Company, 166

Nyline, Sig, 11

Occidental Life Insurance Co. (NC), and Pillsbury Call-A-Computer service, 181

Occupational Safety and Health Act (1970), 215

O'Donnell, Cornelius, 235

Offal. *See* Flour milling industry, by-products; Bran

Ogden (UT), Globe Grain & Milling Co., Pillsbury acquisition of, 131–*132*, 133

Ojibway Indians. *See* Chippewa (Ojibway) Indians

Omaha (NE): Pillsbury plant, calcium cyclamate manufacture, 179; Tidy House Products Co., Pillsbury acquisition of, 172–73

Ontario (Canada), Pillsbury-Canada, Ltd., plants, 164

Ordway, N. G.: on Pillsburys and milling industry, 39

Osell, Don A., 11

Paine, W. W., 79, 83, 85–86; on Pillsbury-Washburn reorganization, 92

Painesville (OH), Pillsbury calcium cyclamate plant, 179

Painters, wages, 36

Panic of 1857, 16

Panic of 1873, 25

Panic of 1893, 53

Partridge, Stanley, 236

Paul Erasmi, G. M. B. H. *See* Erasco (West Germany)

Pearl Harbor (1941), 137

Peavey (Minneapolis), 60

Peavey, F. H., 60

Pemtom (Minneapolis): Pillsbury purchase of interest (1970), 189–90; Pillsbury sale of (1975), 207

PepsiCo, 213

Perkins, John H., 237

Peterson, Hjalmar, 124–25

Peterson, James R., 195–97, 207, 237

Philippines, Pillsbury flour mill interests in, 175

Phoenix mill (Minneapolis), Pillsbury acquisition of, *100*–101

Pike, Zebulon, 13

Pillsbury, Alfred F., 63, 76, *96*–97, 133, 235; and Pillsbury-Washburn American Management Committee, 64, 75, 234; retirement, 131

Pillsbury & Hulbert Elevator Co. *See* Minneapolis & Northern Elevator Co.

Pillsbury brothers, 110; and formation Pillsbury Flour Mills, Inc., 111

Pillsbury Building (Minneapolis), 50, *141*, 209

Pillsbury-Canada, Ltd., 164

Pillsbury, Charles A., 9, 11, *17*, 21–22, 25–26, 29, 32, 37, 39, 43, 45–*46*, 47, 64, 71, 120, 129, 157, 225, 235; and American Management Committee, 47, 234; and dam and power plant construction, 55, 69; and introduction of roller mill, 27–28; and Leiter and wheat market, 60– 61; and quality control, *Northwestern Miller* on, 35; and wheat mixing in flour, 35; arrival in Minneapolis, 13, 16, 19; at Pillsbury-Washburn, 50, 52; early life of, 13, 17, 19; founds C. A. Pillsbury & Co., 20; importance of, to flour industry, 64; Minneapolis Flouring Mill, purchase of interest in, 3; on A mill production, 31; on McIntyre takeover, 63–64; on marketing, 56; on middlings purifier, 22, 25; on mill-

ing industry, 39; on product quality, 65; on profits, 59, 61, 64–65; on sale of flour mills, 41–42; on wheat inventory and purchase, 52– 53, 80; Taylor Brothers mill, purchase of interest in, 20

Pillsbury, Charles S., *96*–97, 234–35; and Pillsbury-Washburn receivership, 76, 78–79, 82

Pillsbury Company, The (1958–　) (*See also* Bennigan's®; Charles A. Pillsbury Co.; JJ. Muggs; Pillsbury Farms; Pillsbury-Occidental; Poppin Fresh® Pie Shops; S & A Restaurant Corp; *and following Pillsbury acquisitions*: American Barge Company (1981); American Beauty Macaroni Co. (1977); Apollo Foods (1984); Azteca® Corn Products Corp. (1984); Bachman's European Flower Markets (1971); *Bon Appetit* (1970); *Bon Voyage* (1970); Burger King·(1967); Cora (Mexico, 1968); Doria, S. A. (Switzerland, 1962); Erasco (West Germany, 1962); Etablissements Brossard, S. A. (France, 1968); Etablissements Gringoire, S. A. (France, 1961); Fox Deluxe Foods, Inc. (1976); Georgia Broilers, Inc. (1961); Gibbs Goodies (1961); Green Giant Co. (1978); Häagen-Dazs® (1983); Hammonds Sauce Co., Ltd. (England, 1982); H. J. Green & Co. (England, 1962); Milani (Venezuela, 1965); Molinos Caracas Maracaibo, S. A. "Mocama" (1960); Pemtom (1970); Pioneer Food Industries, Inc. (1979); Sedutto® Ice Cream Corp. (1984); Souverain Cellars, Inc. (1972); Speas Co. (1978); Steak and Ale Restaurants of America, Inc. (1976); Tidy House Products Co. (1960); Totino's Finer Foods, Inc. (1975); White Wings Pty., Ltd. (Australia, 1961); Wickes Corp. agricultural division (1982); Wilton Enterprises, Inc. (1974)

—acquisitions (*See also*, e.g., Agri-products group, acquisitions; *and* above), 189–90, 203, 205, 207, 222, 225, 227

—advertisements and advertising, 191; and appeal to minorities, *216*–217; Funny Face, *178*– 179; television, *204*–205, *212*–213, *216*–217

—agri-products group, 179, 208, 223; by-products, 201; commodities division, 171, 185, 225; earnings, 171, 191, 198–99, 201–202, 217, 221, 223, 225, 227; feed merchandising (*See* commodities division); formula feed division (*See* Pillsbury Farms; protein division); grain merchandising division, 169, *170*–*171*, 198– 99, 201, *223*; hydroprocessing, 201; profits, 198, 225; products, *200*–201; reorganization of, 179; Spoor on profits of, 225; transportation fleet, 200–*201*

—and corporate responsibility, *214*–215, 228

—and food relief, *214*–215

—and government regulations, 191

—and portfolio balance, 217

—and product safety, 190–91

—and separate business concept, 184–85

—board, and board selection process, 208, 245

—capital investment, 171

—charitable donations, 215, 228

—compared with competition, 157, 193, 229

—computer systems, development and use of, 180–81

—consumer products group, 179, 181, 185, 202, 207–208, 221; acquisitions, 199, 201–202, 211, 213, 217, 222; and banning calcium cyclamate, effect of, 187; competition, 217, 222, *228*; earnings, 191, 198–99, 202, 217; expansion, 187; frozen foods, 172–73, 180, 202, 222; grocery products, 172, 180, 184, 199; management, 184; market share, 222; Poppin' Fresh®

Pillsbury Company, The
—consumer products group (continued)
Pillsbury Dough Boy, 180; products, 179, *187*, 199, 201, 222; publications, 189; refrigerated dough, 179–80, 183–84; sales, 221; success of, 221
—dividends, 227
—earnings, 172, 181, 185, 190–91, 197–98, 202–203, 215
—employees, number of, 228
—executives and executive structure (*See also* individuals), 184, 195–98, 236–37
—exports, 166, *173*; and Public Law 480, 166
—flour mills and milling, *118*–19, 189, 225; acquisitions, *188*–189; A mill, National Register of Historic Buildings, *224*–225; bakery and industrial flour, sales of, 172, 177; earnings, 167, 172, 177; exports, 119, *173*; mill relocation, 177; plants, *188*–189; products, 177; profits, 177; turbo process, 167, 177
—food products, return to, Spoor and, 207–208
—formulation of food products, 190
—FTC case, 177, 244
—growth, 185, 228–29
—headquarters (Minneapolis), *209–210*, 211
—Home Service Center, director, *186*–187
—industrial group (*See also* Agri-products group), 179, 184
—institutional foods division (*See also* Agri-products group; Consumer products group), 167
—international group, 181, 184–85, 202, 205; acquisitions, 189, *173*, 175, 225; Far East, 227; licensing agreements and technical assistance, 166; management, 184; profitability, 166–67; refrigerated dough, 202
—labeling (*See also* Advertising), 179, 190
—labor relations (*See also* and corporate responsibility), 171
—management, 183–84, 195–96, 199, 213
—100th anniversary year (1969), 185
—organizational structure, 165–66
—packaging, *167*
—Political Action Committee, formation, 215
—profits, 171–72, *191–192*, 198, *228, 230*
—protein division (*See also* Pillsbury Farms), 181; products, 176
—research and development, 183, 187, 199; laboratories, 209, 211; management, 199
—restaurant group (*See also, e.g.,* Burger King), 208, 219, 221, 228; acquisitions, 189, 193, 217; competition, 217, *228*; earnings, 191, 198; formation of, 181–83; growth, 199; profits, 198; success of, 217
—sales, 189–90, 197, 203, 215, 227
—shares, 171, 181, 197, 202–203, 227
—Spoor and success of, 217, 227–28
—stock splits, 181, 203, 227
Pillsbury Company, The v. Federal Trade Commission, 177, 244
Pillsbury Dough Boys (orchestra), 115
Pillsbury, Edmund P., 147, 234
Pillsbury Family, and milling industry, N. G. Ordway on, 39
Pillsbury Farms (*See also* acquisition J-M Poultry Packing Co., Inc.), 169, 176–77, 184–87; earnings, 185, 190, 198; plants, *168–169*, 176; products, 198; profits, 181; sale of (1974), 198
Pillsbury Feed Mills, *136*–137; advertisements, *137*
Pillsbury Flour Mills Company (1909–1923) (*See also* Pillsbury-Washburn Company; *and acquisitions*: Island Warehouse Corp.; Minneapolis & Northern Elevator Co.; Phoenix mill), 85–86, 90–92, 95, 129

—advertisements and advertising, *99*; ca. WWI, 105
—and formation Pillsbury Flour Mills, Inc., 111, 113
—*Carry-On*, 103
—delivery trucks, *100*–101
—dividends, 107, 109
—early difficulties of, 97–98
—earnings, 107
—flour: and commercial bakeries, 101–102; flour sacks, uses for, *87*; Loring and expansion of products, 101
—incorporated in Minneapolis, 122
—laboratory, *98*–99
—mills of: *108*–109, *110*; A mill, *98*–99, 101, 105, *110*–111; Anchor mill, 101, 105, 109; B mill, 109; Lincoln mill, 101, 105; Palisade, 101; Phoenix, conversion, *100*–101
—move, rumors of, 101
—officers, 90, 93, 97
—products, 107; animal feed, *106*–107; cereals, *106*–107; grocery, 102; Loring and expansion of, 101; non-wheat, *103*, 105; quality control, *98*–99
—profits, 102, 107
—relationship with Pillsbury-Washburn Co., 92–93, 107, 109–111, 113; and receivership, 97–98
—shares, 109
—supply houses, *100*–101
—veterans, employment of, *104–105*
—warehouses, 101
—WWI, war effort, *103*, 105
Pillsbury Flour Mills Company (1935–1944) (*See also acquisitions*: Globe Grain and Milling Company; Pillsbury Feed Mills; Pillsbury Soy Mills)
—acquisitions, 131, 137
—advertisements and advertising, *128*–129, 141
—Ann Pillsbury, creation of, 143
—board of directors, 127, 235–36
—*Business Week* on diversification of, 139
—competition, 131, 133, 135
—depression and, 122, 124–25
—diversification of, 139, 141
—dividends, 126, 135
—earnings, 126–27, 135
—employee benefits, 122, *123*–124
—employee relations, P. W. Pillsbury and, 139
—employees, number of, 127
—executives, 124–25, 127, 129, 131, 235–37
—feed mills and formula feed (*See also* Pillsbury Feed Mills), 131, 135, 137
—flour, 137, 144; enriched, 137; packaging, 143
—food research laboratories, *134*–135, 139
—Home Service Center, *134*–135
—incorporated in Delaware, 122
—mills of, 131, 139; capacity, 133
—Minneapolis headquarters, moved, *140*–141
—name change, to Pillsbury Mills, Inc. (1944), 141
—packaging, 139
—products, 129, 133
—profits, 127
—recipe books, *140*–141
—soybean plants, 137
—strikes and lockouts, 124–25
—trade-union movement and, 124–25
—war effort, WWII, 137, *138*–139
—wheat, processing taxes, 122
Pillsbury Flour Mills, Inc. (1923–1935) (*See also acquisitions*: Harvey Paper Co. (1928); Pillsbury-Astoria Flour Milling Co.; Pillsbury Feed Mills Co.; Pillsbury Soy Mills; Unity Mills Distributing Co.)

—acquisitions, 119, 137
—advertisements and advertising, 94–95, *112–113*, *114*–115; radio, 115
—and strikes and lockouts, 124–25
—and wheat processing tax, 122
—competition, 113, 115–16
—depression and, 120–22
—distributors, 9, 119
—dividends, 113, 120
—earnings, 119
—elevators, 117
—executives, 87, 120–21
—expansion, Loring and rumors of, 116–17
—exports, 119
—flour: exports, 113; packaging, 115
—flour bag factory, *118*–119
—formation of, 111, 113
—layoffs, 125
—mills of, 9, 113, *117–118*, 119–20; Astoria (OR) mill, 113, 120; Atchison mill, 113, 116; Buffalo (NY), 113, 116; Enid (OK), *117*; capacity of, 119; use in depression, 120
—name change, to Pillsbury Mills, Inc. (1944), 141
—operating company, for Pillsbury-Washburn reorganization, 86–88; and plant improvement, 87
—packaging, 115, 121
—Pillsbury Flour Mills Company merged into, 122, 124
—profits, 113, *126*
—products, 113, 115; control, and bakery research department, 113; ''specialty,'' 121
—recipe books, *139–140*, 141
—reorganization (1935), 122, 124
—sales: organization, 115–16; policies, 121; ''specialty,'' and accounting system, 121
—seventy-fifth anniversary, *140*–141
—shares, 111, 116, 120
—stock: and depression, 120; conversion, 119
Pillsbury, Fred C., *25*, 45, 235; and C. A. Pillsbury & Co., 25, 234; and experiments with bran, 32; and introduction of roller mill, 27; and Northwestern Consolidated Milling Co., 50
Pillsbury, George A., *17*, 21, 47, 234–35; death of, 64; early life of, *18*–20; on sale of mills, 42
Pillsbury, George S., 11, 155, 184–85, 234, 236
Pillsbury Holdings (Canada), Ltd., 176, 184; and Latin and South American holdings and agreements, 175; management, 184
Pillsbury International, acquisitions of, 189
Pillsbury, John S. (first), *16*, 19, 21, 24, 47, 63–64, 71, 234–35; and C. A. Pillsbury & Co., 20; and construction of Pillsbury A mill, 28; early career of, 15–17, 19–20; governor of Minnesota, 16, 24–25
Pillsbury, John S. (second), 76, 79, 83, 235; and Pillsbury-Washburn receivership, 87, 90, *97*; as chairman of board, 120, 125, 127, 131, 133, 155; on competitive position of northern mills, 116; on Loring, 120
Pillsbury, John S., Jr., board member, 166, 236
Pillsbury Management Systems, discontinued (1971), 190
Pillsbury Mills, Inc. (1944–1958) (*See also acquisitions*: American Home Products Corp., Duff Baking Mix Division; Ballard & Ballard Co., Inc.; Copeland Flour Mills, Ltd. (Canada); Kellogg-Pillsbury Canada, Ltd.; Renown Mills, Ltd.)
—acquisitions, 151, *152*–153, *154*–155, 158–59, 162; Canadian, and price fluctuations and exports, 153
—advertisements and advertising, *142*, 143–44;

expansion of, 164; Poppin' Fresh® Pillsbury Dough Boy, *156–157*; television, *164*
—and Pillsbury family, 155
—bakery premix plant, *147–148*, 149
—board, 144
—budgeting systems, 145
—bulk premix division, 144
—competition, 144, 161–62, 165
—controller's office, 166
—diversification, post WWII, 141
—exports, 155
—feed mills, *147*
—flour and cereal division, 144
—formula feed division, expansion of, 145, 147, 153
—FTC case, 159, 161
—grain division, 145, 147, *148–149*
—grocery products (and consumer foods) division, 145, 147, 153, 157, *162–163*, 164–65
—Home Service Center, 164
—human relations department, 166
—Kraft, distributors for, 164
—management: incentive pay program, 145; structure and growth, 165–66
—mixes: home-mix products, 161–62, *163*, 165; market success of, 145–47, 149, 164
—name change, to The Pillsbury Company (1958), 166
—overseas division, 144
—packaging, 159
—Pillsbury Bake-Off® contest, 149, *150–151*, 164
—products, *145–146*, 149, 164–65; development of, Gerot and, 162
—profits, 151, *154–155*, 165
—recipes, 164
—refrigerated dough products and division, *156–157*, *160–162*, 164
—reorganization, post WWII, 144–47; (1958), 165–66
—research and development department, 166
—stock, 141
Pillsbury Mindanao Flour Mills Co. (Philippines), 175
Pillsbury-Occidental Company, Call-A-Computer service, 181; sold (1971), 190
Pillsbury People, 147
Pillsbury, Philip W., 11, *130–131*, *140–141*, *150–151*, 208, 232, 236; and diversification, 139, 141, 143, 232; and employee relations, 139; and food research laboratory, 135; and profits, *154–155*; and sales strategy, 144, 146–47; as president, 129, 131, 137, 153; co-chairman of board, 179–80, 183; changes during presidency, summed up, 155; early career of, 129, 131; on grain division, 147; retirement, 149, 155; war effort and, 137
Pillsbury Soy Mills, organization of, 137
Pillsbury, Susan M., Mrs. Fred B. Snyder, 234
Pillsbury v. Skidmore and Bull, 32
Pillsbury-Washburn Flour Mills Co., Ltd. (1889–1909) (*See also acquisitions*: Minneapolis & Northern Elevator Co.; St. Anthony Falls Water Power Co.; *and* Pillsbury Flour Mills Co., 1909–1923), 129
—advertisements and advertising, *48–49, 54,* 56, *58, 67,* 68–69, *70–71*; anti-trust, *62–63*; during receivership, *74–75*, *84–85*, 88
—American Management Committee, 47, 235
—and strikes and lockouts, 66
—assets, 45
—British-American relationship, 60–61, 63
—*Carry-On*, 51
—cookbooks, *70–71*

—delivery vans, *68–69*
—dividends, 47, 49–50, 53, 59, 66; postponed, 72–73
—domicile change proposed, 72–73
—earnings, 52–53, 59, 61, 64–66
—employees, *51*
—exports, 58, 69
—*Financial Times* on, 49
—flour: packers, *67*; trains, *56–57*
—McIntyre takeover attempt, 63–64
—marketing, 56–*57*
—mills: A mill, 49, 56, *77*, 82; capacity, 49, 56, 66; production, 49
—parade floats, *9*
—products, *54–56*; quality of, C. A. Pillsbury on, 65
—profits, 49–50, 59, 64–65, *72*; Spencer on, 69, 71
—prospectus, *43*, 47, 49
—recipes, *71*; contests, *56*
—receivership, 73, *74–76*, *78–80*, 82–83, 85; *American Banker* on, 80; American interests, 83, 85–86, 89; and reorganization, 83, 85, 92–93; assets, 82–83; English interests, 83, 85–89; fraud, as cause of, 88–90
—relationship with Pillsbury Flour Mills Co. (1909–1923), 86–88, 90, 91–92, 107, 109–111, 113
—shares, 45–47, 50, 66
—wage reductions, 53
—waterpower companies: exempted from receivership, 82; expansion of, 55, 69; profits, 55
—wheat inventory, 59–60, 66
—wheat purchase and futures, 152–53; Canadian, in bond, 69
Pinchin, R. J., 236
Pioneer Food Industries, Inc. (AR), Pillsbury acquisition of (1979), 225
Piper, Harry C., 236
Polaroid Corp., 213
Poppin Fresh® Pie Shops, 189, *191*, 201; earnings, 191; expansion, 202
Poppin' Fresh® Pillsbury Dough Boy, 180
Powell, Meredith B., 11
Powell, William J., 196, 233, 237, 253
Price, Emory J., 236
Price freeze, effect of (1973), 198
Processed Prepared Foods, on success of Pillsbury consumer foods, 221
Proctor and Gamble, 199; cake mix market, 173; Duncan Hines cake mix, 165; compared to Pillsbury, 157, 193, 229
Profit-sharing, Pillsbury and, 36; C. A. Pillsbury on, 36
Public Law 480 (1954), and Pillsbury exports, 166
Purdy, Myron, 79

Quaker Oats: compared to Pillsbury, 157, 193, 229; majority interest in Stokely-Van Camp, Inc., 222
Quinn, Charles P., 11

Railroads: and flour distribution, 56; flour trains, *56–57*; in Minnesota, and growth of milling industry, 16; rate structures, effect on flour exports, 95
Raleigh (NC), Pillsbury-Occidental Co., Call-A-Computer service, 181
Ralston-Purina, 165; compared with Pillsbury, 157, 193, 229
Rankin, J. L., 236
Rapp, J. Cy, 236

Renown Mill, Ltd. (Canada), Pillsbury acquisition of, 153
Review of Reviews, 36
Rockwell, Norman, 194–95
Roller mill "gradual reduction process," *27*; introduction of, 26–27; impact of, 28
Roosevelt, Eleanor, *150–151*
Roosevelt, Franklin D., 121
Rose, Charles D., 59, 63
Rose, E. T., 47, 235
Rosewall, Arthur A., 197
Ruble, Kenneth D., 11
Russell Miller Milling Co., 37

Sacramento (CA), Pillsbury mills, 177
Safford, Arthur T., 63
St. Anthony (MN): early flour and gristmills in, 15; flour mills, increase in number of, 16; incorporation of (1855), 15; J. S. Pillsbury and, 17; settlement of, 15
St. Anthony Falls Water Power Co., 16; Pillsbury acquisition of, *43*, 45–46; profits, 49
St. Louis (MO): Pillsbury flour mill in, *188–189*; winter wheat, and dominance of in milling industry, 20–21
St. Paul & Pacific Railroad, 16
S & A Restaurant Corp. (*See also* Bennigan's®; JJ. Muggs®; Steak and Ale Restaurants of America, Inc.), The Pillsbury Company and, 219, 221
San Salvador, Pillsbury company licensing agreements in, 167
Sawmills, in Minnesota, 13, 15
Schoelhorn, Robert A., 237
Schoenhofen, Leo H., 236
Schoonmaker, Frank, 207
Scott, Walter D., 208, 213, 237
Sears, 201
Security National Bank, 76
Sedutto® Ice Cream Corp., Pillsbury acquisition of (1984), 222
Sella, George J., Jr., 237
Shenandoah (IA), Tidy House Products Co., Pillsbury acquisition of (1960), 172–73
Sioux (Dakota) Indians, treaties, 13
Skinner, Thomas, 90, 93
Smith, Donald N., 208, 213; and Burger King success, 217
Smith, George T., 22; and middlings purifier, 28
Snowbrand Company (Tokyo), and Pillsbury marketing Totino's® Crisp Crust Pizza, 227
Snyder, John P., 234
Snyder, John P., Jr., 155, 234, 236
Souverain Cellars, Inc. (CA): acquisition of Frank Schoonmaker Selections, Inc., 207; Pillsbury acquisition of (1972), 193; sold, 207
Soybeans, 137, 143
Speas Co., Pillsbury acquisition of (1978), 211; losses, 221; sold (1981), 221
Speculation, in wheat, rumored, 50, 52
Spencer, Frank, 61, 75, 235; and Pillsbury-Washburn receivership, 83, 88; on flour milling profits, 71; on Pillsbury-Washburn dividends, 66; on Pillsbury-Washburn receivership, *81*; on waterpower development and profits, 69, 71
Sperry Flour Co., acquired by General Mills, 133
Spoor, William H., 11, 176, 195–*197*, 202, 205, 209, 213, 217, 219, 228–29, 236; and corporate responsibility, commitment to, 215; and diversification, 207; and plan for company performance improvement, 196–98; career of, 184, 195–96, 207, 232–33; on agri-products group profits, 225; on Green Giant acquisition, 213;

Spoor, William H. (continued)
   on return to food products, 207–208; success of
   consumer foods, 221; success, reasons for,
   217, 227–28
Springfield (IL), Pillsbury mills and plants in,
   118–119, 147–*148*, 149, 162, 177, 189
Springfield Twenty-Five Year Club, 173
Spring wheat: and Minneapolis milling industry,
   20; flour, use of middlings purifier and market
   share of, 22; milling of, difficulties, 20–22; use
   of, 39
Stafford, John M., Green Giant and, 213; Pills-
   bury career of, 213, 228, 233, 237
Steak and Ale Restaurants of America, Inc., 203,
   205, *206–207*, 219, 221; and tied house laws,
   207; Pillsbury acquisition of (1976), 203, 205
Steam engines, installed in Pillsbury mills, 31
Steen, Herman: on baking flours, profits, 113; on
   Ballard & Ballard Co., Inc., 151; on milling
   profits, 36, 39
Stevens, Samuel N., 144, 236
Stevenson, Adlai, 147
Stock market, crash (1929), 119
Stokely-Van Camp, Inc.: Pillsbury bid for, 22;
   Quaker Oats majority interest, 222
Strikes and lockouts, flour mill workers, 66, 124–
   25
Stringer, Edward C., 11
Sullivan, Ed, *164*
Swedish-American Bank of Minneapolis, 86, 92

Tariff Act (1897), 69
Taylor Brothers Mill (Minneapolis), *20*–21; mid-
   dlings purifier installed, 22, 25; Pillsbury ac-
   quisition of (1871), 20
Tidy House Products Co.: household products di-
   vision sold, 179; Pillsbury acquisition of
   (1960), 172–73, 179; products, *172*
Thomson, J. Cameron, 236
Thorne, Gilbert G., and Pillsbury-Washburn re-
   ceivership, 82
Thurcroft (England), Pillsbury refrigerated dough
   plant, 202
Thye, Edward J., 141
"Today's Children" (radio program), Pillsbury
   ads, *114*–115
Totino, James, 203
Totino, Rose, 203, *204–205*
Totino's Finer Foods, Inc. (Fridley, MN): plants,
   203; Pillsbury acquisition of (1975), 203; suc-
   cess of, 203, 205
Totino's Italian Kitchen, 203
Touche, George A., 83
Touche, Niven & Co., 82–83
Trademarks, of flour: Pillsbury, and lawsuits, 32
Trade-union movement, and milling industry, 53
Trucks, electric, Pillsbury-Washburn use of,
   68–69
Turner, C. A. P., and renovation Pillsbury A
   mill, 99
Twin Cities Marathon, Pillsbury support of, *214*
Twin City Rapid Transit Co., 55; sublease of
   Pillsbury-Washburn dam power, 69

United States: Panic of 1857, 16; Panic of 1873,
   25; Panic of 1893, 53; Panic of 1907, 72
United States (government): and regulation of
   business, 191; Army Quartermaster Corps,
   Pillsbury supplier for, WWII, 139; Council of
   National Defense, 102; Food and Drug Administration, regulations of, 105, 107, 179, 187;
   food control, WWI, Hoover and, 102, 105,
   107; Millers' Committee, 102, 105; Pillsbury

product safety system, use of, 190–91; National
   Labor Relations Board, 124; Office of Man-
   agement and Budget, 208; Office of Price Ad-
   ministration, 165; reservations, military, in
   Minnesota, 13, 15; Tariff Act (1897), 69; trea-
   ties, with Sioux and Chippewa Indians, 13;
   Wagner Act (1935), 124
United States Flour Milling Co., 64, 97

Venezuela: Pillsbury flour interests in, and market loss, 173, 175

Wagner Act (1935), 124
Wall Street Journal, 213
Wallin, Winston R., 213, 215, 217, 219, 237; and
   consumer foods, success of, 221; and Green
   Giant acquisition, 221; career of, 208, 228
Washburn A mill (Minneapolis), 27, 35, 42; ca-
   pacity, 25; explosion, 25–26; use of middlings
   purifier, 22
Washburn B and C mills (Minneapolis), 42; roller
   mill process, 27
Washburn, C. C., 22, 26, 42, 45–47; and roller
   mills process, use of, 27
Washburn Crosby Co., 80, 133; capacity, 49;
   products, 55
Washburn Mill Co., 41, 45; Lincoln mill (Anoka,
   MN), 42, *44*; Palisade mill, 42, *44*; profits, 49;
   sale of, 41–*43*, 45–46
Washburn, William D., 42, 45–*46*, 47, 235;
   American manager, Pillsbury-Washburn, 65,
   76, 79; congressman, 47; U.S. senator, 47
Watson & Co. (Minneapolis), 92
Weight Watchers International, Inc., 202
Wellsburg (WV), Pillsbury flour bag factory,
   118–119; Harvey Paper Co., Pillsbury acquisi-
   tion of (1928), *118*–119
Wendy's, 219
Wheat (*See also* Spring wheat; Winter wheat):
   cultivation, increase and milling industry
   growth, 16; exports, shipping of, 16; market,
   Leiter and Pillsbury and, 60–61; mixing of, in
   flour, 35; prices, 36, 52–53, 61, 102, 121–22;
   processing, taxes on, 122; purchase and distribution, 35, 52–53; regulation of, WWI and,
   102, 105, 107; supply, 16; transportation of,
   15–16
Whelan, Ralph, 76, 83, 124–25; and Pillsbury-
   Washburn receivership, 87, 92–93
Whitehead, John C., 205, 237
Whiting, Harrison H., *120*, 143, 235; and Pillsbury employee benefits, 122; career of, *120*–
   122, 131, 183; death of, 124
White Wings Pty., Ltd. (Australia), Pillsbury interest acquired (1961), and divestment of, *174*–
   175, 225
Wichita (KS), Pillsbury elevators, 117
Wickes Corp. agricultural division, Pillsbury ac-
   quisition of (1982), 225
Wilson, Woodrow, 102
Wilton Enterprises (Chicago), Pillsbury acquisi-
   tion of (1974), 199, 201
Winter wheat: dominance of, in market, 20–21,
   95; products, 199, 201; Turkey Red, introduction of, 95
World War I: civilian contributions, Pillsbury
   and, 105; regulation of wheat and, 102, 105,
   107
World War II, wheat supply and government regulation, 137
Wray, Peter G., 205, 237
Wyman, Thomas H., CBS career of, 213; Pillsbury career of, 213, 237

Yerxa, Dwight K., 236
Young, Harry F., 236

Zabriskie, George A., 235

WILLIAM J. POWELL, a graduate of Carleton College and the University of Minnesota Law School, maintained a private legal practice in southeastern Minnesota and served in the armed services before working with the Minneapolis and St. Louis Railway Company. In 1960 he joined The Pillsbury Company, becoming the firm's chief legal officer in 1964. In 1973, he was named senior vice-president and elected to the company's board of directors. He retired in 1979.

Pillsbury's B E S T   Pillsbury's B E S T   Pillsbury's B E S T

Pillsbury's B E S T   Pillsbury's B E S T   Pillsbury's B E S T

Pillsbury's B E S T   Pillsbury's B E S T   Pillsbury's B E S T